RIVER OF ENTERPRISE

MIDWESTERN HISTORY AND CULTURE
General Editors
James H. Madison and Andrew R. L. Cayton

RIVER

THE COMMERCIAL ORIGINS

OF

OF REGIONAL IDENTITY IN THE

ENTERPRISE

OHIO VALLEY, 1790–1850

KIM M. GRUENWALD

INDIANA
University Press
Bloomington & Indianapolis

Portions of chapters 1 and 2 were published in different form as
"Marietta's Example of a Settlement Pattern in the Ohio Country:
A Reinterpretation," *Ohio History* 105 (Summer–Autumn 1996):
125–44.

This book is a publication of

Indiana University Press
601 North Morton Street
Bloomington, Indiana 47404-3797 USA

http://iupress.indiana.edu

Telephone orders   800-842-6796
Fax orders   812-855-7931
Orders by email   iuporder@indiana.edu

The paper used in this publication meets the minimum
requirements of American National Standard for Information
Sciences—Permanence of Paper for Printed Library
Materials, ANSI Z39.48-1984.

Manufactured in the United States of America

Library of Congress Cataloging-in-Publication Data

Gruenwald, Kim M. (Kim Marie)
  River of enterprise : the commercial origins of regional identity in
  the Ohio Valley, 1790–1850 / Kim M. Gruenwald.
     p. cm. — (Midwestern history and culture)
  Includes bibliographical references and index.
  ISBN 0-253-34132-9 (alk. paper)
  1. Regionalism— Ohio River Valley— History. 2. Frontier and
pioneer life—Ohio River Valley. 3. Ohio River Valley—Social
conditions. 4. Ohio River Valley—Economic conditions. 5. Ohio
River Valley—Commerce—Social aspects—History. 6. Merchants—
Ohio River Valley—History. 7. Pioneers—Ohio River Valley—
History. 8. Woodbridge family. 9. Merchants—Ohio—Marietta—
Biography. 10. Pioneers—Ohio—Marietta—Biography. I. Title.
II. Series.
  F518 .G78 2002
  977'.02—dc21
                                                    2002000809

  1 2 3 4 5 07 06 05 04 03 02

TO
MOM AND KELLY

CONTENTS

MAPS

ACKNOWLEDGMENTS

A number of institutions helped make this book possible. The History Department at the University of Colorado furnished a Douglas A. Bean Fellowship to fund summer research, and a Dean's Small Grant provided funds for a December trip to Ohio archives while I worked on my dissertation. Kent State University gave me release time from teaching to devote all my attention to the manuscript during my third spring through a Research Council Academic Year Research and Creative Activity Appointment. The Division of Research and Graduate Studies has also funded a number of weeklong visits to regional archives through research travel grants. The Filson Historical Society in Louisville, Kentucky, honored me with a Filson Fellowship in the summer of 1998, and I never enjoyed a week at a research center more.

The staffs at every research institution I visited proved most professional, helpful, and friendly as I hunted down any and all information on the Woodbridge family: the American Antiquarian Society, the Baker Library at the Harvard Business School, the Cincinnati Historical Society, the Connecticut Historical Society, the Connecticut State Library, the Dawes Memorial Library at Marietta College, the Detroit Public Library, the Filson Historical Society, the Historical Society of Pennsylvania, the Massachusetts Historical Society, the Ohio Historical Society, the Regional History Collection at West Virginia University, the Washington County Historical Society, the Special Collections at Western Kentucky University, and the Western Reserve Historical Society.

A few individuals deserve special mention. On my first trip to Ohio via car and campground, Gary Arnold allowed me to enter and work in the reading room when he arrived for his workday an hour before the Ohio Historical Society opened each morning. Likewise, Sandra Neyman allowed me access to Special Collections at Marietta College when they were closed for Christmas break one December. At the Filson Historical Society, Nelson Dawson, Jim Holmberg, Trace Kirkwood, and Rebecca Rice made a week in Kentucky go by very quickly and smoothly with much laughter and good fellowship. As I searched for just the right illustrations for the book and wrote to obtain permission to quote from manuscript collections, Duryea Kemp at the Ohio Historical Society and Tim Mahoney at Harvard's Baker Library were especially helpful. At Indiana University Press Bob Sloan, Jane Lyle, Tony Brewer, and Jimmée Greco have made the difficult process of publishing a book look easy.

Kent State University has been a great place to make a start in the historical profession. My colleagues and the staff at the History Department have been wonderful, especially my mentor, John Jameson, and my good friend Isolde Thyrêt. Dr. Thyrêt also offered her expertise as a photographer—it is she who took the photograph of the picture of Dudley Woodbridge Jr. that appears in chapter 7. Julio Pino showed me area bookstores, and Shirley Wajda introduced me to the work of Yi-Fu Tuan. Michael Hradesky of the Geography Department produced the maps.

The following scholars made invaluable comments on the dissertation, conference papers, article manuscripts, or book chapters: Michael A. Bellesiles, Wayne K. Durrill, John Mack Faragher, Craig Friend, Patricia Nelson Limerick, James Madison, Ralph Mann, Cathy Matson, Peter Onuf, Elizabeth A. Perkins, Ken Wheeler, and Marion Nelson Winship. Eric Hinderaker read a chapter early on and, later, two versions of the book manuscript (a heroic undertaking indeed), and his comments helped me tighten and strengthen the argument. His phone call on the eve of preparing my tenure file buoyed me immeasurably. Andrew R. L. (Drew) Cayton has provided support for many years: he met with and advised me when I came to Ohio for my first plunge into the archives, he read and commented on my dissertation after I defended it, he read book manuscript chapters for me one summer, and he read the whole manuscript and made the sort of criticisms that helps one bring one's topic into better focus. Stephen Aron's insights challenged me to put the argument and its context into their final form. Virginia Anderson has become a good friend since graduate school, and my first years in the profession have been made easier by her support and advice. As for my advisor, Fred Anderson, under his tutelage I became an historian. He has been a combination of stern taskmaster, vigorous mentor, gracious protocol officer, and now, happily, friend. I can't thank him enough. Fred and Drew collaborated on the title.

My family has been very supportive ever since I entered graduate school, and I feel lucky to have been surrounded by such a fine group of parents, siblings, siblings-in-law, nieces, nephews, aunts, uncles, and grandparents. All of them helped me put my work and my profession in proper perspective in their own individual ways. This book is dedicated to my mother and my sister because they have provided so many different kinds of support over the years that giving them thanks in words alone would be impossible.

INTRODUCTION

Dudley Woodbridge moved to the newly settled town of Marietta at the confluence of the Ohio and Muskingum rivers in 1789. A merchant from Norwich, Connecticut, he often wrote of going "across the mountains" when planning a trip. His son, Dudley Jr., used that phrase too, but more commonly referred to the region as "the Western Country." His son, in turn, called Ohio "the Buckeye State." Why they called Ohio by three different names indicates more than changing fashion. It offers a clue to the evolving role the Ohio River played in each of their lives and in the development of the new United States.

What often comes to mind when one considers the Ohio's role in American history is Harriet Beecher Stowe's fictional slave Eliza crossing the icy river to freedom with a child in her arms and a pack of dogs nipping at her heels. Since that time, Americans have visualized the Ohio River as the boundary between freedom and slavery, between North and South. This image has laid the foundation for much of the history of the Ohio Valley. Early scholars wrote of hardy pioneers battling the wilderness far from the security of their old homes. With slavery excluded north of the river, they shed old values and fashioned new ones in a laboratory of democracy. One group of scholars did resist splitting the valley's history along a north/south axis, but they erected a temporal divide. In the decades following World War II, economic historians focused on the transportation revolution, concentrating on developments after 1815 and leaving older models to explain the region's early formation.[1]

Recent historians have returned to concentrating on the history of one bank of the Ohio River or the other. Politics have taken center stage in most studies of the states north of the river, and many scholars begin their analysis with the passage of the Northwest Ordinance in 1787. Some of this interest can be traced to the bicentennial of the ordinance itself. Kentucky's history has come back in style as well, and the number of books and dissertations that focus on the first state west of the Appalachian Mountains continues to grow. Much of the recent interest in Kentucky's history can be traced to the emergence of backcountry scholarship over the past fifteen years.[2]

For the most part, though, these studies, old and new, allow political boundaries or economic watersheds to delimit their focus, and thus at times they overlook the way the valley's key geographical feature, the Ohio River itself, bound the trans-Appalachian West together from 1790 to 1830. In recent years many scholars of the trans-Mississippi West have replaced the study of the frontier (especially as "the line between civilization and savagery") with the study of place. They have moved beyond frontier to region in order to highlight themes of western development. Taking this approach for the early republic means putting the Ohio River at the center of the narrative. One scholar has concluded that travelers descending the river hardly ever described it as a boundary between North and South until the 1830s, but what of the people who made the valley home—people like the Woodbridges?[3]

Merchants such as Dudley Woodbridge, his son, and his grandson have been the subject of few studies of the Ohio Valley because most histories of the early West take the viewpoint of farmers. The two best overviews of the trans-Appalachian frontier start by dividing northern and southern expansion into separate chapters, and then go on to emphasize the similarities as well as the differences in the lives of everyday settlers on both sides of the Ohio River. One historian labeled the place "an agricultural world," and indeed farmers far outnumbered merchants. But the way business entrepreneurs view the world can provide us with significant insight into the growth of the new nation. Merchants made the economy work because they controlled capital and credit. All goods went through their hands to markets they managed—agricultural goods to towns and cities, raw materials to artisans, and manufactured goods to laborers and farmers. In general, they wielded influence far out of proportion to their numbers. For the Ohio Valley, the perceptions of merchants prove to be especially important to understanding the place as a region because they interacted with the economy on a variety of levels: locally, through farmers who bought goods and paid with cash and barter; regionally, through western producers of raw materials such as salt, cotton, tobacco, iron, and lead; and nationally, through eastern suppliers of manufactured goods. By its very nature, their worldview was an integrated one.[4]

The mercantile pursuits of the Woodbridge family of Marietta, Ohio, followed such a pattern of integration. The Woodbridges' account books, blotters, invoice books, journals, ledgers, and letter books can be found at the Ohio Historical Society in Columbus and the Regional History Collection of West Virginia University in Morgantown. In addition, a wide range of family correspondence is available in the Burton Collection at the Detroit Public Library in Michigan. These collections provide the foundation of this study. Through them one can trace the Woodbridges' mercantile ties to others in southeast Ohio, along the Ohio River, and back east to Philadelphia. A merchant's world was one of connections: connections between East and West, between North and South, and between one western town and its counterparts, large and small, throughout the Ohio Valley. These connections reveal a much more complex world than the vision summoned up by older descriptions, be they those of novelists or historians.

Just as the strategies of the Woodbridges can provide us with a window to view the creation of a regional economy, the changing nature of life in their hometown of Marietta provides us with insight into other regional developments. Marietta occupies a peculiar place in the historiography of the early republic. During the first years of settlement, some described Marietta as a New England village, and most historians since have taken these early visitors at their word that settlers from Massachusetts and Connecticut recreated a traditional Yankee community in the wilderness. The town is always mentioned as the first permanent white settlement north of the Ohio authorized by the new nation, but then scholars move on to the history of the Miami and Scioto valleys as more representative of early Ohio. Good reasons exist to do so. The spectacular success of Cincinnati makes Marietta's gains seem modest by comparison, and the smaller town's history becomes lost in the shuffle. In addition, southern-born settlers and settlers from the mid-Atlantic region heavily outnumbered New Englanders during the first decades of the state's history to the west of Marietta, and most of them were Jeffersonian Republicans. The New Englanders banded together in response, forming the staunch Federalist opposition to statehood in 1803.[5]

But the vast majority of westerners lived in communities the size of Marietta and the settlements that made up its hinterland rather than in cities like Cincinnati. Marietta's history is also all the more interesting for its New England beginnings, for as Marietta grew and changed, as the newly independent people from all regions of colonial America worked together to create a commercial economy in the Ohio Valley, the story of the town's evolution serves to highlight many of the important transformations taking place in the United States during the decades that followed the American Revolution. Marietta's story also highlights the rise and fall of towns as new modes of transportation replaced older ones.

This study seeks to explain the changing meaning and role of the Ohio River in the lives of three generations of valley settlers: the first, to whom it was the land "across the mountains," born in a world dominated by imperial competition between Great Britain and France; the second, who called it "the Western Country," raised during the era of the American Revolution; and the third, born in "the Buckeye State," who comprised the first generation of American citizens to come of age west of the Appalachian Mountains. From 1790 to 1830 the Ohio River helped create a regional identity in the West on both banks as Americans strove to create an empire based upon the ties of commerce. Only as the commercial world began to give way to an emerging industrial economy, and as artificial transportation networks such as canals and railroads supplanted the river, did those living on the northern shore begin to define the Ohio as the boundary between North and South.

My story begins in the late eighteenth century as Americans devised strategies to acquire a region they had long coveted: the fertile lands between the Appalachian Mountains and the Mississippi River. It encompasses the Ohio River's valley, from the headwaters at Pittsburgh to the falls at Louisville—a series of rapids that represented the only major interruption (other than seasonal) in the river's navigation during the first half of the nineteenth century. Because the process of extinguishing Native American land titles in Indiana and Illinois below the falls took longer than it did in Ohio, the Euro-American population along the lower third of the Ohio's course grew slowly during most of the years covered by this study. This book ends in 1850, when the coming of railroads signaled the final shift from the dominance of commercial schemes to the world of manufacturing.[6]

Part 1, "Across the Mountains," examines the strategies of North American colonists who coveted the Ohio Valley as space, a vast expanse that seemed to promise the status of landowner to all white householders. The process by which newly independent Euro-Americans would lay claim to the Ohio Valley is the subject of the first chapter: men like Dudley Woodbridge promoted westward expansion by establishing towns like Marietta as portals hundreds of miles inland through which settlers would pass. The second chapter compares the vital roles that land speculators, farmers, and merchants played in making the construction of such gateways a success. For this generation, the Ohio River represented access to the interior of the continent.

Part 2, "The Western Country," traces the emergence of a regional consciousness in an Ohio Valley transformed by commerce and white settlement. A three-tiered system of towns grew up: entrepôts, the subregional hubs that made up the entrepôts' hinterlands, and the small towns that comprised the hinterlands of those subregional hubs. Chapter 3 details how Dudley Woodbridge Jr. helped transform Marietta into a subregional hub within Pittsburgh's orbit, even as others were doing the same in the hinterlands of Lexington, Kentucky, and Cincinnati, Ohio. The fourth and fifth chapters trace the links merchants forged between East and West, and among western hubs and entrepôts that tied both shores together to create a regional economy. Chapter 6 probes the sense of place that informed westerners' view of their world: attitudes that led them to protest eastern banking policies and embrace the transportation revolution all along the Ohio's banks, north and south, in the years before and after the Panic of 1819. Dudley Woodbridge Jr.'s generation regarded the Ohio Valley as home.

Part 3, "The Buckeye State," reveals how the relationship between neighbors across the river cooled. During the 1820s and 1830s the transportation revolution set in motion economic and demographic changes that lessened many residents' dependence on the Ohio River. Chapter 7 focuses on the economic transformation that brought about social and political realignments in Ohio. The eighth chapter details how residents of the Ohio's northern bank increasingly came to define themselves as fundamentally different from those living to the south. As the river lost its dominance over life in the region, the grandsons of Dudley Woodbridge and others of their generation came to regard the Ohio River as the boundary between North and South.

This new model of regional development in the Ohio Valley reveals the central role commerce played in the expansion of the United States. The strategies town boosters, railroads, and entrepreneurs employed and the roles they played in settling the lands west of the Mississippi were first tested upon the river systems of the trans-Appalachian West. A regional perspective likewise uncovers important similarities between the strategies of northerners and southerners immediately following the Revolution—similarities that allowed them to begin the critical process of establishing a continental empire together before expansion in the era of the Mexican War tore the nation apart. As farmers sought competency and merchants sought profits, the new United States came of age as both nationalism and individualism flourished in the West.

Such a model also reveals much about the course of the market revolution. Scholars studying the transformation of New England's economy during the first half of the nineteenth century of necessity focus upon intrusive changes made in long-settled areas. But in the Ohio Valley, towns and rural hinterlands grew together, and each half of the economy supported the other as merchants and farmers settled the region side by side. Forty years ago historian Richard Wade was the first to assert that "the towns were the spearheads of the frontier." But Wade's excellent study of Pittsburgh, Cincinnati, Lexington, Louisville, and St. Louis is really five stories that run parallel to one another.[7] By contrast, this study takes as its focus intersections—the connections between western towns, large and small. Only by revealing the commercial network merchants created along the Ohio River and its tributaries and adding it to the oft-told tale of pioneer farmers can a full account of the settling of the Western Country emerge.

The evolution of the Ohio's role in the lives of three generations of early Americans make it clear that reading backward from Harriet Beecher Stowe's mid-nineteenth-century image of the river to see only an inevitable division obscures our understanding of the early development of the Ohio Valley as a region. We must learn to read the Ohio Valley forward from the world envisioned by the merchants and farmers who claimed it for the new United States in the decades following the American Revolution.

PART I ACROSS THE MOUNTAINS

Across the Mountains

Ohio

Western Reserve

Greenville Treaty Line

Zane's Trace

Virginia Military District

Seven Ranges

Ohio Company Purchase

Symmes Purchase

not to scale

Norwich

New York

Pittsburgh
Wheeling

Philadelphia

Chillicothe • Marietta

Cincinnati

St. Louis

Louisville

Limestone

Ste. Genevieve

Lexington

Ohio R.

Mississippi R.

Natchez

New Orleans

N

0   400 Miles

Michael Hradesky

Across the Mountains. To Americans of the late eighteenth century, the land across the mountains represented space waiting to be used, and the Ohio River represented access to the heart of the continent.

The Allegheny and Monongahela rivers come together on the western slopes of the Appalachian Mountains to form the Ohio River. Initially, the Ohio flows northwest, but it soon turns southwestward until it reaches the Big Sandy River, the boundary between present-day West Virginia and Kentucky, a little over three hundred miles from its source. Although well watered by many smaller streams, steep, rocky hills dominate this portion of the valley. Only when the Ohio turns north and west once again and flows onward to the boundary of present-day Ohio and Indiana, nearly one hundred and sixty miles farther on, does the topography change. The rich Bluegrass region of central Kentucky lies to the south of this point, and the fertile Miami Valley of western Ohio stretches north. From the Miami confluence, the Ohio falls away to the south and west once more. A hundred miles farther on, the falls of the Ohio break the river's flow in a series of rapids that signal a twenty-foot drop in elevation over three miles. Below that point, the site of present-day Louisville, Kentucky, hills and bluffs gradually give way to flatter ground and open plains, and the Ohio flows placidly for the last four hundred miles of its journey.[1]

Thus does the Ohio River flow nearly a thousand miles to make the Mississippi mighty. Yet a straight line drawn from the Ohio's headwaters to its mouth would be only half as long. The river twists, turns, and meanders through its valley, augmenting its flow with the volume of eighteen major and many more minor tributaries, draining a territory covering over two hundred thousand square miles. The width and depth of the river vary greatly, and two hundred years ago, when the river was full of snags, rocks, gravel, islands, and sand bars, it varied even more. Back then, dozens of kinds of fish inhabited the river, including bass, catfish, crappie, sunfish, and sturgeon. The river valley gave life to a great variety of trees—among them ash, beech, buckeye, cedar, chestnut, elm, hickory, maple, oak, and sycamore.

Deer, elk, wolves, bears, eagles, and other creatures made the valley's plentiful forests their home.[2]

In addition to the abundance of flora and fauna, the Ohio Valley nurtured Native American cultures, peoples tied together by the mighty river into far-reaching networks of trade that lasted more than a millennium and stretched from the Appalachians to the Gulf Coast to the Rocky Mountains. Emptied by the Beaver Wars of the seventeenth century, the fertile valley beckoned to new Indian groups who came to make the valley their home during the first half of the eighteenth century. French and English officials wanted to trade with Ohio Valley Indians, but the colonists of British North America wanted the land itself. By the era of the American Revolution, a river that had united diverse cultures for a thousand years divided warring inhabitants: Delawares and others defended the "Indian coast" to the north, and Euro-Americans defended the "Virginia shore" to the south. These settlers and others would forcibly expel the Native Americans from the Ohio Valley in the years to come.[3]

Despite the fact that Dudley Woodbridge Jr. used the term "Western Country" more often than his father did, the designation was in widespread use during his father's time. But while westerners of the younger man's generation would use the term to refer to home after the turn of the century, to the colonists of British North America it meant something different. To them the Ohio River represented access to the vast interior of North America, and by the mid-eighteenth century, they coveted it. Looking west, they saw "space": a vast unmapped area that "suggest[ed] the future and invite[d] action." Space meant freedom and possibility. Those who promoted the settling of the Western Country described it as a new Eden where farmers could grow more bushels of corn per acre than they could ever have imagined before.[4]

They pushed forward at the expense of Native Americans because they sought competency, or "a degree of comfortable independence." The Europeans and their descendents did not endeavor to accumulate riches so much as they worked to acquire enough land for their families to live above the level of subsistence and to provide for the next generation without being overly dependent on others. North America's natural abundance seemed to hold out the promise of competency to all men. The colonists produced goods not only for their own use and to barter with their neighbors, but also specifically to sell in the nearest market town. Markets meant opportunity, and farmers willingly produced shoes and cider or picked cherries and hauled firewood to make a profit. Engaging in market activities did not mean giving up independence, for patriarchs controlled the labor of their families as well as such means of production as cider presses.[5]

People competed for the resources needed to gain competency, and in England that conflict developed along class lines. During hard times, common people used riots and other rituals of collective protest to demand that the propertied classes provide them with just food prices and rents because of a moral duty to help those dependent on them. But in North America a much higher proportion of men had access to land of their own, and even those who accepted the role of tenant could expect to become landowners some time in the not-too-distant future. Rather than concerning themselves with the legitimacy of entrepreneurs seeking profits at their expense as the English did, the American colonists strove to prevent the rich and powerful from holding a monopoly on opportunities for advancement. Like farmers in the Old World, Americans concerned themselves with the well-being of their families and communities and thus engaged in community rituals. But in America activities such as quilting bees, barn raisings, town meetings, and huskings were intended to preserve peace between competitive neighbors rather than between social classes.[6]

As Americans expanded west, then, the sort of collective action that led to rebellion had a different aim than that in England. Conflict ended in the late-eighteenth- and early-nineteenth-century backcountries of the Carolinas, Pennsylvania, Vermont, and Maine once settlers gained access to the legal and governmental institutions that allowed them to settle differences among themselves and between backcountry and coast. During the American Revolution they bargained for strict proportional representation in the new state governments by threatening to withhold their support from the patriot cause.[7]

In the Ohio Valley ambitious men did seek profits and power rather than competency, of course, but Americans took steps to ensure equality of opportunity. After the Revolution they fashioned strategies of expansion that curbed the development and power of absentee landowners—the Great Proprietors who had plagued the settlers north of Massachusetts did not exist in the Ohio Valley. Tension between East and West continued throughout the first decades of the new nation's existence, but with the promise of the Northwest Ordinance—that territories, once settled, would become full-fledged states—legal and political institutions would be put in place that obviated the need for rebels and vigilantes. Within a generation, religious upheaval and the emergence of political parties indicate that citizens organized to make their voices heard.

This is not to say that all American men truly had an equal opportunity to achieve what they desired in the Ohio Valley, and certainly Native Americans, African Americans, and women did not. Prosperous, well-educated men controlled the government, and speculators controlled the distribution of a large portion of western lands in antebellum America. But a true capitalist system in which an elite few controlled the means of production while others became dependent on selling their labor to earn a wage would not affect the great majority of Americans until after the Civil War. The growing belief that all men had the right to an equal chance at the resources needed to achieve competency crystallized in the rhetoric of revolution, and reality could not dim that goal in the minds of Americans heading for the land across the Appalachian Mountains.[8]

In 1780 an anonymous western settler wrote to a friend about his plans for the future when he lay claim to over two thousand acres of land in Kentucky covered with buckeye, walnut, and cherry trees. He wrote, "I am Confident [my land] will be worth more Money than any lands in this Countrey." The man wrote of the hardships settlers faced— winter, cold, and frostbite—but his "drooping spirits" rose because of "the pleasing prospect" he had of "acquireing a Computant Fortune for my Children."[9] Such, then, was the mindset of the people who set out to make the Ohio Valley their own, a people culturally disposed toward geographical expansion.

After the Revolution the newly independent Americans sought to claim the vast space for their new nation. In 1786 a group of New England veterans of the Revolutionary War formed the Ohio Company of Associates and purchased a million and a half acres of land from the United States the next year at the confluence of the Ohio and Muskingum rivers, just over one hundred and seventy miles below the Ohio's headwaters at Pittsburgh. During the spring of 1788 they established the town of Marietta there. The work of speculators, trailblazers, and farmers would be needed to turn their dreams into reality, but it would be the commercial connections created by merchants that lay the foundation for the new United States' continental empire.

1

Claiming Space

In December of 1788 Dudley Woodbridge, a merchant of Norwich, Connecticut, wrote to his brother-in-law, James Backus, a surveyor in the employ of the Ohio Company, asking for information about the company's purchase. Business is "exceeding dull, & Money grows scarcer," Woodbridge complained. He wanted James to send him a detailed report about "the prospects of business" in the West, including answers to the following questions:

> Where can vessels go, and have the least land carriage—Philadelphia, Virginia, or where[?] [A]re vessels suffered to go down & up the Mississippi unmolested, how far can a vessel of a hundred tons get up the Ohio, are materials for ship-building plenty and good[?] . . . [I]s the navigation down the rivers safe and good[?] [W]hat is the demand for goods and what *kinds* will best answer, with the *prices* of *liquors etc.* there, what is the price per ton for land carriage, from Philadelphia or your nearest seaport, what are the remittances that will be made for goods, cash or produce, if produce, what kind and the price? In short, I should be glad of a particular & minute information with regard to what does now or may relate to the *mercantile line.*[1]

Apparently Woodbridge was pleased with the young man's response, for he moved to the fledgling town of Marietta the next summer and immediately began speculating in land and seeking out men interested in erecting gristmills and sawmills. Together they poured their energy and capital into the development of the company purchase of land in the interest of connecting East and West and making the area attractive to farmers.[2]

In their quest for opportunity, newly independent Americans such as Dudley Woodbridge and the founders of the Ohio Company went about conquering the Ohio Valley in a very particular way. Rather than slowly pushing their way out from older settlements, entrepreneurs and speculators began planting towns hundreds of miles inland to act as magnets to farmers, promising them access to both goods and markets. Their vision also attracted men who wished to be at the forefront of creating a continental empire. Because they intended to create and control a trade route that penetrated deep into the heart of the continent, merchants played a central role in most plans. War with Ohio Valley Indians erupted within a few years of settlement, but the Euro-Americans won control of the southern portion of the territory north of the river in 1795, and Marietta then became a portal through which settlers came west.

I

Born in Stonington, Connecticut, in 1747, Dudley Woodbridge moved to the port of Norwich in 1770, established himself as a lawyer, married the daughter of a prominent iron manufacturer, and turned to mercantile pursuits soon thereafter. When they married, Dudley Woodbridge was twenty-seven and Lucy Backus was seventeen. Woodbridge discontinued most of his law work and set up shop as a middleman between New York and Boston overseas merchants and Connecticut farmers and traders. Connecticut's exports went almost exclusively to the West Indies and other communities on the Atlantic coast, for the colonists produced nothing that Europeans particularly wanted. Overshadowed by long-established New York, Boston, and Philadelphia merchants, those in smaller ports imported little directly from England. But provisioning the British and the Continental armies during the American Revolution created a sharp increase in the demand for local produce.[3]

During the Revolutionary War, Woodbridge primarily occupied himself with marketing beef, pork, sugar, corn, oats, flax, and wood, while importing whatever he could to run a store, including rum, cloth, wine, and tea. He either traded directly with merchants, or if he could turn a larger profit by doing so, he instructed agents in Boston and New York to sell his produce, and then he paid the importers with cash for goods he retailed in Norwich. An account with Silvester Gilbert of Hebron for any goods and rum that Woodbridge could supply indicates that he supplied country merchants with goods to sell. In addition, Woodbridge made contacts farther afield, sending apples, cheese, walnuts, and cider to Elisha Hinman in Williamsburg, Virginia, in exchange for tobacco in 1782.[4]

Clearly, though, Dudley Woodbridge had greater ambitions. In 1786 he acquired a quarter interest in the schooner *Elizabeth* and added others thereafter. Owning his own ships brought a whole new host of commercial activities for him to engage in. He had to pay for insurance and the maintenance of the ships, and he had to pay the captain and crew. Woodbridge became busy enough to hire a lawyer to follow up on his debtors instead of taking care of it himself in the late 1780s. But owning schooners brought new headaches. Seamen jumped ship, and new hands had to be hired. A shipment of horses became ill with distemper on the voyage to the Caribbean and could not be sold for a profit. Fog delayed another shipment of horses, keeping it in port and forcing Woodbridge to buy additional feed. Once he dispatched seventeen horses and sixteen oxen to the West Indies only to find that six ships full of stock had arrived ahead of them, glutting the market.[5]

In the years following the Revolution, American merchants like Woodbridge often found their path to the West Indies blocked by the English, and so they decided to find an alternate route to the Atlantic world down the Mississippi through New Orleans. Philadelphia merchants had been busy establishing their own niche at the Ohio's headwaters for some time. As Kentucky's population grew during the 1770s and 1780s, some eastern firms began to launch trading ventures west. A few sent goods by wagon to Fort Pitt, where their agents exchanged them for furs, skins, flour, and tobacco in western Pennsylvania and Virginia, Kentucky, and Illinois before sending the new cargo on to New Orleans to be sold there or shipped to other markets. One pair, the partnership of Reed and Forde, set up a store in both western Virginia and Natchez to facilitate their commercial plans. They also speculated in land, hoping to make their fortunes as settlers poured into the region following the Revolution. One visitor wrote that the "major part of merchants settled at Pittsburgh, or in the environs, are the partners, or else the factors, belonging to the houses at Philadelphia." A Frenchman named Louis Tarascon confirmed this view, reporting that the town housed thirty stores in 1799, but for the most part the men who ran them worked for Philadelphia or Baltimore merchants rather than owning the stores themselves.[6]

Dudley Woodbridge's brother-in-law painted a rosy picture of life in the Western Country downriver from Pittsburgh. James Backus reported that the Indians were friendly, and one family had even stayed in town to help them plant corn. The younger man believed that a treaty with the Ohio tribes was only a few months away. James also reported that settlers were flocking in by the boatload, and he asked his father to send him ten pounds of nails and one hundred pairs of shoes that he could sell for a tidy profit. He sent along the names of four Ohio Company shareholders (three of whom appeared in the Norwich business records of his brother-in-law) and urged his family to buy their shares to sell later for a much higher price.[7] And so Dudley Woodbridge decided that joining the Ohio Company of Associates in their endeavors represented his best chance to forward his mercantile goals.

II

During the Revolutionary War, Congress had used force to evict squatters north of the Ohio in an effort to appease the Delaware Indians. The army burned cabins and ran settlers off the land but failed to deter others determined to cross the Ohio from Kentucky and western Virginia. Because of such attempts to control the banks of the Ohio, the valley was as well known to the military as to the squatters themselves, and army officers knew the lands were rapidly being settled. In September of 1783 a group of Continental officers began to formulate plans of their own for making use of the Ohio Valley—plans that did not include letting it fill up with squatters. Led by the army's chief engineer, Brigadier General Rufus Putnam, they petitioned Congress to grant the land to them in the tradition of military bounty lands. Putnam argued in the petition and elsewhere that by allowing his group to set up a permanent settlement on the Ohio, the new American government would gain a buffer against the British and the Spanish, as well as a line of communication between East and West through the Great Lakes. Putnam emphasized that if settlement was not carried out in an orderly fashion, a European power might gain control of the area. Nearly all the petitioners, as officers and members of the Society of Cincinnati, intended to make their settlement a bulwark of national authority in the West.[8]

When their push for bounty lands met with no success, Rufus Putnam and a group of fellow veterans created the Ohio Company of Associates in 1786. Membership was open to anyone who could purchase a share of stock for one thousand dollars in continental securities or ten dollars in gold, whether they had served in the military or not. This allowed men to turn depreciated securities into something of value—land. They limited the number of shares one person could buy to five to insure that professional speculators could not cash in—thus preserving the speculative advantage for themselves.[9]

The man who lobbied Congress on behalf of the company and negotiated the purchase was the Reverend Manasseh Cutler, a Connecticut-born Yale graduate. In 1787 he published a pamphlet extolling the virtues of the Ohio Country. Hoping to lure settlers with his prose, he wrote of the fertility of western soil, the navigability of western rivers, and the various paths by which produce could be taken to Atlantic markets—north to the Great Lakes and south to New Orleans. To Cutler, the role of the Ohio Company itself was clear:

> The first settlement will inbosom many men of the most liberal minds—well versed in the world, in business and every useful science. . . . The people in the Kentucky and Illinois countries are rapidly increasing . . . on seeing examples of

government, science, and regular industry, follow them into the neighbour-
hood of their own country, they would favour their children with these advan-
tages, and revive the ideas of order, citizenship, and the useful sciences.

Cutler intended for the Ohio Company's settlement to be a shining example
of civilization and order in the West, and eastern leaders apparently warmed
to his words.[10]

The Confederation Congress sold land to the Ohio Company because
they believed that the New Englanders would help impose order in the West.
Eastern policy makers wanted the lands west of the Appalachians for the
new United States for both strategic and economic reasons, but they dis-
trusted the people who lived there. In their view, western hunters and squatters lived like savages, and easterners often described them in the same terms
they used for Native Americans. National leaders intended for East and West
to remain united by common interests by promoting commerce and attract-
ing settlers intent on improving the land. Northerners and southerners at
the national level found themselves in agreement on many issues. Both saw
the need for surveys prior to settlement, the creation of compact communities, and the recruitment of industrious, market-oriented settlers. Friction
between the backcountry and the eastern seaboard had been seething for a
generation, and the chaos of overlapping land claims in the southern backcountry had taught them a valuable lesson. Sectionalism may have caused
more friction if squatters had not already been moving north of the Ohio
River, forcing Congress to act quickly or lose control of the region.[11]

The result of their concerns was the Northwest Ordinance of 1787, a
document with two faces. In order to attract the right kind of settlers, it
promised freedom of religion, due process of law and full civil liberties, support for public education, representative governments, and a process by
which territories would eventually become states. Revolutionary principles
did have a hand in the formation of these policies, but promising westerners
they would be citizens was also seen as an important step in securing their
loyalty. Intending to prevent the scattered pattern of settlement that squatters left behind, eastern policy makers granted land in townships to cluster
settlers together for defense and sought sites that would give farmers ready
access to markets. In this vein, the ordinance can be read as a text that de-
scribes careful planning and control. Under the new settlement scheme, settlers would live in close proximity to each other so that they could be
properly socialized and educated. They would need to work together, and
public schooling would transform savages into educated citizens.[12]

The New Englanders who settled the company's lands made the decision to move west for a variety of reasons. The economy had suffered since
the end of the Revolutionary War, and the land could no longer support

New England's growing population. As debt rose and the number of fore-closures increased, the volatility that sparked Shays' Rebellion made life all the more uncertain. For over a century and a half, migrating to new lands in search of competency had represented an important strategy among New Englanders who sought to maintain family independence and to ensure the next generation's access to land. In the 1790s farmers from Massachusetts, Connecticut, and Rhode Island would move once again, but much farther than their colonial counterparts ever had, as many crossed the Appalachian Mountains to settle in the Ohio Valley.[13]

Most of the prominent men who moved west had lost capital during and after the war, and, in some ways, they wanted to recreate the more or-derly world they had known before. Joseph Gilman of New Hampshire was one such man. When chaotic currency conditions led to the decline in value of state securities, he lost much of his property in the late 1780s. Gilman had provided clothing and blankets to the troops of his home state during the conflict, but he could not collect on many of these debts after the Peace of Paris, and his economic status collapsed. Joseph Gilman intended to make a new start in the West, away from the eyes of neighbors who had witnessed his ruin.[14]

Neither Rufus Putnam nor his associates planned to create an egalitar-ian society. They expected ties to the national government to secure their own individual social status, for the ex-army officers longed for the respect they seemed to have lost in the postwar world. As members of the Society of Cincinnati, many received federal appointments in the new territorial gov-ernment. Rufus Putnam himself sought an increase in status. Putnam was born in 1738, but his father died when Rufus was eight. He apprenticed as a millwright and enlisted three times during the Seven Years' War, rising from private to ensign by war's end. Putnam preferred soldiering but was forced to utilize his other skills to erect sawmills while on campaign. After the war he used his pay to buy land and established himself as both a millwright and surveyor. His reputation as a builder followed him to the next war, and he became an engineer, was promoted, and was eventually made a brigadier general in, and chief engineer of, the Continental Army during the Ameri-can Revolution. Putnam made the most of his relationship with his fellow Freemason and veteran George Washington, who eventually appointed him surveyor-general of the United States in 1796. As a director of the Ohio Company, Putnam controlled the patronage system in what would become Washington County, Ohio.[15]

Like Gilman, Rufus Putnam wanted to restore a sense of order to his world, but he had bold plans for the future as well. Putnam envisioned an urbanized West "fully integrate[d] . . . into the Atlantic cultural and commercial community." Putnam's West would have an interdependent relationship with Atlantic culture and society rather than an independent one, but the Ohio settlements would be no mere colony of the East. Putnam planned to promote manufacturing in his scheme, and churches and schools would stabilize society. The as-yet-unnamed city of Marietta was to be the hub of western commercial and cultural exchange with the East. Putnam and his associates knew that farmers would provide the foundation of the western economy but wanted them to support urban areas of industry and commerce. Rather than an agrarian paradise, Putnam envisioned a complex, economically diverse society.[16]

Such a vision was bound to attract men with ambitions beyond those of ordinary farmers. A cousin of Rufus Putnam, Israel Putnam Jr. of Connecticut, moved to Ohio at age fifty in an effort to ensure that his children and grandchildren would have enough land to make them comfortable and independent. But he realized that one of his sons, David, had different aspirations. In urging the young man to join him in the West, Israel emphasized opportunity rather than land or security. He wrote his son that Marietta would be the center of government in the Northwest Territory, noting that four out of five territorial judges lived there. The older man recognized that David wanted to be where important decisions were being made.[17]

Joseph Gilman also had a son who responded to the lure of being in the thick of plans for the nation's future. When Joseph's financial difficulties forced him to move west in 1788, the twenty-two-year-old Benjamin Ives Gilman accompanied him. The younger man wrote his eastern fiancée, Hannah Robins, a year later that Marietta already had the look of an old settlement: "Those people who wish it have not only the necessaries but the luxuries of life in as great plenty here as in N[ew] England." He also bragged of how quickly the settlers cleared the land and planted crops. Soon thereafter, he returned east briefly to marry Hannah, brought her to Ohio, and then set about establishing a mercantile business.[18]

Benjamin Ives Gilman opened a store at Fort Harmar, across the Muskingum from Marietta, shortly thereafter. One of his many plans involved financing a fleet of ocean-going vessels to be built from the wealth of materials found in the western woods and floated down the Ohio and Mississippi rivers to connect the Ohio Valley to the Atlantic trade world. Gilman also wanted to participate in the growth of the new nation. He sought an active role in the government of the Northwest Territory by writing to a relative in Congress, seeking territorial appointments. He eventually served as clerk for the Washington County Court of Common Pleas.[19]

Rufus Putnam and the Ohio Company set plans in motion to prepare the land for settlement once Congress agreed to sell. In late 1787 an advance party which included surveyors, carpenters, laborers, and a blacksmith stopped and stayed the winter at Sumrill's ferry, thirty miles south of Pittsburgh on the Youghiogheny River. There the men turned their attention to the building of boats, so that when Putnam and a group of reinforcements joined them the next spring, the entire group could proceed to the mouth of the Muskingum, where they landed on 7 April 1788. The men immediately began surveying, clearing the land of trees, building log cabins, and planting crops. Settlers with families trickled in until the population reached nearly two hundred by summer's end, though their numbers were very small compared to the eighteen thousand men, women, and children who passed their settlement while descending the Ohio that year in nine hundred boats, looking for land farther downstream. The Mariettans began building a blockhouse called Campus Martius a half-mile inland, but it took three years to complete.[20]

The Reverend Manasseh Cutler had expressed his wish very early on that settlers be northerners rather than southerners. He argued that they would work harder, not being used to idleness. But when Cutler visited Marietta that first summer, he found friendly relations ongoing between the neighbors north and south of the Ohio River. Virginians and New Englanders worshipped together at Campus Martius on Sunday mornings, and during the first hard winters in Ohio, the New England settlers depended on the men and women south of the river in western Virginia for corn and meat as well as local medical know-how.[21]

Over the course of the next spring and summer, the Ohio Company established a settlement fourteen miles down the Ohio at Belpre. They also built a blockhouse twenty miles up the Muskingum at the site of present-day Beverly and a mill nearby on Wolf Creek; together these settlements came to be called Waterford. One hundred and fifty men came to the Ohio Company's lands in 1789, one-third of them with families.[22]

As Marietta grew, the Ohio River itself proved to be as important an actor in the drama of settlement as the people themselves. An agent for a group of company stockholders, Thomas Wallcut, kept a journal of his stay in Marietta over the winter of 1790. His account shows that the river's moods were often central to planning one's day, for from the end of January through March, Wallcut typically prefaced each day's account with a comment on the rise and fall of the Muskingum and Ohio rivers. Three men left for New Orleans in a boat loaded with flour on 24 January. The agent and a friend accompanied them as far as Belpre, intending to talk with Ohio Company members and seek news of how an exploring party had fared. Two days later Wallcut spotted "a Canoe of hunters . . . going up with meat to sell at Marietta" but decided to walk home with a few com-

FORT HARMER
In 1590 By JosGilman.

Fort Harmar. The Ohio Company pioneers benefited from the protection of the army at Fort Harmar on the opposite bank of the Muskingum River and the neighborliness of Virginians on the opposite bank of the Ohio River. The site of Marietta, except for the tip of the land settlers called "the Point," is out of the picture to the left. *From S. P. Hildreth,* Pioneer History *(Cincinnati: H. W. Derby and Co., 1848), courtesy of the Ohio Historical Society.*

panions. Some days proved mild and others quite cold in the weeks that followed.[23]

Wallcut provides clear pictures of some of the perils of life on the Ohio River. On 7 February a group of men taking millstones up the Muskingum River lost their boat. Another group lost a raft of boards they were bringing down to Marietta from Wolf Creek. The next day a messenger came up from Belpre to inform them that the craft with the millstones had been stopped. It could not be retrieved, however, because both rivers had become "choked with Ice." A few days later, the ice carried away the boat and millstones south where they were spotted by hunters near the mouth of the Kanawha River "amidst a large cake of Ice," from which they could not be recovered. Men from Wolf Creek attempted to bring another raft of boards on the twenty-third "but left part on an island coming down." On 6 March Wallcut reported that some of the boards had been recovered when the river fell.

Ice came from upstream because heavy rains and an early thaw to the north and east made the rivers rise as February wore on. Water invaded the homes of many residents by the middle of the month, and those on higher ground had to shelter their neighbors. Yet it was not so ill a flood as to bring no good: Wallcut reported that when the water swept through town on the nineteenth, it carried away "fences, barrels & everything that will float so that some are busy in towing the timber off their garden lots to go down the stream which saves a vast deal of labour." The river subsided and a boat dropped off mail on its way to the Miami River on 20 February. But within a few days the river became impossible to navigate once again because of high winds. The men spent this time clearing the roads of timber and repairing bridges destroyed in the flood. On the morning of the twenty-sixth, a family seeking lands to the south of the Ohio stopped at Marietta, as did a boat with a shipment of flour for two merchants. Two more keelboats loaded with flour for New Orleans floated by, and three more passed the next day.

In many ways, Marietta's future depended on the sufferance of the Ohio River itself. Not only was it central to the grand schemes of Ohio Company leaders, but the settlers had to learn how the river's character changed from season to season. Ice did not represent the only danger. Dudley Woodbridge reported that a man dispatched to take a message upriver to Wheeling on the southern bank in western Virginia drowned along with his horse while attempting to ford one of the Ohio's many tributaries.[24] Settlers had to adapt to life in the West, and the Ohio could trap the unwary.

The Ohio Company's plans convinced men like Dudley Woodbridge to come west to make their fortune. In addition to his account of the peoples' daily dealings with the river, Thomas Wallcut also recorded some particulars of a debating society that met on snowy evenings. At the end of one such meeting, men put forward possible topics for the next as follows:

> Whether the Am[erican] States have contravarient to the regulations of the Span[ish] Gov[ernmen]t a right founded in the Customs & Laws of Nations to navigate the Mississippi from its source to its mouth—No 1—Parsons.

> No 2 "Is the Police of the City of Marietta equal to the good Gov[ernmen]t of the same & what alteration, if any is necessary to that purpose" Prince.

> No 3 Whether Capital punishment ought ever to be instituted; if admitted ought it to be inflicted in any other case than where the criminal is guilty of murder—Fearing.

Wallcut's own question completed the list:

> No 4—Is the popular opinion true that the Interests of the farmer, the mechanic & the merchant are one & the same inseparably connected, or does this supposed one[ne]ss [of] interest exist any where but in the brains of speculative theorists or prejudiced politicians—or in other words is it not necessary in the nature of things & to preserve harmony in a system that some one Interest or

principle should predominate[;] if so which principle or interest that should be must be another question—TW.

Last came the result of the vote: "No 1 was elected."[25]

The list leads readers to the unsurprising conclusion that while a visitor might wish to discuss political theory, actual settlers were more concerned with law and order in their new home. But Wallcut's journal also sheds light on the aspirations of some of Marietta's earliest residents, revealing goals beyond those of recreating a New England village in the wilderness. Manasseh Cutler and other founders of the Ohio Company had won over the Confederation Congress with rhetoric about establishing an orderly, civilized settlement that would serve as a model for others. But the choice of debate topics—navigation of the Mississippi River—indicates that there were men who came west who had just as great an interest in their own economic plans.

Rufus Putnam quickly put into action his plans to establish Marietta as a portal that would promote the settlement of the Ohio Valley. When he first arrived at the confluence of the Ohio and Muskingum rivers, he sized up the area with a critical eye. The first "market," he wrote one associate, would be the wave of new settlers and the army. With his vision of Marietta as the hub of western settlement in mind, Putnam concerned himself with how to best lay out settlements and roads to bring produce into the city, and he tried to decide where the Ohio Company should plant "farming towns."[26]

Rufus Putnam's concerns were echoed in other locations, for commerce was to play a key role in the planning of western settlement. The same year Putnam oversaw the laying out of Marietta, John Cleves Symmes, a New Jersey judge and congressman, negotiated the purchase of a million acres of land from Congress between the Great and Little Miami rivers. The tract lay over 450 river miles from the Ohio's headwaters and opposite the Licking River that flowed north from central Kentucky, providing access to the Bluegrass region. The next spring Symmes inspected his lands, looking for just the right spot to establish a town. He reported to one of his partners the following:

> The extent of country spreading for many miles on both sides of the G[reat] Miami, is beyond all dispute equal, I believe superior in point of soil, water, & timber, to any tract of equal contents to be found in the United States. From this Egypt on Miami, in a very few years will be poured down its stream to the Ohio, the products of the country, from two hundred miles above the mouth of the G[reat] Miami; which may be principally collected at a trading town, low down on the banks of that river: here no rival city or town can divide the trade of the river.

But Symmes did not choose wisely, for he sold the site of present-day Cincinnati that same year to a man who formed a partnership with a pair of Kentuckians who intended to take advantage of the commercial possibilities kindled by Kentucky's rapid growth.[27]

With commerce central to so many plans, Rufus Putnam attracted merchants to his new settlement. Readers can turn to Wallcut's journal once more to gain a glimpse of Dudley Woodbridge's first winter in the West. He reported that Woodbridge presided over a Court of Quarter Sessions in early February, and on the morning of the twenty-first, Wallcut went to Woodbridge's store to pick up his mail and some sugar. Woodbridge was one of the merchants who received a load of flour a few days later. Thomas Wallcut could not know it, but Dudley Woodbridge and his son, Dudley Woodbridge Jr., were to play important roles in Marietta's future.

III

Woodbridge's letter seeking the particulars of "the prospects of business" in the Ohio Valley suggests careful planning, but in a separate letter to her brother, Lucy confided that she felt her husband's plan was one "verry hastily formed." Still, she wrote, "I feel reconcile'd myself to any step that will promote the interest of my family." Lucy worried that her children would not be able to make good in crowded, economically depressed Norwich. "It will be painful parting with the connections I must leave behind me," she wrote, "but the society of our friends but poorly compensates for the want of a subsistence."[28]

Woodbridge visited young Backus in the late spring of 1789, just before James embarked on a series of surveys for the Ohio Company. Dudley asked James to report on good lands to invest in and instructed him to buy shares from nonresident shareholders. Woodbridge planned to speculate in land, mills, and mines, using Backus's advance knowledge of soil and resources to his advantage. He would later import mill machinery from his father-in-law's ironworks back east. Woodbridge also discussed going into business with prominent Ohio Company stockholders such as Samuel Parsons and Griffin Greene. Parsons was the man who would suggest the topic of the legality of navigating the Mississippi River to the debating society the following winter. Marietta's prospects pleased Dudley Woodbridge, and he decided he could make his fortune there.[29]

Woodbridge left Norwich for good to set up shop in the West in early August of 1789. Lucy stayed behind to supervise the closing up of their business and their home. A young apprentice named Cushing who lived with the Woodbridges in order to learn the mercantile business kept a journal of his actions from 4 August until all was done on 5 September. Cushing closed out the business by settling the accounts with Woodbridge's customers and creditors, dealing with both in cash and goods. He also had to dispose of leftover merchandise, which included everything from violin strings to old cider barrels. More than one customer gave him strenuous arguments over the amounts due on account, but Cushing had only Woodbridge's day books to go by, and on a few occasions he refused to settle until Woodbridge himself could act. Cushing felt anxious and assured Woodbridge that he was doing his best and consulting Lucy at every turn.[30]

Cushing's diary reveals that Lucy functioned as a deputy husband in Dudley's business while he was away, and she displayed business acumen in her dealings with customers. Despite caring for six young children, Lucy kept a close eye on the young man, consulting with him every two or three days. He gave her the larger cash payments whenever they came in, and Lucy herself made decisions that were beyond an apprentice like Cushing. Apparently well versed in business practices, Lucy knew when to take cash and when to use credit. On 14 August Cushing recorded that "with Mrs. Woodbridge's consent I sold Dan Harris the barrel of rum . . . as she had rather have the money than let it go to pay debts which could be paid in notes." Lucy checked Cushing's invoices and inventory records, and she took charge of the keys, books, and building when Cushing finished closing out the business.

Lucy Woodbridge followed her husband to Ohio with some of their children in late September and arrived in Marietta in early November. As yet her husband owned no property. Woodbridge rented a home and shop, keeping a constant eye out for property to buy. The move had cost him most of what he had, but Woodbridge remained confident that he could make profitable business deals and alliances in Marietta. With his business knowledge, his experience as a lawyer, and his connections within the Ohio Company through his brother-in-law, Woodbridge must have felt that he had an excellent chance of succeeding.[31]

When Lucy first arrived, she anticipated that the first winter would be a lean one. She wrote her parents that "Mr W—has a few goods which if they were paid for might do something towards providing for his family but the profits on so small a quantity cannot I think furnish us with much more than a liveing for the winter." But her husband "flatter[ed]" her with the notion that he intended to buy a farm. Like any good eighteenth-century American, she believed that only land could insure competency and true independence for her family. And, she continued, "I hope it will be in my power to get one of my own[, for] I shall then feel secure." If she herself owned land, so much the better.[32]

Despite Lucy's fears, her husband's plans for a combination of land speculation and entrepreneurship were part of an emerging process of westward expansion that had taken shape during the latter half of the eighteenth century as men interested in commercial development began to take a keen interest in the settlement of the backcountry. Prosperous New York and Pennsylvania investors began speculating in lands in the northern Susquehanna Valley in the 1770s. Landlords and entrepreneurs sold land or rented it to tenants, erected mills, and built roads between the frontier and coastal ports. A trading center grew up near the Susquehanna's headwaters, and political leaders allocated public money to the construction of roads and ferries.[33]

This method of pushing westward worked especially well in the Ohio Valley because the river and its tributaries provided a commercial highway that would link settlements together and provide passage to markets in New Orleans. The development of the lands where the Allegheny and Monongahela rivers join to create the Ohio—the site of Pittsburgh, Pennsylvania—furnishes the earliest example. George Washington recognized the strategic value of the place in 1753 during a diplomatic mission that preceded his first disastrous military campaign against the French. Ten years later the Treaty of Paris finally confirmed British ownership of the region. Colonel John Campbell platted four squares to form a town along the Monongahela in 1764, but the settlement grew slowly. After the Penns ordered a new survey, Pittsburgh's first permanent settlers began arriving in the 1780s and 1790s. Many of them were traders seeking profit by outfitting others heading farther west and bartering for furs and skins.[34]

But Pittsburgh proved to be much more than a way station. It also functioned as a hub of settlement for the region. By the early 1780s more than thirty-three thousand people inhabited western Pennsylvania, and that number tripled by the turn of the century. Speculators bought large blocks of land, platted towns, and sold off lots. Most town proprietors had business interests spanning the spectrum from mills and ferries to ironworks and glassworks. They did all they could to attract artisans and professionals to their locales. Dudley Woodbridge intended to do the same in southeastern Ohio.[35]

Other towns grew up in the Ohio Valley farther west. Like Pittsburgh, they began as military outposts but became commercial centers after the American Revolution. A group of men scouting Kentucky in 1775 named the site of Lexington after receiving news of the famous opening skirmish of the war earlier that year. As the only major city in the early West not located on a major river, Lexington served as a center for overland migration, outfitting settlers heading for western Kentucky and Tennessee. Settlement began in 1779 when Robert Patterson and twenty-five others built a block-house, surveyed the town, and petitioned the Virginia assembly for legal status, which came in 1781.[36]

George Rogers Clark established Louisville at the falls of the Ohio in 1778 by bringing twenty families to create a permanent camp from which he could harass British forces and their American Indian allies to the north. In 1780 the settlers petitioned Virginia's government for town status, and Virginia granted title to a group of trustees appointed by the assembly. Located at the only break in the Ohio's navigation, all goods went through Louisville, and trading parties tied up to wait days, weeks, and even months for a rise in the river that made passage over the rapids possible. One observer reported that during the first six months of 1802, eighty-five thousand barrels of flour passed through the town, two-thirds of it from Kentucky and the remainder from Ohio and the Monongahela and Allegheny valleys in western Pennsylvania.[37]

IV

Rivalry between settlements along the western rivers proved fierce. In 1789 John Cleves Symmes reported that "a *number* of towns are building on the banks of the Ohio from Pittsburgh to Louisville, and even further down the river. [E]very one of these will be aiming at some importance." Symmes complained that residents of Limestone, a settlement on the Ohio's southern bank fifty miles upriver from his purchase, lied to immigrants, telling them that settlers in southwestern Ohio had all been killed by Native Americans or had fled, scaring them into choosing Kentucky for their new homes instead.[38]

But the residents of Limestone proved to be prophetic. Before the settlements of Cincinnati and Marietta were three years old, the outbreak of war with the Delaware Indians and their allies interrupted all the carefully laid plans of the people settling Ohio. During the 1780s the American army had established numerous forts in the Western Country, but it lacked the troops to enforce peace. They tried to curtail squatters and protect surveyors, but constant warfare between whites and Ohio Indians made the region a battleground much of the time. In the late 1780s some Delaware leaders and others negotiated peace at Fort Harmar. But many of the Ohio Indians, including the Shawnee and the Miamis farther west, refused to abide by a treaty in which they had taken no part. During the fall of 1789 rumors of raids and murders traveled up and down the Ohio's length.[39]

As tensions rose the next spring between the settlers and the Ohio Indians, John Cleves Symmes reported to an eastern associate that settlers were "hovering along the Ohio's banks, fearful to go farther back into the country." This is our chance, he wrote, to sell many town lots. But war would curtail these plans, and Symmes eventually retreated back east.[40]

That summer, white and Indian attacks continued unabated. Colonel Josiah Harmar led troops from Fort Washington (at the site of present-day Cincinnati) against Indian villages in northeastern Indiana. They burned two settlements but achieved no real victory. Another expedition of fourteen hundred, led north by Arthur St. Clair the next year, resulted in nearly one thousand dead or wounded. The United States attempted to return to the policy of negotiating peace over the next two years. But with confidence inspired by earlier victories and British support from Canada, the Ohio Indians refused to consider anything less than a boundary between whites and Indians at the Ohio River itself.

Marietta's settlers lived under siege. During the winter of 1791, one short year after Wallcut's rather uneventful stay, Indians attacked the Big Bottom, a settlement thirteen miles up the Muskingum River, killing twelve. Afterward, settlers abandoned the outer settlements and retreated to blockhouses and stockades in Marietta and Belpre. Dudley Woodbridge's business remained fairly healthy during the war, thanks to opportunities it furnished: he supplied goods to the army and members of the local militia in exchange for their pay vouchers and sold goods to the army directly as well. In 1794 Woodbridge noted that "[m]y principle remittance is by militia order." He also received army warrants that aided him in his quest to speculate in land.[41] Most of the fighting took place to the west of Marietta, and goods came through Pennsylvania and down the Ohio unimpeded.

Westerners clearly expected the federal government to come to their aid. In addition to the Indian wars, rumors circulated of war with Spain, and in early 1794 Woodbridge wrote a friend that if the United States did not go to war with the British, he "must quit the Ohio." He later wrote another associate that the proximity of Canada lay behind his fears; unless the United States sent more troops, the family would leave, rather than risk becoming British subjects.[42]

Woodbridge did not know it when he wrote, but the worst of the fighting would be over before the summer was out. During the fall and winter of 1793–1794, General Anthony Wayne established Fort Greenville about one hundred miles north of Cincinnati and continued to train his men there. With better troops, better preparation, and carefully secured supply lines, Wayne defeated the Ohio Valley Indians at the Battle of Fallen Timbers on 20 August 1794. One year later at the Treaty of Greenville, Native Americans ceded lands in the southern and eastern part of the Northwest Territory to the United States.

After returning to Ohio in 1795, Symmes wrote his eastern associate that with the conclusion of the war, the township his friend owned had been "reduced [by] more than one-half of its numbers of inhabitants . . . and the cabins are of late deserted by dozens in a street." The people left to find other lands farther back in the woods. Early the next year Symmes noted that some Native Americans had appeared, interested in trading skins, but Cincinnati's twenty merchants had no interest in doing business with them. "The President's plan of fixing traders and stores of Indian goods along the frontiers," he wrote, "I think is very judicious."[43] Obviously Symmes concluded that whites and Indians could not live side by side, sharing the land.

Peace had come at last to southern Ohio. During the war itself, traveler and botanist André Michaux passed through Pittsburgh, counted 250 houses, and noted that the number increased yearly. He reported that the ditches in which the French entrenched themselves at Fort Duquesne were still visible, but Americans were destroying the British fort that came after and using the bricks to build houses. After the war in 1796 another traveler, Francis Baily, observed that everything destined for the Ohio Valley passed through Pittsburgh: "Through this town is the great channel of emigration to those countries lying on each side of the Ohio." Most Pittsburgh residents were either storekeepers or artisans. They occupied themselves with building boats and packing provisions for the stream of immigrants passing through on their way west. Pittsburgh had become a portal indeed and would serve as the main entrepôt to southeastern Ohio and western Virginia in the decades to come. The town's population more than tripled to over fifteen hundred during the last decade of the eighteenth century.[44]

Peace came to Kentucky, too. As the commercial center of the Bluegrass region, Lexington's population grew from eight hundred thirty-five in 1790 to nearly eighteen hundred ten years later. Perhaps a quarter of that number was slaves. The town was larger than Pittsburgh and twice the size of Cincinnati. At the falls of the Ohio, Louisville grew more slowly. Its population stood at fewer than four hundred in 1800, and there, too, perhaps a quarter of the residents were slaves.[45]

The history of Marietta's first years brings into focus the emerging image of frontier settlements as portals rather than hedges or barriers during the early republic. In the earlier colonial period, people thought of "the frontier" as the point of the colonists' farthest expansion into the wilderness, making it either a buffer against Indian attack, a backcountry isolated from the mainstream of the life of the colony, or a hinterland that absorbed goods from coastal communities. The Marietta settlers, on the other hand, crossed the Appalachian Mountains and put themselves near the headwaters of a mighty transport system that flowed to the west, away from the old world and on to a "new" continent. They intended to create a gateway through which those moving farther west could pass. Although eastern merchants supplied them with wares, westerners intended to make their own profits by selling in New Orleans rather than simply exchanging their produce for finished goods. Dudley Woodbridge, Rufus Putnam, and John Cleves Symmes envisioned a mighty future nation by looking westward down the river, not back over their shoulders to the Atlantic coast. The interior of the continent was there for the taking, and they planned to be at the forefront of that effort. The first residents of Marietta, Ohio, planned to harness a river to claim a continent, not simply to carve a New England village out of the wilderness.

2

Planting a Place

Having ousted the Native Americans who called the Ohio Valley home, white inhabitants could at last turn their full attention to settling the region. Different groups had different roles to play, but the goals and the methods they used to accomplish them meshed together well as they strove to transform space into a place to call home. Speculators made the land accessible, trailblazers opened up routes to the interior, farmers came west to establish new family nuclei, and merchants provided the links between East and West necessary to keep farmers supplied with goods and to allow a commercial economy to grow. When the election of Thomas Jefferson cut off the patronage network of Marietta's Federalists, it would prove to be the commercial networks of merchants such as Dudley Woodbridge that allowed the town to flourish.

I

Of land speculators who based their operations in Marietta, Benjamin Ives Gilman proved to be the most prominent, eclipsing the older men who had originated the venture. In 1795 he wrote his kinsman in Congress to express his hope that "Whenever Congress opens their Lands for Sale . . . it will be under such restrictions, as will prevent Speculators, with large Capitals from engrossing." But in 1810, just fifteen years later, Gilman stood sixth on a list of men who owned the most acreage in Ohio. The top man owned over forty-one thousand acres, and Gilman only a little over half that much, but he led the list of men with the most individual pieces of property—127 in all. Much of the capital needed for his speculations came from Congressman Nicholas Gilman, but the total cannot be ascertained.[1]

Four of the five men who held more acres than the Mariettan had begun their careers as surveyors, acquiring their first property as payment for locating and surveying land for others. Like Gilman, all four had come to Ohio in the 1790s, but much of their land lay within the Virginia Military

District and the Connecticut Western Reserve. In addition to the Ohio Company Purchase in the southeastern corner and Symmes's purchase in the southwestern corner of what would soon become the state of Ohio, Congress had set aside over 3.3 million acres in the northeastern corner for the state of Connecticut to compensate it for ceding its western claims, and over 4.2 million acres in the south-central portion to the state of Virginia for the same reason and to help that state satisfy all the soldiers with military warrant claims. The lands of the Western Reserve, which contained the site of present-day Cleveland, and the lands of the Virginia Military District, which contained the site of present-day Chillicothe, ended up in the hands of ordinary farmers and townsmen—but not before they had first passed through the possession of men like Gilman.[2]

But speculators served an important purpose in the process of westward expansion. They sold land to farmers on credit, lobbied for public money and public education, supported business enterprise and manufacturing, and pushed for more and better roads. Their aim was to get rich, but the only reliable way to achieve that goal was by helping communities become established. And when public lands opened up and people had a wider choice of where they would settle, Gilman would find himself with tens of thousands of acres he could not sell. Nathaniel Massie, the chief organizer of speculation in the Virginia Military District, found himself in similar straits, and John Cleves Symmes ran afoul of the federal government over the title to his land. Land speculators took risks and often failed to realize as large a profit as they had hoped, but in the meantime, they furthered the cause of westward expansion.[3]

One of the speculators' activities that met with some success involved their demands for improved transportation. With the end of the Indian wars of the 1790s, they pushed for a road to facilitate entry into the lands of southern Ohio. The man who provided that road was Ebenezer Zane. In the company of his brothers, Zane had done some exploring in western Virginia in 1769, and he took a fancy to the land where Wheeling Creek flows to the Ohio. They staked a claim, returned the next year with their families, planted crops, and built a settlement. Later, Zane utilized Virginia's land laws to claim two four-hundred-acre plots and preempt another thousand acres because he had settled there before 1778. Over the next few years he would purchase ten thousand more acres, including the land on which present-day Wheeling, West Virginia, now stands. During the late 1780s he sold much of his land to other settlers.[4]

Being a speculator himself, Ebenezer Zane saw the possibilities of making his settlement the terminus of a road that would provide access to the Ohio Company Purchase and the Virginia Military District. In 1796 he petitioned

Congress to allow him to blaze a trail from Wheeling to Limestone, Kentucky, arguing that the road would help not only individuals, but the public as a whole. Zane also noted that ferries would be needed where the road intersected the Ohio's major tributaries to the north—the Muskingum, Hocking, and Scioto rivers. Zane promised to blaze a trail and build ferries if the government would give him the title to a six-hundred-and-forty-acre tract of land at each river crossing in exchange for military warrants in his possession. Congress quickly agreed, and Zane began his endeavor that summer.

Zane had hunted and explored the woods of southeastern Ohio for years and led survey parties as well, and his brother had participated in military expeditions there against Native Americans. With the help of his brother, his son-in-law, and a Native American ally, Ebenezer Zane blazed marks on trees and cleared underbrush, branches, and fallen trees from his path. Whenever they could, the men incorporated old trails over which the American Indians and the British had traded before the Seven Years' War, as well as paths cleared by later armies. The men completed the trail during the summers of 1796 and 1797, but for nearly a decade Zane's Trace remained a path fit only for people and horses rather than wagons.

Eventually Zane got the ferries up and running as well, and Congress granted him his land in 1800. Zane had picked his spots to cross the river's most important northern tributaries very carefully to ensure that his land would be valuable for its commercial possibilities. His tract on the Muskingum lay where Licking Creek entered the larger river, and then he aimed the trace at a ford on the Hocking. Zane's tract on the Scioto stood opposite Chillicothe, established in the Virginia Military District by Nathaniel Massie in 1796. Zane never developed this tract and later sold it.

Speculators like Gilman and Massie founded towns and pushed for trailblazers like Zane to establish roads to their settlements in order to attract the largest group of new residents: farmers. The Ohio Company sold 817 shares of stock, but less than a third were purchased by people who settled in Ohio. Those intent on speculation bought the rest and sold them to others who chose Washington County as their new home.[5]

When the settlers arrived, building lean-tos or erecting tents for shelter represented their first priority; others in the area helped them build log cabins later. In both Ohio and Kentucky, settlers utilized buckeye trees because their soft wood made them easy to fell and split. The first cabins usually consisted of one room covered by a roof made of boards. Later, a loft would be added to house growing broods of children. Settlers used more boards to put up shelves and hung their clothing on wall pegs. They made their own tables, benches, and beds and fashioned chimneys from clay soil reinforced by sticks.[6]

Planting the first crop was all-important. The settlers cleared the land by felling what trees they could and girdling the others—cutting a groove around a tree to kill it. During the early years most settlers planted corn. It fed the family and the stock and could be turned into whiskey. Most added turnips to their diet, and visitors reported that New Englanders also grew pumpkins in abundance. Hunting and trapping deer, bear, opossums, and wild turkeys and gathering nuts and fruit from the woods rounded out the frontier diet.[7]

Planning for and surviving the winter took up all the settlers' time during their first year in the West. Once past the initial stage, most tried to obtain livestock, especially a milk cow, as well as hogs who could take care of themselves by foraging in the woods. By the third year, settlers began to think about marketing surplus crops. The first market usually involved newly arriving immigrants who came west with a little cash to purchase their first supply of food, seed, and tools. As life improved, frame houses replaced log cabins.[8]

The farmers who settled on Ohio Company lands went about securing their homes—creating a place—through traditional extended kin networks. Men came west accompanied by brothers and sons, and daughters and sons-in-law followed patriarchs. William Dana, a Continental Army captain from Massachusetts, had sunk all his capital into continental currency in 1788. When that depreciated, he was forced to move to Amherst, New Hampshire, where his brother lived. He rented a farm there, and earned extra cash as a carpenter and deputy sheriff. In 1789 he decided to move to the banks of the Ohio to become a landowner once more. A young man of twenty-four named Joseph Barker married Dana's eldest child, Elizabeth, and they followed Captain Dana to the Ohio Valley. Other examples abound. Israel Putnam Jr. came to Marietta with his grown sons, and Ichabod Nye followed his father-in-law, Benjamin Tupper, to Marietta. The Alcocks, Corners, and Thornileys came all the way from England to settle in Ohio; each family included a father, a mother, nearly grown children, and grown children with families of their own.[9] Although they corresponded with other family members left behind, these men and women set up new family nuclei in the West and together built tight-knit local communities.

If a young man did not have money to purchase land, he could agree to settle a donation tract—a hundred-acre plot given to anyone willing to live on the far outskirts of the settlement and aid in protecting Marietta from American Indians. The head of one of the most successful and persistent of the New England families to reside in Washington County got his start in just such a manner, although he had family in the area to provide help if needed.

Despite sharing William's surname, Benjamin Dana's ties were to the Putnams—he was the nephew of Israel Putnam Jr. and thus David Putnam's cousin.[10]

Benjamin Dana left behind a journal that reveals just how families and neighbors worked together to make their local communities grow. Dana came to Ohio in the spring of 1794 in the company of another cousin, David's brother, Israel Putnam III. David and Israel's father, a stockholder in the Ohio Company, had removed to Belpre only a short time before. Benjamin managed to farm his donation tract as a single man with no children by providing labor to area farmers who in turn lent him oxen and equipment. In May Dana plowed and planted corn for Timothy Goodale one day and another farmer the next. He planted corn for a man named Davis and then helped Goodale build a fence. The next week he plowed his own land and planted corn, then he helped a farmer named Pierce. Davis helped Dana with his land the following day, then Dana spent time planting corn for a man named Loring, and then for Goodale again. One day Dana helped Captain Miles raise a barn, attending a ball there afterward. Other social events combined with work included shooting and exploring trips with other men on Sundays. He used Miles's oxen one day and Putnam's hoes another. Dana worked on the Curtis farm, and Curtis worked on Dana's the next week. After the harvest, Dana delivered his corn by boat to Cincinnati and traveled on to New York. He returned to Ohio the next year and obtained land in Waterford, where he settled down to raise a family.[11]

In addition to the networks of exchange between family and neighbors, Dana's diary reveals a life of toil. The task of making such a life livable fell to merchants who provided farmers with access to the kinds of goods they needed to maintain a reasonable level of comfort. In addition to necessities such as tools and cloth, merchants provided the settlers with looking glasses, pins, china, gloves, shadow boxes, inkstands, candlesticks, hooks, buttons, locks, and chocolate.[12]

Farmers wanted something besides subsistence as they built new homes in the West, and it was their local merchants who provided what they craved. In and about Louisville, Kentucky, in the 1790s, customers eagerly sought British tableware, pewter, and tea, and one farmer exchanged surplus corn for a set of cups and saucers. Rather than relying solely on homespun, farmers' wives demanded British textiles, even if they had to pay for cloth with butter and other produce. Consumer goods probably served pioneers in a variety ways—as proof of elite status in a society in flux, as signs of hospitality and neighborliness, as a link to the past they had left behind, and as a representation of their belief that in the future, life would be better and more refined in the West.[13]

But even though demand for goods was high, setting up shop in the West proved to be anything but a simple task. The journal of one merchant who sought to make a fortune in the Ohio Valley reveals the rhythms of trade that existed there in the late eighteenth century. Like Thomas Wallcut, Boston merchant John May acted as an agent for a group of Ohio Company stockholders. He visited Marietta in 1788 and had the first frame house constructed there. May returned home for the winter but came west once more in 1789 to establish a business in Wheeling, western Virginia, ninety miles from the amenities of Pittsburgh and a little over halfway to Marietta. He rented half a building in which another merchant had set up shop at the opposite end. In his journal, May noted that boats going up and down the Ohio stopped there, and "I am handy to the farmers and can watch the marketts of Marietta and send them supplies of provisions when wanted." May had come west with an associate named Breck but took a dislike to him early on. He sent Breck on to Marietta with a portion of the goods to sell what he could and send back pertinent news from time to time.[14]

May opened for business on 13 August, and over the next few days, many men from the surrounding neighborhood came in to look over his goods, but few made purchases. The early half of the second week passed in much the same manner, but on Thursday he reported that changes in the moon had "opperated on the feelings of the women," and they came by his store, spending approximately six pounds in cash between them. That Saturday, he spent the whole day exchanging goods for furs and deerskins. During his third week of business, he prepared and packed the pelts but did little other business. The fourth week proved slower still.

May's second month of business opened with a good day as people from Marietta came upriver and spent about twelve pounds cash in his store. During that fifth week, he pickled some peaches his landlord had brought in to sell to the ladies down the river. Business picked up near the end of his sixth week. That Thursday he outfitted two boats heading for Kentucky, and on Friday he once again did a steady trade of goods for pelts. The next week passed without incident. He did a little trade at the beginning of the eighth week, and that Saturday he took in seventy deerskins and two hundred pounds of ginseng.

May's interest in ginseng grew out of the beginning of the China trade in the new United States during the 1780s. The roots of the ginseng plant were much sought after in China for their medicinal qualities. Jesuit missionaries first reported ginseng growing in North America in the early eighteenth century. Under the mercantilist system, residents of the English colonies had to trade ginseng through London. Immediately after the Revolution, however, American merchants discovered that cargoes of ginseng sent to China could be exchanged very favorably for tea and other goods. Profits were large, and Philadelphia's China trade began.[15]

May's business really took off during his final month, which began in early October. He sold some goods at retail, but mostly traded for fourteen hundred pounds of pelts and over a ton of ginseng. Once he traded for butter, presumably to sell to his neighbors. During that last month, he spent his days either in trade or in preparing and packing the pelts and ginseng for shipment. Breck, his associate, returned from Marietta at the end of May's third month on the Ohio and arranged to purchase the remaining goods for 190 pounds cash. A week before May was due to depart, "a Mrs [Dudley] Woodbridg[e] and young family from Norwich arrived," and the next day he "assisted in fitting out" the group as they headed for Marietta. Over the next week May settled all his accounts and set out for the East on 5 November. He shipped the goods by wagon and rode the whole way on horseback, stopping to do business in Baltimore, Philadelphia, and New York before arriving home in Boston on 16 December.

May's journal reveals that some weeks proved very busy for western merchants and others tediously slow. There was some cash to be had, but most of his trade took the form of barter. Because May never returned, however, in order to examine the ups and downs of a mercantile venture that flourished in the Ohio Valley, we must turn to the career of Dudley Woodbridge.

Like May's, Woodbridge's earliest business consisted mostly of local barter. He received much whiskey as payment for goods, and in turn sold the liquor to men working in town, many in the employ of the Ohio Company. The townsmen paid Woodbridge in work—plowing a garden, doctoring a cow, killing a calf, bringing in stock, carting rails, or drawing millstones. Some paid with venison, which, like the whiskey, Woodbridge sold in Marietta to other residents. Transactions between three parties were quite common. After Henry Rockwell bought tea, a looking glass, and other goods from Woodbridge in exchange for work carting, a third man paid Woodbridge for his goods with a note he held from Rockwell, thus increasing Rockwell's debt to Woodbridge. Similar transactions appear in the books of merchants in other Ohio towns and in Kentucky as well.[16]

Besides the goods Woodbridge received from local hunters and farmers, he also sold cloth, tools, thread, tobacco, powder, wine, and coffee, which he obtained at six to twelve month's credit from his Philadelphia counterparts. He generally paid his eastern accounts when he made his twice-yearly journeys to Philadelphia to purchase goods, and other western merchants did the same. It took between three and four weeks for large covered wagons pulled by four-horse teams to bring goods from the East. One traveler com-

The Honorable Dudley Woodbridge (1747–1823). *Courtesy of the Ohio Historical Society.*

plained that his group had broken seven axletrees while crossing the mountains. Goods were unloaded and stored at Pittsburgh when the river ran low or froze over. During the spring and fall, when the Ohio was navigable, goods would be loaded onto boats and shipped down river.[17]

In the decade before he moved west, Woodbridge bought his goods from merchants in Boston and New York. He transferred some hardware and dry goods (textiles and goods made of cloth) from his store in Norwich to Marietta in the fall of 1789 and began stocking his new establishment with goods from Philadelphia. The majority of his business dealings went through the Adgate family by way of the firms of Westcott and Adgate, Andrew Adgate, and Webster, Adgate and White. Daniel Adgate apparently served as a western agent in Pittsburgh for all three firms, handling storage and transportation of goods from there to the Ohio Country. Woodbridge also acquired whiskey, flour, butter, and livestock from his neighbors, other western merchants, and traders on the Ohio River.[18]

John May had shipped ginseng and pelts east over the Appalachian Mountains, but such a plan was only worth the expense because those articles brought in high profits in relation to their weight. Most western merchants shipped flour, whiskey, and other bulky items to Atlantic markets west and south down the Ohio and Mississippi rivers through New Orleans. Before the arrival of steamboats, virtually all traffic on western rivers went downstream. A trip upstream from New Orleans to Louisville took three arduous months or more. In 1807 more than eighteen hundred boats arrived in New Orleans from the north, but only eleven departed back up the river.[19]

As Woodbridge attempted to establish his business, he had to overcome a series of obstacles. Woodbridge estimated that a shipment which arrived a month late in the spring of 1793 cost him two hundred dollars in sales. The limited market during the Indian wars meant that competition between merchants was keen, and whoever received their goods first made what money was to be had. The main army sometimes moved through, heading west, days before a big shipment arrived—those sales were lost, although the local militia represented a continual market during the summer. Another time Woodbridge wrote that goods he had ordered in January "did not arrive seasonably to answer a particular purpose for which I designed them," indicating that, once again, he took a loss.[20]

Reliable shipping presented a problem as well. Woodbridge believed that shipments arrived late because the middleman in Pittsburgh did not get them out on time. Once he complained that his Pittsburgh correspondent had carelessly stored his goods in a damp cellar, and when they finally arrived, the dry goods were wet, the tea was musty, and many goods had sustained other damage. In October of that same year, he lamented that none of his communications to Philadelphia had been received. Woodbridge speculated that due to the yellow fever epidemic, his messengers had refused to enter the city and simply "scattered" his letters. No matter how good his markets were, Woodbridge was at the mercy of forces beyond his control— middlemen in Philadelphia and Pittsburgh, sickness in eastern cities, wagoners taking his goods across Pennsylvania, and ship captains on the Ohio River. But he was not the only one to suffer. After one particularly lengthy period without supplies, Woodbridge wrote that "our women have not a shoe to their feet nor any tea to drink."[21]

A merchant named Charles Greene provided Woodbridge's main competition. When trade was slack in the summer of 1793, Woodbridge wrote that business would have been even worse if Greene had not taken his goods farther down the river. At another time, Woodbridge referred to Greene getting shipments on time and scooping sales while Woodbridge's sat in a warehouse at the Ohio's headwaters. In a different letter Woodbridge complained that Greene sold linen cheaper than he could and speculated that rapid price fluctuations had allowed Greene to buy at a lower price.[22]

Such times did pass, however. By 1800 Woodbridge's ledgers indicate that the first stage of his business had ended as farmers flooded into the Ohio Company's lands. Rather than exchanging goods for army vouchers or work from company employees, Woodbridge began to take in larger quantities of corn, rye, oats, and wheat.[23]

Perhaps Woodbridge's most important contribution to his community involved helping craftsmen become established. General merchants created a diversified economy by helping artisans make a start. Woodbridge had tin brought in, and the whitesmith paid his account with cups, providing Woodbridge with goods to sell. Coopers paid with barrels, blacksmiths with nails and horseshoeing services, tailors with coats and trousers, and tanners with leather. At the other end of the territory, the firm of Smith and Findlay also traded tin for cups. When artisans first came into their Cincinnati store, the partners carefully wrote down their specialty, taking note of the arrival of a brick maker, a butcher, a saddler, a carpenter, an artificer, a tailor, a shoemaker, and a rope maker between the spring of 1796 and the fall of 1797. Woodbridge listed occupations next to his customers' names, too.[24]

Smith and Findlay did additional business outfitting traders with eastern goods, typically charging them 25 percent of the total price for the service, in addition to transport costs. One of their customers, a man named John Matthews, bought eighty pounds worth of goods from the firm in May 1796, with smaller purchases to follow in the coming months. He paid back most of the cost by the next summer with an equal amount of raccoon, bear, beaver, and wildcat furs on the one hand, and cash on the other. The final twenty pounds of Matthews's payment consisted mostly of three due bills from another Smith and Findlay customer who first owed Matthews but ended up in deeper debt to the two partners, as well as a small note on Matthews himself for the balance.[25]

By 1800, then, Cincinnati and Marietta had become real, if small, towns with merchants and artisans who serviced the needs of farmers in hinterlands that stretched along the Ohio, Muskingum, Kanawha, Licking, and Miami rivers and the smaller creeks that flowed into them. Southern Ohio blossomed after the Indian wars, with speculators like Gilman and Massie, trailblazers like Zane, farmers like Dana, merchants like Woodbridge, Smith, and Findlay, and traders like Matthews all playing vital roles in the region's development.

II

Woodbridge's Marietta did not grow to be the commercial hub of the Ohio Valley, but Smith and Findlay's Cincinnati would indeed emerge as the "Queen City" of the West in the decades that followed—at least in part because the federal government established Fort Washington there during the war with the Ohio Indians in 1792. At the center of military operations in the West, early Cincinnati merchants reaped economic windfalls as suppliers of an army, the needs of which Woodbridge could only serve when it happened to pass through his town. Even after the Treaty of Greenville, the infusion of cash fueled the growth of trade. Between 1 June 1796 and 31 May 1797, Smith and Findlay handled over twenty-two hundred transactions. Army officers, their families, and the United States itself (in the form of building and office supplies) accounted for a little over three hundred of them. A substantial number of the rest of the transactions—it is not clear precisely how many—involved ordinary soldiers. Large quantities of paper money went through the partners' hands, and they received many "crowns," or specie, as well.[26] But most important for Cincinnati, land in the Miami Valley proved to be flatter and richer than that of the lower Muskingum Valley above Marietta. As soon as the United States expelled Native Americans from southern Ohio completely, boats bypassed the Ohio Company Purchase and headed farther west.

Rufus Putnam's world came under siege in 1800 with the election of Thomas Jefferson, and then collapsed altogether in 1803 when Ohio became a state. Putnam had controlled local politics in Washington County and Marietta from 1790 to 1803, and with the power of a federal appointment as surveyor-general and a judgeship behind him, Putnam served as the town's principal leader. He appointed some officers, and his recommendations to Governor St. Clair and Congress carried weight for other territorial posts. But settlers poured in from the backwoods of Virginia and the mid-Atlantic states. They settled along the Miami and Scioto river valleys in the 1790s, and many of them would later become Jeffersonian Republicans. These men had no ties to the federal government, and they wanted to establish local control within Ohio. They sought to replace the federal patronage system with local competition for offices—building their own patronage system in the process. After the election of Jefferson as president, they called for frequent elections and an Ohio state government based on a strong legislative and a weak executive branch.[27]

While the Virginians wanted statehood as soon as possible, New Englanders did not. The Revolutionary War veterans who settled in Marietta may have owed their political appointments to Governor St. Clair's patronage, but they also kept national goals in mind for western settlement. They worried that the Virginians were too committed to localism to make virtuous, responsible citizens. For his part, St. Clair believed the Virginians were too selfish and materialistic to take charge of so important an undertaking as the settlement of the West. In 1801 the electors of Marietta met and resolved to oppose statehood on the grounds that Ohio's society had not yet developed a stable order and needed to remain under the paternalistic eye of St. Clair and the federal Congress. But the more numerous Jeffersonian Republicans carried the day, and Ohio became a state in 1803.[28]

The Revolution of 1800 shook Marietta's political structure to its very foundations. Some men who had owed their offices to Putnam began opposing the old general shortly thereafter. They sided with the Virginians in territorial politics, and when the southerners emerged as winners, these men received appointments in the new state government. Rufus Putnam brought his own political career to a close when Jefferson replaced him as surveyor-general of the United States in September of 1803.[29]

Despite his disappointment, Rufus Putnam stayed in Marietta for the rest of his days. Benjamin Ives Gilman, another Federalist, did not. Gilman had ambitious plans for Marietta, but his attitudes changed after 1808 when Jefferson's embargo destroyed his shipbuilding enterprise. On the effects of the embargo, Lucy Woodbridge wrote, "our streets are as empty and our countenances as sober as if we were a remote Yankee village, and our days a continuous Sunday." That same year, Gilman's daughter Jane, Dudley Woodbridge Jr.'s wife, died in childbirth, and soon after, Benjamin's father, Joseph, died as well. Although Benjamin had initially reassured his fiancée that Marietta had the look of a New England town, he began to complain that Marietta now had all the problems of a "new settlement," including poor schools. He began to see Marietta as a failed experiment, and his discontent grew as his fortunes declined. Perhaps Gilman felt that the national government had abandoned him (the navy refused to buy his surplus ships in 1808); it had clearly abandoned Marietta. In 1812 he returned to Philadelphia and went into the business there, leaving behind his plans to be part of the building of the new nation. While visiting sons who had pushed on to settle in Illinois, he fell ill and died at age sixty-eight in 1833.[30]

Benjamin Ives Gilman believed that he pursued the national interest, not as a poor relative, but as a leader. With the ties between early Marietta leaders and the Federalist government, he and others could make some claim to being central to the planning of what the new nation would be, rather than just an appendage to the older states. Undoubtedly he would have understood perfectly the lament of another land speculator—John Cleves Symmes. When Symmes ran into problems establishing the validity of his purchase in the southwestern corner of the Ohio territory, he defended his claim by asserting that men like him "push[ed] forward to make settlements . . . extend[ing] the empire of the United States and reclaim[ing] from savage men and beasts a country that may one day prove the brightest jewel in the regalia of the nation."[31] When Gilman's ties to the federal government disappeared, like Symmes he must have felt betrayed, and his hopes withered.

Marietta failed to become all that Woodbridge hoped for, too, but he stayed anyway. He had served as a territorial judge and lost his political clout at the same time Putnam and Gilman did. Perhaps he persisted because, like Putnam, he had reached an age when retirement seemed attractive—Gilman was still a fairly young man. But in addition, Woodbridge had forged other ties to the outside world. His son, Dudley Woodbridge Jr., thirteen years Benjamin's junior, would improve on his father's business practices and help create new links between East and West and within the West itself. When the Federalists lost control of the national government, and Ohio's government as well, it was the commercial connections of Woodbridge, his son, and their fellow merchants that would allow Marietta to survive, grow, and change. Connections based on credit and markets proved to be more flexible and adaptable than the political links of the Federalists had been.

As speculators, trailblazers, entrepreneurs, and settlers all worked to settle the southeastern corner of the Ohio Territory, Marietta's early history reveals the different but complementary goals and strategies of farmers and merchants. The expansion of farmers involved a search for security as they sought the independent status of landowner. The farmers' independence—the competency they valued above all—depended in many ways on the support they received from kin and neighbors. Farmers came west to set up new core families who survived with the aid of local neighborhood networks and flourished with the aid of merchants. In contrast, the expansion of merchants was wholly speculative. They moved west seeking profits, and in the process, they extended networks of trade that bound regions together by links of capital and credit. Merchants created the connections that would insure that the United States would be more than a collection of isolated villages. Federal leaders thus found their dreams of expanding the new nation fulfilled not in politics, but in business, for commercial connections between East and West had long been forged by the time Ohio attained statehood. When merchants like Dudley Woodbridge helped settle a town like Marietta, that town became part of an economic network. Because of the eastern links of western merchants, the new United States could set out to claim a continental empire and still survive as a nation.

PART II THE WESTERN COUNTRY

The Western Country. During the first three decades of the nineteenth century, residents considered the Ohio Valley to be a place—their home. The commercial world of the Ohio River united the people on both banks as westerners. Limestone, Kentucky, had become Maysville; Springfield, opposite of Zanesville on the Muskingum, would later be part of that city; and Harmar is now part of Marietta.

The

Indiana

Illinois

Wabash River

Vincennes

Ohio River

Greenville

Green River

Russelville

Mississippi River

Nashville

Murfreesboro

Tennessee

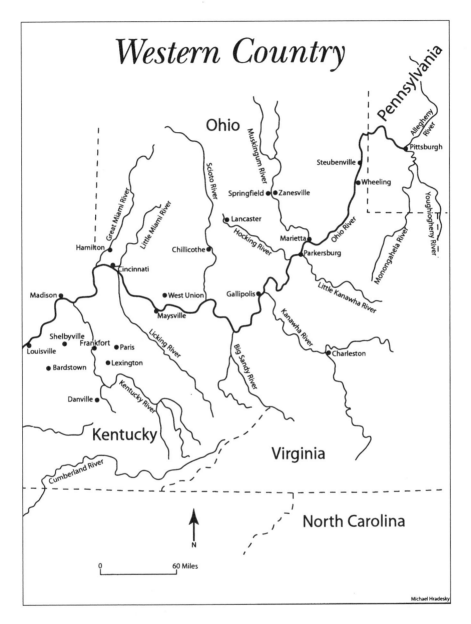

Western Country

Pennsylvania

Ohio

Muskingum River

Scioto River

Great Miami River

Little Miami River

Steubenville

Pittsburgh

Allegheny River

Wheeling

Springfield ● ● Zanesville

Lancaster

Hocking River

Marietta

Ohio River

Youghiogheny River

Hamilton

Chillicothe

Parkersburg

Monongahela River

Cincinnati

Little Kanawha River

Madison

West Union

Gallipolis

Maysville

Kanawha River

Licking River

Shelbyville

Frankfort ● Paris

Louisville

Bardstown

Lexington

Big Sandy River

Charleston

Danville

Kentucky River

Kentucky

Virginia

Cumberland River

North Carolina

N

0   60 Miles

Michael Hradesky

By the turn of the century, the ex-colonists had succeeded in exiling the Ohio Indians from their homes. The land across the mountains now rested firmly in the hands of the new United States, laying the foundation for an inland empire, and the trickle of settlers down the Ohio would become a flood. As Rufus Putnam and others intended, newly independent Americans followed them west through portals, and the new settlers began the process of transforming space into place—home, where people live, work, and raise families. One aspect of a peoples' sense of place is "pragmatic"—it grows from the way in which their economy functions.[1] As they adapted to life in the West, the second generation of Mariettans would create a riverine economic network in which the Ohio River served as the heart of their world. They would come to call home "the Western Country," an inclusive term that signified their ties to people and communities north and south of the Ohio all along the river's length.

The commercial economy westerners built upon the Ohio River and its tributaries rested on the relationship between three levels of urban development. The first order of towns were small, local communities which contained not much more than a mill and perhaps a country store where farmers could buy goods and exchange news. The second order of towns were subregional hubs. Merchants in these medium-sized towns gathered produce for export from the small communities that made up their hinterlands and imported eastern goods to supply the country shopkeepers. In turn, subregional hubs made up the hinterlands of the third order of towns—larger towns or cities that served as entrepôts to the region. Merchants in these cities supplied settlers with what they needed as they made the last leg of the journey to their new homes.[2]

This network grew because merchants like Dudley Woodbridge Jr. focused their energy on building connections. The first stage of economic growth involved establishing towns and hinterlands and connecting them to entrepôts and the East. Woodbridge made Marietta a subregional hub for southeastern Ohio and northwestern Virginia. The second stage of economic growth involved connecting subregional hubs to other entrepôts and hubs within the Ohio Valley. During the second decade of the nineteenth century, Dudley Woodbridge Jr.'s mercantile business expanded to encompass the Ohio Valley from Pittsburgh to Louisville. The regional economy created by Woodbridge and others like him bound westerners together, north and south across the river.

❧

3

Creating a Subregional Hub

At eighteen years of age in early January of 1797, Dudley Woodbridge Jr. embarked on a buying trip from Marietta to Philadelphia at the behest of his father. He safely crossed the Ohio River on his way to Wheeling, eighty miles upstream on the river's eastern shore in western Virginia. But two days later he encountered difficulties crossing one of the Ohio's many tributaries. He recounted this event to his father in a matter-of-fact report written a month later:

> [I] attempted to [ford] Grave Creek, rode in, the current very swift, my horse swam & cou'd not get up the opposite bank, wheeled about, I jumped off & the current carried me about 7 rods before I cou'd make the shore my boots being full of water & my clothes heavy, I caught hold of a twig which gave way and I went in head and ears but finally got out, rode 12 miles to Wheeling Creek & dryd myself.[1]

Thus did Dudley Woodbridge Jr. survive his baptism in western waters and his initiation into the hazardous life of making one's living on the Ohio River during the opening decades of the nineteenth century.

Dudley Woodbridge Jr. played a key role in turning Marietta into one of the second order of western towns—a subregional hub in the hinterland of Pittsburgh, Pennsylvania. In order to accomplish this, Woodbridge engaged in a ceaseless quest for connections. Getting a start in the West meant gaining a toehold in the business of an established entrepreneur—an endeavor in which having a merchant father put him a step ahead of the competition. Once settled, Woodbridge found farmers and artisans looking to him to market their surpluses and import eastern manufactured goods. Dudley Woodbridge Jr. would also find that running a business involved nurturing a wide variety of human bonds, from overseeing clerks and dealing with shopkeepers in Marietta's hinterland to directing the men who ran branches of the central firm in other locales. By 1810 merchants in the town of Marietta, Ohio, provided services for others in communities along the Muskingum

River and its tributaries, along a section of the Ohio itself, and in towns in northwestern Virginia as well.

I

The first set of connections a young man wishing to become a merchant in the West had to foster were those that would grant him entry into the world of commerce. Family ties provided the surest path.

Dudley Woodbridge expected his sons Dudley and William to join him in the business. Eleven when his family left for Ohio, Dudley Woodbridge Jr. remained back East to attend school in Connecticut. In the fall of 1794, as Dudley's sixteenth birthday approached, his father began to make plans to place his training in the hands of the firm Webster, Adgate and White in Philadelphia. He made the necessary arrangements the following January and sent for the young man. A year later the seventeen year old had charge of his father's store on the banks of the Ohio for the first time while the elder Woodbridge made a trip to Philadelphia. Father wrote son from the East with the following advice: "I feel not a little anxious how you may get along in [the] Business of Recording & Store together with the Collections necessary to be made, should you have more business than you can attend to, It will be well to get some Person to assist you in Recording[,] you will consult your Mama who to get."[2]

Woodbridge also advised his son to consult with Mr. Gilman or his Uncle Matthew Backus about collecting debts but added, "in all matters I wish you to consult & Advise with your Mama." Lucy had proven her capacity for business long before; her husband thought her at least as capable of supervising their eager young son as any well-established Philadelphia merchant. Nor would his mother fade from sight once Dudley Woodbridge Jr. assumed the reins of power. In the fall of 1802 she wrote her son William that with Dudleys junior and senior out of town, "my time is so wholly occupied with the store, sister is obliged to seek amusements abroad."[3]

Dudley Woodbridge Jr. learned to master the rules of trade, though not without difficulty. In the summer of 1796 Lucy wrote William that "Dudley has the happiness to meet your Papa's approbation—he is extremely attentive to business." Two weeks later she told him that Dudley would write soon if he had time, but that he was "very busy in the store." However, father was not always pleased with son. Not long after Dudley's near drowning in Grave Creek, the elder Woodbridge sent additional instructions on to Philadelphia, warning the novice to pick goods slowly. "Be not in too great a hurry," the seasoned veteran wrote; "the sales [here] are rather dull, especially [for] *highpriced, damaged* goods. . . . [Choose only] *well selected goods.*" Dudley

Woodbridge seems to have been a stern father. When informing William of the actions of a third son, John (known to the family as Jack), Lucy wrote that he was "stepping out of the track [his father] had marked." Little evidence survives of Dudley's attitude toward the older man, but while on another trip to Philadelphia in the summer of 1798, he did send a revealing letter to his brother. He wrote William that he had just spent hours reading and answering one of Papa's "lengthy letters." Dudley had been tempted to buy some things in the East for himself, he wrote, but "was fearful of Papa's fits of economy."[4]

Dudley Woodbridge had commenced his new life in Ohio within a year of Marietta's founding. While at war with Ohio's Native Americans in the early 1790s, Mariettans had turned their town into a fortified outpost. But by the time Dudley Woodbridge Jr. arrived, the war had ended and settlers were pouring into the countryside. Instead of a fort, the younger man found that Marietta had become the hub of settlement for southeastern Ohio. While preparing to take over the family business, he discovered that his father could barely keep up with the demand for goods. Woodbridge once sent instructions to his son in Philadelphia to "get a good supply of tin ware—tin cups especially, vast numbers are going into the woods."[5]

Others in the West took a similar path in their quest to become merchants. In 1795 Cincinnati merchant Abijah Hunt brought his twenty-two-year-old cousin, John Hunt, to establish a branch store in Lexington, Kentucky. Both put up a stake of two thousand dollars, and Abijah picked goods to sell in Philadelphia with John looking on. Most of the goods came from another cousin, John's brother, also a merchant. Abijah, with his excellent connections in the East, planned to keep the younger man stocked with goods as the new business grew.[6]

Other examples abound. In 1791 Nathaniel Hart wrote a letter from Lexington, Kentucky, to his uncle, stating that he liked the mercantile business and hoped to make the store "more profitable" to the older man soon. A man named James Trotter came to Kentucky in the 1780s and soon settled in Lexington to set up shop. He retired in 1797, and the firm came under the control of his twenty-five- and nineteen-year-old sons, Samuel and George. A little more than a decade later, Jonathan H. Hanna, an established merchant of Frankfort, Kentucky, wrote twenty-one-year-old George W. Meriwether, offering to pay good wages if the young man would run his Frankfort or Shelbyville store while he traveled east. Hanna assured Meriwether that once the young man acquired mercantile training, he would be ready to act as a full-fledged merchant upon Hanna's return. The next spring, Meriwether established his own store in Louisville, starting with nearly two thousand dollars worth of goods bought from the older man at six-month's credit.[7]

One factor did set the Woodbridges apart, however, and gave Dudley Jr. a significant advantage over rivals: the partnership of Harman Blennerhassett. Blennerhassett had arrived in Marietta in the fall of 1797 bearing a letter of introduction from Pittsburgh businessman Edward Turner. A second letter to the elder Woodbridge stated that "he is a man whom I know to be worth at least 25,000 [pounds]. Could you persuade him to set down among you I think it would be a great acquisition as monied men will give a celebrity to the settlement and consequently enhance its value." Blennerhassett proved to be the youngest son of a noted Irish family who, through the deaths of his elder brothers, had inherited a large estate. He traveled in Europe for a time, before returning to marry a niece, Margaret Agnew, thirteen years younger than he. His family was upset over the marriage as well as his support of the French Revolution, so the thirty-two-year-old Blennerhassett sold the family estates for one hundred sixty thousand dollars and sailed for New York in 1796.[8]

The elder Woodbridge and the Irishman soon became partners, and Dudley Sr.'s brother-in-law, Matthew Backus, sold Blennerhassett an island in the middle of the Ohio a few miles below Marietta so that he could officially call Virginia home and acquire slaves. It was through Blennerhassett's money and name that the Woodbridges began their association with two Philadelphia merchants who would be their most important creditors and suppliers for some time to come—Joseph Clark and Joseph S. Lewis. Intent on speculating in land, Dudley Woodbridge pulled out of the partnership and handed the business over to his son in June of 1798.[9]

Dudley Woodbridge Jr. was then a young man of nineteen and barely three years out of his apprenticeship in Philadelphia. Blennerhassett was fifteen years his senior, but the younger man ran the business and made all the significant decisions. The name of the company was, in fact, Dudley Woodbridge Jr. and Company, and the younger Woodbridge proved to be every bit as ambitious as his father. Perhaps James Backus experienced a queer sense of déjà vu upon reading the following letter written in 1799 by his nephew. Only a little more than a decade had passed since his brother-in-law had sent him a similarly staccato request for information:

> I must beg you to inform one of the necessary machinery of a rope walk, the number of men that are employed in one to advantage, the probability of being able to procure workmen in Connecticut, the price of wages, the length of time it will require a certain number of men to make into cordage a ton of hemp, the supposed expense per ton of manufacturing hemp into rope yarns—will you give me information (by post) of the above particulars as soon as you can conveniently?

And just as profit had been his father's primary motivation for moving west, Dudley wrote that he was trying to "form a variety of *plans* to grow *rich*."[10] It may have been his father's thinking and doing that gave him the ready-made connections and credit Dudley Woodbridge Jr. needed to implement his schemes, but what he did with that opportunity would be up to him.

II

Once a young merchant acquired his training and established a relationship with creditors, he next turned his attention to embedding himself in the web of exchange among his neighbors, the local farmers and artisans.

By 1810 Ohio landowners made up between 45 and 50 percent of the adult male population. The proportion of those who owned land in Marietta's Washington County stood at 43 percent. Nine out of ten Ohio landowners claimed less than 480 acres, but in rural areas, nearly every farmer had a farm of at least 40 acres. Those who rented did not expect to be tenants for more than a few years, and speculators who needed their labor allowed them access to land in exchange for work clearing and improving tracts and for a share of the crops, meaning that those without cash could make a start in the West. By 1825 57 percent of the adult men in Ohio owned land, but fewer than half of the 1810 landowners still resided in the state. In both Ohio and Kentucky, settlers displayed a high degree of mobility.[11]

African Americans made up a portion of Washington County's population from the very beginning, but they owned far less land than their white neighbors. The first African Americans came as servants with the initial wave of Ohio Company settlers and owned no land at all. By 1810 only forty-eight of Washington County's nearly six thousand residents were African American. Over half of them lived in Marietta itself, but only five were listed as heads of household. Other than the families of those five, all other African Americans listed on the census lived as dependents in white households, most of them singly, others in groups of two or three—some were clearly slaves in all but name. In 1802 one S. R. Wilson of western Virginia freed a sixteen-year-old black boy named Bob. Dudley Woodbridge Jr. then paid Wilson two hundred dollars for the privilege of making him an indentured servant until Bob reached the age of twenty-one. Of the five black household heads in Washington County, only one, Richard Fisher of Salem township, owned land. Fisher, a mulatto from Maryland, presided over a family of eight. Another household head known as "Dinah Black-woman" included three others in her household, and one other family numbered four.[12]

George Harvey, *Spring #2: Burning Fallen Trees in a Girdled Clearing—Western Scene,* Yale University Art Gallery, Mabel Brady Garvan Collection. Farmers sold the potash that resulted from burning trees to local merchants, or they exchanged it for goods. *Courtesy of the Yale University Art Gallery.*

Whether land owners or tenants, farmers initially concentrated their energy on raising hogs and corn. Piglets came along in larger numbers and at a much faster pace than calves, and instead of consuming hay, pigs foraged in the woods for acorns and nuts. As farmers sweated and toiled to clear the land, corn grew well in partially cleared fields, and families consumed most of what they grew in the form of corn bread, mush, and hominy. The market in New Orleans stood ready to absorb as much cornmeal as they could send, but unless dried and packed carefully in barrels, it molded. Corn exports usually took the form of whisky, beef, or pork. As they cleared their fields and burned the timber, farmers could sell the resulting potash to local merchants for a little cash. The merchants in turn sold it to manufacturers of soap and glass.[13]

Once farmers had guaranteed their livelihood, they turned to wheat as a cash crop. They grew wheat only in fields that had been well worked and previously used to cultivate corn, oats, or other grains. While corn grew best in the rich river bottoms of the Miami and Scioto valleys, wheat grew best in the drier hills of the eastern half of the state, north of Washington County. During the first decade of the nineteenth century, flour proved to be Ohio's biggest export as war in Europe drove up prices. Farmers and merchants shipped flour down the Ohio on flatboats in 196-pound barrels, or they sent the flour south as hard biscuits.[14]

Farmers also planted orchards as soon as they could. Apples could be pressed into cider or sold in New Orleans. Many grew peaches because the trees matured very quickly, producing fruit in just three years, and farmers could exchange peach brandy for goods with local merchants. Ohioans also cultivated pears, plums, and cherries.[15]

Just like their eastern counterparts, Ohio farmers did not focus on producing goods exclusively for either use or market—instead they did both. Mixed in with their corn, many farmers grew flax. Farm wives turned the plant fibers into cloth for family use, and they traded the "country linen" to local merchants. Linseed oil could also be bartered to men who sought it for export. Farmers grew rye to produce whiskey that could be drunk or sold, and they grew oats to feed their horses.[16]

Settlers south of the Ohio in Kentucky did the same. Women there produced their own brand of country linen to barter with merchants—"tow linen" made from hemp fibers. Other settlers gathered and dried ginseng for cash. One westerner remembered that his family and others mixed hunting with the production of saltpeter—a chemical used in the making of gunpowder. They gathered nitrates from the soil, boiled it in vats, and once the "soup" crystallized, they cooled and dried it, loaded it onto packhorses, and took it to "market." When prices were high, they stepped up production, and when prices were low, they concentrated on other endeavors.[17]

The nature of exchange between Woodbridge and his neighbors can be found in a ledger that covers the merchant's Marietta store from 1802 to 1805.[18] It contains the accounts of five hundred customers in Ohio and western Virginia. Half of the customers had to scrape together their payments from more than one source of income. Although only 20 percent of all customers who bought on credit used cash to pay their total bill, 57 percent of them used cash to pay Woodbridge at least once. Sixty-six customers (13 percent) paid some or all of their accounts with credit for labor, the majority of them under the generic categories of "work" and "hauling."

Nearly 10 percent of the customers paid their accounts with skins and furs, and another 10 percent took advantage of Marietta's boat-building industry to barter hemp. About 5 percent of the customers paid with finished goods that required a certain amount of labor—sugar, country linen, tallow, whiskey, peach brandy, and cheese. Merchants charged lower prices for goods to those who paid cash or who traded goods that they could sell easily for cash—items such as those listed above. Perhaps that is why less than 10 percent bartered agricultural products, including flax, oats, wheat, flour, hay, hay seed, clover seed, pork, beef, mutton, hogs, cattle, horses, melons, and apples. There was a market for all these goods, but prices in New Orleans fluctuated wildly on such perishables, and a profit was by no means guaranteed for merchants. Thus merchants usually charged more for their wares when farmers bartered with country produce.[19]

One in five Woodbridge customers paid with orders to be collected from third parties and notes on third parties that the merchant accepted at a discount. Many of these men worked for boatbuilder Joseph Barker or had dealings with Woodbridge's partner, Harman Blennerhassett, who paid others to build and furnish a mansion on his island. The dealings of such men obviously had a positive effect on the area's economy. Woodbridge accepted these orders and charged them to Barker's and Blennerhassett's accounts. He also lent cash to a dozen individuals, required sixty-five of his customers to sign notes for what they owed, and lodged thirty-two accounts with lawyers for collection.

Farmers were not the only customers to show up in the Woodbridge ledgers. Among those who paid in work between 1802 and 1805 were a tailor, a joiner, a comb maker, four smiths, four shoemakers, two saddlers, and two coopers who bartered their crafts and services for goods. In 1801 Dudley Woodbridge Jr. sold a store he owned in Waterford to a man named Levi Allen in exchange for $150 worth of blacksmith work. He supplied Allen with iron from western Pennsylvania, and Allen provided Woodbridge with axes, ploughs, and chains to sell. In 1806 Woodbridge lent money to Michael Graham of Wheeling to help him establish a ropewalk.[20]

There are two ledgers available for merchants in Kentucky that provide a comparison to Woodbridge's business in Ohio and western Virginia. The first was kept by an anonymous merchant in Mason County from 1797 to 1799, and contains the accounts of two hundred eleven customers. Only sixty-one (29 percent) of the customers scraped together their payments from more than one source of income. Though only 16 percent of all the customers who bought on credit used cash to pay their total bill, ninety-three (44 percent) of them used cash to pay the Kentucky merchant at least once. Thirty-four (16 percent) of the accounts contained transactions utilizing third-party notes, cash, and assumptions—a little lower than the 20 percent of Woodbridge customers, though comparable to the Marietta totals if the Ohio town's two largest employers (Blennerhassett and Barker) are excluded. A little over 10 percent of Woodbridge customers bartered with their labor, compared to a little under 10 percent in Mason County, while a similarly small proportion of customers paid with agricultural produce.[21]

The second ledger is that of Daniel Halstead, a merchant of Lexington, Kentucky, who dealt in tobacco for more than a decade beginning in 1807. From June 1809 to January 1810, nearly two-thirds of the customers (two hundred of them) did not make a payment and had their totals posted to another ledger. Nearly one-third of those who did pay used cash at least once. Sixteen bartered tobacco, one paid with a large crop of cotton, and a smaller number of customers utilized whiskey, salt, butter, and cloth. Halstead kept a separate book for his larger tobacco transactions and also accepted as payment the work of shoemakers and coopers.[22]

A few key differences between the ledgers become immediately apparent. First, one of the Mason County customers paid with the "work of a negro," and another with the "hire of a negro girl." There were slaves in northern Kentucky, though it is important to note that the wealthiest Mariettans had black servants of their own—servants with little chance to aspire to a better future. Second, the Mason County ledger seems to have covered a time when sickness invaded the area, for forty-three (20 percent) of the Mason County customers bought medicine only. It is difficult to know what impact that had on the merchant's business or on the settlers' ability to pay. Third, Halstead's ledger covers only seven months in a world in which most people (both farmers and merchants alike) met their obligations only once or twice a year. Despite these differences, a comparison of the ledgers does yield important information.

In terms of the availability of cash in the West, Halstead's numbers are the lowest but also the most suspect, because the ledger covers such a short span of time. The ledgers from Marietta, Ohio, and Mason County, Kentucky, seem to indicate that nearly half of all local customers who bought goods on credit had access to cash at one time or another, a total that includes slightly more than half of the Ohioans and slightly less than the half of the Kentuckians.[23]

Although nearly six of ten Woodbridge credit customers used cash at least once between 1802 and 1805, the amounts were typically very small. Despite this, the firm's cash account in the ledger states that Woodbridge took in $945 in sales in 1803, as well as nearly $7,000 cash for debts. Cash sales rose to $4,202 the next year, while the firm collected nearly $8,000 for debts. Turning from the ledger to a blotter covering the months of November 1804 to April 1805, it becomes apparent that Woodbridge took in some cash for sales every day—the amounts are listed in a space at the top of the day's business without names beside them. Presumably these were people not listed in the ledgers because they were not customers who bought on credit; or perhaps many of them were the same people, but occasionally they came in to buy something and paid at the time without paying off any of their debt. Marietta's location on the Ohio may have affected cash sales, though, for Woodbridge chided a man who ran a branch store at Waterford for selling too many goods for credit while taking in too little cash.[24]

There are other points of comparison between the settlers of Ohio and Kentucky involving the way westerners paid their accounts. First, the Mason County ledger seems to indicate that fewer Kentuckians than Mariettans had to use more than one method of payment, but this does not necessarily represent a more specialized economy. In the two years covered by the Mason County ledger nearly one-third of the one hundred fifty customers who were left made no payments at all, "settled" in an unknown fashion, or ran away. Second, 16 percent of Halstead customers paid with tobacco, an item that was considered equal in value to cash when exchanged for goods, a ratio comparable to the nearly 20 percent of Woodbridge customers who paid with cash-equivalent items of their own—hemp, furs, and skins. In both cases they outnumbered the number of customers who bartered with grains, stock, or meat.

Settlers came west ready to engage in commercial agriculture, but the distance from markets and the hazards of wagon and keelboat transportation often defeated them. At this stage of development, settlers ate most of the crops and stock they produced, and sold any surplus to newcomers or traded with neighbors. Merchants were intent on establishing markets, and farmers were willing to participate, producing goods for both use and market, but the full flowering of a commercial economy would come later.[25]

Relations between merchants and farmers did not always run smoothly. One obstacle to the growth of a commercial economy lay in the inability of settlers to pay, and the settlers themselves could not have liked the willingness of merchants to use lawyers to collect debts. Dudley Woodbridge Jr. once complained to Harman Blennerhassett that because "the practice of not paying debts has become so universally in vogue in and about this place," they never had more than a fraction of the proceeds of their sales on hand to use in other pursuits. But because suing men for debts was usually a slow and expensive process, when some customers paid nothing on their accounts for a year or more, Woodbridge simply transferred them to the next ledger when the old one was full. However, when in need of cash, Woodbridge twice ordered his partners in locations outside Marietta to lodge every past-due account on their books with a lawyer for collection. Farmers must have disliked the fact that when merchants sold goods on credit, the prices were much higher than goods sold for cash. The farmers grumbled, but some took advantage of the system to get things they needed without settling up for years, and other never paid at all. Merchants undoubtedly thought the high markup was necessary to protect themselves from heavy losses. [26]

Despite such signs of occasional acrimony between creditors and debtors, there is evidence that Woodbridge and the local farmers joined forces to further their economic interests by improving trade routes between town and country. In February of 1806 the citizens of Marietta organized a lottery for the purpose of constructing a bridge over the Little Muskingum River east of town. Most of the subscribers made their pledges in corn, whiskey, and labor; each pledge usually amounted to less than five dollars. Not surprisingly, most of those with cash to pledge were the town dwellers—merchants and professionals such as the Greenes, Gilmans, and Putnams. As it turned out, however, most of the cash came from the Woodbridges.[27]

Though Woodbridge and the farmers worked together to build a bridge, at other times and in other places western entrepreneurs and small holders disagreed about the path commercial development should take. In 1789 a large-scale landowner attempted to have a gristmill built on a river in Kentucky. Local residents opposed his plans, but their reasons topple the traditional explanation of wealthy capitalist versus independent farmers. Court records reveal that both sides had similar concerns. Opponents felt that the disruption of navigation caused by the mill would hamper their efforts to get tobacco to an inspection station and on to market; they seemed more concerned about tobacco, a better cash crop than corn, than having a mill to grind their grain. The two sides disagreed over whether policy should favor large or small holders, but they shared a similar market orientation.[28]

III

If a town like Marietta was to become a subregional hub rather than re-main a village with a country store or two, merchants like Dudley Wood-bridge Jr. had to create a set of connections that reached beyond the limits of their townships. To make his business grow, Dudley Woodbridge Jr. had to be an adept manager of people, whether he was instructing clerks and agents or convincing country storekeepers that he could supply them with goods. The creation of a subregional hub involved fueling the development of the town's hinterland by looking for other locations that seemed to promise growth and establishing branch stores in those locations to take advantage of emerging markets.

Because success in commerce depended so heavily on connections, as-piring merchants needed to develop skills in handling people. Dudley Woodbridge Jr. believed that a merchant who was quiet, bashful, or reserved was bound to fail. Merchants should be polite and obliging to customers. A merchant had to be sociable, pleasant, and agreeable. Running a business in the Ohio Valley involved a talent for speculation, a willingness to take risks, attention to detail, knowledge of markets, and a knack for working with people. Woodbridge's sister, Lucy, divorced her husband in 1796 and raised her son, William, in her parents' home, where the boy had ample opportu-nity to observe both his grandfather and uncle in action. At age twenty, he turned his back on trade, calling the work "drudgery" and stating that "none but those of a superior cast can hope for eminence or respectability." It is not clear if William judged his uncle to be of a superior cast or believed that Dudley lacked eminence and respectability. At any rate, Woodbridge himself seemed to thrive on the work that went into running a successful commer-cial operation.[29]

Dudley Woodbridge Jr. did have trouble on occasion living up to his own image of the ideal merchant. He admitted to his brother William that he tended to worry about situations and dwell on problems. Woodbridge also had, in his own words, a "hasty irritable temper." Once he fought with a man named Gardiner, a supplier of furs. During the dispute, Woodbridge "took up a cow skin [whip] to give him a flogging." Gardiner apparently reached for a knife, and Woodbridge began to throttle him. When the local printer tried to break the two men apart, Gardiner punched Woodbridge in the face and retreated to his office, where he "indulged himself in abusing" the merchant through the door. More than two decades later, the members of his local church nominated Woodbridge for a position of leadership, but he declined, declaring himself unfit. A short time later, the fifty-five-year-old wrote the following to one of the church's leading men:

> On Friday last I met with an entire unlooked for opposition from Mr. Holden to the moving of my warehouse which I had made engagements & preparation to have removal & in a publick conversation between us many were shown what was in me—The public evidence which I then gave that [I] was soon angry & easily provoked, have fully confirmed me in the opinion that it is not my duty to take a place for which I am not qualified.[30]

Still, Woodbridge did the best he could, and to judge by the scope of his connections and the esteem he enjoyed among his neighbors in his old age, Dudley Woodbridge Jr. mostly succeeded in controlling his temper and engendered trust in those who associated with him.

The men Woodbridge dealt with most often were his own clerks. When he took a short trip to the Hocking River in early May of 1800, Woodbridge left Mr. Dyer in charge of the store. Woodbridge instructed Dyer to sell goods for cash only for the most part, although he could extend credit to a short list of preferred customers. Woodbridge told the clerk to sleep in the store, but to take no candles inside at night. He would caution others in a similar manner in the years to come. Later that month, it was Dyer who did the traveling. He was to descend the Ohio to the mouth of the Scioto and deliver letters, to wait for replies, and to go on to Cincinnati to post them. While in Cincinnati, Dyer was to get a deed recorded without letting a rival know of Woodbridge's intentions.[31]

Woodbridge also sent clerks on excursions to Pittsburgh. In May of 1804 Woodbridge directed Henry Mills to take charge of Philadelphia goods that had been forwarded to Ebenezer Denny, the man who received and stored the firm's stock while awaiting a rise in the river. Mills was to examine the packages for damage and make sure all the goods had arrived safely. Woodbridge informed Mills that Denny had paid the wagoners who had brought the goods west, so the clerk had only to bring Denny's bill home with him. He instructed Mills to procure a boat, load the goods, buy a quantity of nails, and start for home. As he descended the river, the clerk was to stop at Steubenville for flour and at Wheeling to pick up a wayward trunk of books that Woodbridge's partner had been trying to trace for some time.[32]

In addition to instructing clerks, Woodbridge also developed relationships with traders. In the summer of 1799 he began sending letters to men in other settlements along the rivers that flowed to the Ohio or the Muskingum, offering to supply goods, whiskey, powder, and lead for them to sell in exchange for furs and skins, cash, and salt. In July and August he sent one load of goods out with a man named Silas Bingham, and a second with James White. The two men were to return any goods they could not sell, presumably in the fall, and in exchange they would receive 20 percent of the sales they did make. Other men took loads of goods that they were to trade specifically for furs to be delivered at Philadelphia.[33]

But Woodbridge soon moved on to fostering relationships with more settled storekeepers. During 1802 and 1803 he and his father's old rival, Charles Greene, exchanged goods on a regular basis. Woodbridge provided Greene with hardware, textiles, glass, shoes, wine, whiskey, hemp, and codfish. Greene provided Woodbridge with rope, nails, glue, knives, and, once, a draft. In 1804 Dudley Woodbridge Jr. bought specific goods in Philadelphia for Increase Matthews of Springfield, north of Marietta on the Muskingum. He wrote:

> Our terms follow—provided you send a memorandum of the principal articles wanted before the goods are purchased and the money is paid in Phila. at the time of purchase we shou'd charge 10 percent on the cost and carriage—or we will furnish you with groceries at 60 days credit for 15 percent advance on cost and carriage, with dry goods on 6 months credit for 20 percent advance on cost and carriage—shou'd the money be remitted to Phila. before the payments become due—interest would be allowed at 1 percent advance for paying the money in Phila.

However, most agreements were more general and seemed to involve simply supplying others with a broad selection of goods. Woodbridge offered to supply one Simon Converse on six months credit at a 25 percent advance, with a 5 percent discount if the goods were paid for within six months. Woodbridge wrote Converse that he would accept hemp, cash, or skins and furs as payment. Woodbridge offered goods to a Gallipolis merchant named Fletcher; once again the advance was 25 percent.[34]

Merchants in other western towns provided similar services. During the first decade of the nineteenth century, Lexington merchants Samuel and George Trotter supplied eastern goods to shopkeepers in Danville, Greensburgh, Maysville (formerly known as Limestone), and Paris, Kentucky; Chillicothe and West Union, Ohio; and Ste. Genevieve on the Missouri bank of the Mississippi River. Frederick Hine, one of the Trotters' customers, opened stores in both Russellville, Kentucky, and Robertson City, Tennessee. Almost a decade later, the Louisville firm of Southard and Starr shipped textiles, sugar, coffee, tea, whiskey, brandy, paper, and straw hats to the firm of Jacobs and LeRoy in Vincennes, Indiana. The Indiana firm sold some of the goods on consignment and paid the Kentucky firm a 5 percent commission for supplying the rest.[35]

Merchants like Woodbridge did more than simply supply others with goods, however. One common way for an ambitious merchant to expand the scope of his influence involved establishing branch stores within a town's hinterland. Such tactics were well known in colonial Connecticut, where the elder Dudley Woodbridge had gotten his start. When Dudley Woodbridge Jr. arrived in Marietta, most merchants still located their operations in town, and indeed the Woodbridge general store would remain a fixture there for decades. But Woodbridge wanted to extend his reach beyond the confines of Marietta.[36]

Young Woodbridge set up stores in strategic locations using partners, providing farmers with local stores where they could sell their crops and buy goods. One of his earliest associates was Simon Converse's brother, James. The two men first opened a store in Waterford where Converse sold most of the goods on credit, and it took Woodbridge years to collect all the money owed. Converse then moved on to a new location, the town of Lancaster on the Hocking River. The site of the town was one of the sections granted to Ebenezer Zane by the federal government for his work in cutting Zane's Trace in 1796 and 1797. Because of the ford, the spot needed no ferry. Zane did not plat the town until 1800, but German settlers from Lancaster, Pennsylvania, had lived in the vicinity for a few years, and so Zane named the town New Lancaster. Later residents shortened the name by dropping the "New." Zane held back a few town lots for artisans, offering to give land free to the first blacksmith, carpenter, and tanner who lived and plied their trade in town for four years.[37]

The population of Lancaster lagged behind Marietta's during the first decades of the nineteenth century, and in 1811 the entire town consisted of only one hundred houses, eleven stores, nine taverns, and a population of perhaps 350. But numbers do not tell the whole story. As Zane originally intended, the town sat at the northern-most point of keelboat navigation on the Hocking. With stores established by Dudley Woodbridge Jr. and others, Lancaster came to serve as a place where farmers from the surrounding countryside could come to barter for goods and send their produce seventy miles south to the Ohio River and on to New Orleans. Thus merchants in subregional hubs such as Marietta helped their towns' hinterlands grow.[38]

Another early Woodbridge partner was Joseph F. Munro. Munro's father had come to Ohio with one of the first Ohio Company parties, leaving his son back east. In 1796 at age fourteen, Munro joined his father but later recalled that his paternal parent seemed disinterested in his future, so the young man moved on to Cincinnati. Five years later Munro was back in southeastern Ohio, where he entered into a partnership to sell goods in

Chillicothe with a man named John Matthews. Competition proved fierce in the heart of the Virginia Military District, however, prompting Munro to move to Lancaster. But he later complained to Matthews that his assortment of goods was too scanty and poor to compete with other merchants. The men ended their partnership soon thereafter, and Munro partnered with Woodbridge instead. With Blennerhassett's capital backing him, Woodbridge apparently had no trouble supplying his partners with a large and varied stock.[39]

The association between Munro and Woodbridge expanded, and Woodbridge made commercial connections with other men as well. In early 1802 Woodbridge "made a contract" with Munro to open a store at Licking. That fall, it was Munro who made the trip to Philadelphia to buy goods. Woodbridge wrote James Converse that Munro was to use some of the goods to "establish a temporary store down the river (for the purpose of purchasing pork & lard)." Woodbridge hoped to hire James's brother Royal to take charge of the store at Licking until spring. He would pay Royal nine dollars a month. Not much stock remained, according to Woodbridge, but Royal was to sell only for cash and expend most of his energy on collecting debts that Munro already had on the books. Other men who operated stores in partnership with Dudley Woodbridge Jr. included Nathaniel S. Cushing, Augustus Stone, and Thomas L. Pierce.[40]

At times Woodbridge found these relationships to be exasperating. His letters to James Converse in Lancaster indicate that his associate often wrote that one trader or another had come and taken all his business. Woodbridge replied with soothing words, telling Converse just to keep on selling and business would turn out all right. In February of 1802 he instructed Converse not to worry about others underselling him because they would end up out of business. Woodbridge advised his partner to calculate what it cost to get goods and price them accordingly—he would make more profit than the others in the end. Counseling his partner not to be "frightened" by other merchants, Woodbridge told Converse to "keep on in the old way." A year later, Converse still sent anxious letters, and Woodbridge's tone changed as he replied that Converse's problems came from an inability to follow instructions. Apparently Converse often threatened to move away and quit, but Dudley wrote that he would simply find another "storekeeper."[41]

Despite the rocky road their association often traveled, Woodbridge supplied the anxious Converse with goods one way or another for many years to come, even after their partnership ended and Converse settled in Zanesville. In addition, James's brothers, Wright, Simon, and Daniel Converse, also participated, in one way or another, in Woodbridge's mercantile network. Daniel shipped goods and acted as a courier, Wright went as far away as Kentucky in search of furs for the firm to buy, and Simon seems to have been a procurer of furs as well. In the fall of 1805 Woodbridge wrote to Simon Converse to tell him that he wanted to establish a store at either Lancaster or Gallipolis. Woodbridge offered Converse three options: he would sell Converse goods outright, he would pay Converse wages as a storekeeper, or the two could be partners, selling jointly.[42]

Strategies similar to Dudley Woodbridge Jr.'s can be found among merchants throughout the West. John Hunt's store in Lexington functioned as a branch of Abijah's Cincinnati business, and in the late 1790s the cousins opened new branches in Danville, Frankfort, and Shelbyville, Kentucky. A decade later Frankfort merchant Jonathan H. Hanna wrote a letter referring to his Shelbyville store. In 1815 Lexington land speculator Richard Clough Anderson pondered the idea of establishing a store "in the country near Oxmoor on the road . . . [to] increase the value of [my] land." In 1818 Nashville merchant Andrew Hynes established a business with twenty-year-old George Miles, extending his reach south and east to Murfreesboro, Tennessee. Such relationships could also be found throughout the Mississippi Valley in the decades prior to the Civil War.[43]

The branch stores and the country stores of shopkeepers supplied by merchants like Woodbridge, the Hunts, or the Trotters were not always large or well stocked. In the early years, they might consist of a trader with a couple of chests to hold goods that he opened upon demand when customers came. In 1789 John May and another trader operated two "stores" in one building. In 1797 a traveler named Francis Baily stopped at the confluence of the Ohio and Little Miami rivers to find two or three "warehouses," one of which he described simply as a room in a man's home stuffed full of European goods.[44]

William Woodbridge, a lawyer and Dudley's younger brother, rendered the following judgment upon Marietta in 1807: "our little place continues to increase in wealth & population Thanks be to the unremitting activity of our commercial people."[45] Marietta grew into the hub of a busy hinterland in less than a decade, linking area farmers to the Atlantic trade world. The growth of Marietta's role as a subregional hub is revealed by the Woodbridge business records. In addition to Lancaster, Marietta's merchants served a hinterland of eleven towns and townships in Washington County itself, all of them tied to Marietta by waterways and lines of credit. They included the following: Grandview and Newport upstream on the Ohio, Fearing and Salem on Duck Creek, Adams and Waterford on the Muskingum River, Wooster and Wesley on Wolf Creek, and Warren and Belpre downstream on the Ohio. Woodbridge records also indicate that Marietta's hinterland included customers and traders in western Virginia's Wood County.

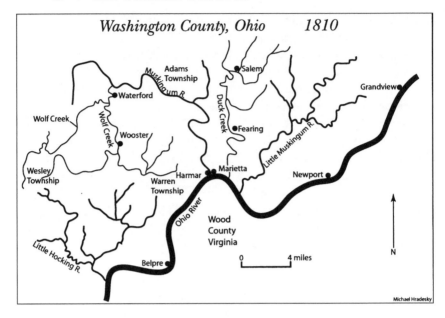

A part of Washington County Ohio in 1810. Fearing quickly became known as Stanleyville, and Wooster eventually became Watertown.

When young Woodbridge first arrived, the firm's ledgers listed people from towns with mills, but an equal number of household heads were listed only by their location: Catts Creek, Duck Creek, Wolf Creek, Little Muskingum, Bull Creek, Federal Creek, and one farm "7 miles up the Ohio." But by 1811 the vast majority of customers were listed by town and township only. In 1810, when Washington County had a human population just shy of six thousand, it boasted over twenty-eight thousand head of stock, including more than seventeen hundred horses, nearly sixty-six hundred cattle, over fourteen thousand hogs, and more than five thousand sheep. Farmers had improved seventeen thousand acres of fields and orchards.[46]

Even before the stimulus of the War of 1812, Washington County residents had established small-scale manufacturing, although most of the goods produced were probably consumed within Marietta's hinterland. In 1810 local looms wove over fifty-two thousand yards of textiles, and residents produced nearly seventy-five hundred yards of wool cloth. Marietta supported three tanneries, and Salem one. Waterford and Belpre entrepreneurs utilized three distilleries to turn corn into whiskey; Grandview, Fearing, and Marietta each had two, and Adams and Newport could boast one distillery apiece. Fearing had the county's only fulling mill, while Marietta claimed the county's only carding machine and ropewalks, as well as nail, hat, and tin plating "factories." Farmers wishing to turn their grain into flour could choose from three gristmills in Fearing, two mills each in Marietta, Adams, and Grandview, or the mills in Belpre, Waterford, and Wooster. Those wishing to turn timber into planks could frequent eleven sawmills spread out among five towns. Marietta had four cabinetmakers, and Adams two. Three of the four county potteries were located in Marietta.[47]

The role merchants played in westward expansion revolved around connections. First, a merchant had to gain access to capital and credit, as well as gain the trust of local farmers and artisans. Then, by fueling the growth of small trading centers in a town's hinterland and by supporting local manufacturing, a merchant could transform a town into a subregional hub. Dudley Woodbridge Jr. proved to be a key player in the evolution of both Marietta and southeastern Ohio.

4

Connecting East and West

Fostering the growth of a town's hinterland in the West depended on a merchant's ability to create connections between his customers and the wider world of capital and goods on the Atlantic seaboard. Nurturing these links involved gathering items for export, transporting them down the Ohio and Mississippi rivers, planning and executing buying trips to Philadelphia, and shepherding consumer goods west over the Appalachian Mountains. The records of Philadelphia merchants reveal that they supplied goods directly to merchants living both north and south of the Ohio River, and that a substantial portion of the goods went through the largest western cities before going on to the smaller towns that made up their hinterlands. In the years prior to the War of 1812, Dudley Woodbridge Jr. would become well acquainted with one of these entrepôts—Pittsburgh, Pennsylvania.

I

In the early 1800s the most important export down the Ohio to New Orleans was flour. According to one observer, during the spring of 1802, eighty-five thousand barrels passed over the falls of the Ohio, with most of them coming from Kentucky and the rest from Ohio and western Pennsylvania. In addition, westerners shipped pork and whiskey, and by the end of the decade, iron, glass, mill and grindstones, apples and cider, and peach brandy.[1]

Some farmers shipped their flour to New Orleans themselves, but as the trip was long and arduous, many others relied on merchants to market their surplus. The farmers received goods for their crops, or a mixture of goods and cash, but rarely cash alone, and one traveler wrote that they complained about just that fact in central Kentucky. But merchants were compelled to send the bulk of specie that came their way east to pay creditors, although they also used it to speculate in land, furs, or other western goods. Merchants acquired flour either directly from farmers or from mills. Once a place was settled enough, a merchant could enter into contracts with neighbors for their produce. Because the population of other Ohio settlements grew faster than the hilly country of Washington County, during the first decade of his career, Dudley Woodbridge Jr. had to go abroad to find enough flour and pork to make up a profitable load of cargo. He bartered goods or paid cash for flour in Steubenville and pork in Cincinnati.[2]

Once a merchant gathered together his produce for export, he next turned his attention to transporting it down the Ohio River to New Orleans. The New Englanders who settled Marietta planned from the beginning to take advantage of the western forests to build ships. Building smaller boats to navigate the Ohio itself proved very profitable in Pittsburgh, Wheeling, and other towns, but Mariettans built two-thirds of the twenty or so ocean-going brigs and schooners manufactured west of the Appalachian Mountains between 1802 and 1807.[3]

Woodbridge and Harman Blennerhassett jumped into shipbuilding with enthusiasm and money but little else. In November of 1801 Dudley Woodbridge Jr. wrote to a Connecticut friend asking about rigging and "any other circumstances you can mention which may be useful to me who am somewhat of a novice in that kind of business." That same month Dudley borrowed a book about the craft from Blennerhassett's impressive library but quickly returned it, explaining that, "the treatise on ship building you were good enough to send me is on account of terms etc. etc. beyond my comprehension." There were plenty of workers in Marietta to build ships, but finding a master workman to direct the labor took months in early 1802. Thereafter hiring a captain posed equally maddening problems. The partners needed a man familiar with the markets in New Orleans but had to check the references of the candidates in the East.[4]

At last they launched the brig *Dominic* with a full load of pork, lard, and other goods in the spring of 1803. The produce gathered by Joseph Munro made up part of the cargo. Unfortunately, the passage proved full of problems, including lost anchors and botched paperwork, as well as silence from the captain. So sparse were his reports that by December the partners feared the ship had been lost. It did arrive in Philadelphia, eventually, but could not be sold there at a profit, so Woodbridge and Blennerhassett found themselves forced to retain ownership for longer than they wished. The experiment proved to be a costly one, and not notably successful. They had invested just over ten thousand dollars in ship and cargo and lost nearly thirty-three hundred dollars of it.[5]

Dudley Woodbridge Jr. and Harman Blennerhassett were hardly the only two men to encounter problems. A boat built at Elizabethtown, Pennsylvania, named *Monongahela Farmer* set sail from Pittsburgh in April of

1801 loaded with 750 barrels of flour, in addition to whiskey, hemp, and skins. When the boat reached Louisville, it had to wait three months for the river to rise enough to make it over the falls. By the time it reached New Orleans, the flour had gone bad and ended up in the hands of a man who used it to manufacture crackers. However, the boat did go on to make many voyages between the east coast, the West Indies, and New Orleans. A Marietta brig named the *St. Clair*, also launched in 1801, made a good profit for its owners as well. But long delays at Louisville were quite common in the years to come, and sometimes cargoes had to be unloaded, floated down the rapids on flatboats, and then loaded onto the brig again after it cleared the falls empty. In April 1807 three Marietta boats wrecked at the falls, although the owners did salvage part of the cargo and at least one of the boats. Boatbuilding died soon thereafter, though, and the Marietta Federalists blamed Jefferson's embargo. But one scholar has speculated that "perhaps the shipbuilders were glad to cast the blame for the wreck of their ships and their hopes upon the broad shoulders of Jefferson." In such ventures, costs simply outweighed benefits.[6]

The real workhorses of river transport in the early years of the nineteenth century were keelboats and flatboats. Keelboats were about ten feet wide and could be as long as eighty feet. Equipped with a mast and sail, most of the boat was roofed over with a cramped deck that circled the top of the hull. Keelboats were virtually the only craft that went upstream within the West before the arrival of steamboats, and indeed continued to do much of the work on the Ohio's shallower tributaries thereafter. Crews either poled the boats against the current or extended a thousand feet of rope from the mast to a tree on shore and pulled the boat forward hand over hand. A crew of eight to twenty men could pole or pull between ten and forty tons of keelboat and cargo upriver at an average rate of six miles a day.[7]

Craft that carried produce and goods downriver (never to return) came in a variety of sizes and went by many names, but were generally known as flatboats. When westerners still feared attacks by Native Americans on shore, the craft were approximately ten feet wide and forty feet long, with a cabin built on deck that enclosed part of the surface. As they expelled the Native Americans from the Ohio Valley, westerners built longer vessels with more open space to accommodate more livestock and larger heaps of cargo.[8]

But what most complicated plans for exporting goods was the changeable nature of the Ohio itself. Each spring, rains and the run-off from snow and ice made the river rise and brought a season of relatively trouble-free navigation—provided one could avoid sandbars and submerged rocks and timber. But the spring rise also brought mixed blessings. One incident of what valley residents called "high water" occurred in early March of 1818. A Marietta clerk wrote his employer, who was making a buying trip back east, the following:

> Before you receive this you will probably hear of the River having been high, it continued rising till [it] overflowed the Town, and several feet higher than the last fresh, measuring two feet on the store floor[.] [T]he Goods I secured by hoisting part aloft and part on the counter, the water got off the floor this morning so that I have been able to clean out and get the principal part of the Goods to their places today[.] [T]he pork and Bacon I secured likewise so that not any article sustained any damage by the water.

By summer, however, the river ran so low that navigation proved impossible for all but the smallest craft. Rains made the river rise again in the fall, but the shipping season did not last as long as the one earlier in the year, and if the weather was dry, it might not come at all. The winter season meant low water and ice.[9]

Although flour made up the bulk of cargo, merchants exported many other things as well. Some of the goods Dudley Woodbridge Jr. specialized in promised enough profit to justify the expense of sending them east by wagon through agents in Pittsburgh instead of downriver through New Orleans. These items included ginseng, hemp, and skins.

In 1799 Dudley Woodbridge Jr. offered between one and four tons of ginseng to Philadelphia merchant Joseph S. Lewis if the price was right. During the following decade, he exported ginseng to the East Indies and Philadelphia, as well as to two merchants in Vermont. Men who managed his branch stores gathered it for him from surrounding farmers. When prices fluctuated in mid-1800, he instructed them to barter for it rather than pay cash. Demand dropped by the end of the decade but picked up again in the 1810s.[10]

Other westerners exported ginseng as well. The southern settlers of western Virginia and Kentucky were especially skilled at spotting the medicinal plant that was so highly valued in China. They could receive cash for the dried root or barter it for store goods at a price comparable to what they could get for corn whiskey. Ginseng could not be cultivated at that time, so it had to be found in the wild, and gathering it was hard work. The roots shrunk to half their original volume when dried. Still, ginseng functioned as a cash crop for westerners. In the East it brought high prices in relation to its weight and twice what western merchants paid for it, justifying the expense of shipping it by wagon over the Appalachians.[11]

Shipments of ginseng had inaugurated the China trade in Philadelphia in the 1780s, and eastern merchants exchanged the ginseng for a variety of

Asian goods. The ones that showed up most frequently in the Woodbridge business records of the 1790s and first two decades of the nineteenth century include Bohea and Hyson tea and nanking cloth, which Americans called "nankeen"—a strong, yellow-brown cotton fabric that was especially useful in making breeches.[12]

Other plants came from south of the river as well. In 1816 a doctor in Marietta informed Woodbridge that snakeroot, also used to make medicine, was in demand in France. Woodbridge began gathering it from merchants he supplied with goods in western Virginia, and a Philadelphia firm took care of the marketing in the East and Europe.[13]

Before Jefferson's embargo, Dudley Woodbridge Jr. also sought hemp. As detailed above, more than 10 percent of his customers between 1802 and 1805 bartered hemp for goods. One year he paid a cash advance to a Virginian named Hamilton Kerr to grow the crop, informing him that if the crop arrived too late to ship, Kerr would have to return the money. Marietta's shipbuilding industry required the hemp for rigging, but Woodbridge also shipped it to Philadelphia by way of Wheeling and Pittsburgh.[14]

The real center for hemp production in the West, however, was Kentucky. Farmers grew it to produce their own brand of country linen or bartered it to merchants for goods, and Lexington entrepreneurs built ropewalks to manufacture cordage. In fact there were more ropewalks in Kentucky in 1810 than any other state, although Massachusetts establishments surpassed Kentucky in pounds of cordage produced. The demand for hemp would wane after the War of 1812 but grow again in later decades, as Kentucky manufacturers produced bagging and cords for cotton producers in the South.[15]

Dudley Woodbridge Jr. also speculated heavily in bear skins. In 1804 he sent agents throughout Ohio and western Virginia seeking to buy them from both white hunters and Native Americans. Woodbridge wrote Philadelphia businessman Benjamin Wilson offering an arrangement by which Wilson would supply the cash for skins and transport, while the westerner used his contacts to acquire them. The two men would then split the profits.[16]

Not all commercial ventures succeeded, however. The time and distance that news of prices and trends had to travel took their toll. Woodbridge and Blennerhassett lost a third of their investment in the brig *Dominic,* and Charles Greene, the elder Woodbridge's rival and the younger man's source of goods needed in a pinch, apparently went bankrupt in 1806.[17] Another example involves Dudley Woodbridge Jr.'s business losses during the War of 1812. In the fall of 1813 he dispatched a river boat captain named Daniel Greene to New Orleans to speculate in cotton and sugar. Greene and Woodbridge both contributed nearly three thousand dollars to the venture. Hearing news of high prices back East after Greene left, Woodbridge borrowed money from others in Marietta in order to take further advantage of the market. Unfortunately, by February news of peace negotiations had drastically lowered prices in Philadelphia. Woodbridge's letters do not make clear how he originally intended to divide the goods between East and West, but he ended up bringing all the goods upriver when eastern prices fell. He consigned some of the sugar to be sold in Cincinnati and tried to unload the rest in Zanesville and Pittsburgh. Woodbridge lost just over eleven hundred dollars on the venture.[18]

Dudley Woodbridge Jr. especially courted disaster in fur trade speculations. In July of 1816 he received a circular from a London merchant claiming that the market was rising again and pelts were needed. Over the next couple of days, he wrote to his brothers who had moved on to Chillicothe and Detroit, asking them to contact area merchants. Woodbridge also wrote to merchants he knew in Kentucky and to another merchant in "St. Louis, Upper Louisiana." Every contact he had made in his eighteen-year career who still survived received a letter. Woodbridge bought furs outright, he purchased them on commission, and he acquired them by giving hunters a cut of the profits. He sank thousands of dollars into this venture, mostly by selling drafts on himself, apparently confident he was about to make a killing.[19]

Unfortunately, news arrived that Woodbridge's London agents, Alex Glennie and Son, had failed soon after he shipped his cargo. Thereafter, he had trouble tracing the fates of his furs. Apparently the Glennies' creditors took control of them and sold them at a one thousand dollar loss, and Woodbridge didn't expect shipments remaining in France and Philadelphia to recoup the price he paid for them in Ohio. He had borrowed a considerable sum from brother William but had to delay paying him back.[20]

Like Woodbridge, Miami Valley merchants who shipped loads of flour and pork to New Orleans ran considerable risks as well. Everyone had to send their goods to market during the seasons of high water, and because the greatest portion of western produce reached New Orleans at roughly the same time, glutted markets proved to be a common occurrence. In addition, if low water delayed shipment, or if flour and pork had been packed incorrectly, they spoiled. Prices fluctuated rapidly—flour could bring as much as twelve dollars a barrel or as little as three dollars; thus a large profit was by no means guaranteed. One study of the Cincinnati market concludes that most of the profits merchants made came from marking up the prices of their eastern goods rather than selling produce for high prices in New Orleans. Merchants charged much higher prices for goods bought with barter as insurance against fluctuating markets. In 1802 the chronicler François

Michaux encountered many farmers in Kentucky who were well aware of what the merchants were about and resented it. When Dudley Woodbridge Jr. was no longer a young man, he wrote his brother Jack that retailing had kept him in business all through his career, when fur speculations and other ventures failed.[21]

II

Assembling and shipping a cargo down the Ohio or across the mountains represented but half of a western merchant's relationship with the Atlantic trade world. Westerners also had to make a trip to Philadelphia once or twice a year to settle accounts and buy goods.

A month or so before departing for the East, Woodbridge would send letters to branch stores and merchants he supplied, asking them to gather together all the cash they could lay their hands on to bankroll the trip. Often, such efforts met with resistance. A Chillicothe merchant ran the following rather sarcastic ad in March of 1807:

> Notice:
> I wish to start to Philadelphia the first of April for a supply of goods, and from experience find it necessary to have money when I start; therefore I request all those indebted to me to be punctual in discharging their accounts before that time, as no further indulgence will be given by,
> H. Fullerton[22]

For western merchants, trips to Philadelphia meant walking around the city comparing goods and prices for a week or more. During the early 1800s many merchants in Philadelphia and New York began to specialize. Some concentrated on hardware or crockery, and among the dry goods merchants, some specialized in wool, cotton, or silk cloth. Woodbridge once warned his agent Thomas Pierce that "a great deal of time & running about will be necessary to obtain goods on tolerable terms."[23]

On one junket to Philadelphia, Kentucky merchant Asa Runyon wrote a letter home to Mayslick that echoed Woodbridge's tone. There was a good supply of dry goods in the city, Runyon wrote, but prices were inconsistent. He reported that "in some Houses some articles are low & others high—I shall take my time & select when & such as I think will best suit our market." Timing could be everything. Runyon noted that prices had risen 10 to 15 percent in some establishments where he had bought goods just a short time before.[24]

One of Dudley Woodbridge Jr.'s agents spent seven days picking out goods in Philadelphia in the fall of 1804, buying over $6,000 worth. Goods bought on credit made up 70 percent of the total—over $4,200 worth. This credit was spread out as follows: to his grocer, Joseph Clark, $2,523 (for tea, sugar, coffee, snuff, raisins, tobacco, pepper, brandy, wine, soap, chocolate, and liquor); to his supplier of saddlery and hardware, Harvey and Worth, $923 (for buttons, gimlets, brass cocks, pocket books, whips, wool cards, shovels, curb bridles, snaffles, saddlebags, and saddles); to his dry goods merchant, Samuel Carswell, $543 (for drab cloth, kersey, and coating); to his crockery merchant, Jonathan Gartland, $183 (for cups and saucers, china, pans, basins, sugar bowls, quart bowls, pitchers, cream pots, sauce pots, plates, teapots, decanters, and tumblers); and to his stationer, John Conrad and Co., $95 (for spelling books, pasteboard, and journals). The nearly $2,000 spent in cash went almost exclusively for a wide variety of cloth and other dry goods in amounts ranging from $25 to $400 at other mercantile houses.[25]

From the beginning of 1801 through the spring of 1806, Woodbridge spent between $1,500 and $5,000 twice a year at Philadelphia, with occasional trips to New York and Baltimore. He made the trip himself on occasion and used agents other times—perhaps his brother Jack, a partner such as Joseph Munro, or a woman identified only as Mrs. Jourdan, apparently a Philadelphia merchant herself. The buyer stayed in Philadelphia from three to ten days, although one week proved most common. Generally, less than one-third of the total outlay was paid at the time. The grocery bill was usually around $1,000, as was the hardware and saddlery bill. The outlay for crockery and stationary usually totaled between $80 and $200 each. Dry goods could be expected to comprise between 40 and 60 percent of the trip's total expenditures, with one large order bought on credit but most paid for in small lots with cash.[26]

One blotter contains the summing up of young Jack Woodbridge's trip on behalf of his brother in the fall of 1805. He utilized credit to buy $2,819.70 worth of goods and spent $1,103.23 in cash. His personal expenses for the trip totaled $109.37. Shipping the goods west from Philadelphia involved $6.66 in coopering and portage, $447.29 in wagon bills, $30 in freight charges to shift the cargo from Wheeling to Marietta, and $2.50 to shift the goods from shore to store. Thus freight and other expenses made up $595.82 of the grand total of $4,518.55—a little less than 15 percent.[27] This total lends credence to the conclusion that a high markup could result in a good profit.

During the first decade of the nineteenth century, Woodbridge usually instructed his suppliers to send the goods he had purchased to grocer Joseph Clark, who arranged for the shipment west of other merchandise in addition to his own. Months later from Marietta, Woodbridge would often send a large draft to Clark and instruct the grocer to distribute payments to other

Invoice book, BWC, box 35, folder 2. On these pages are part of the particulars of a trip to Philadelphia in the fall of 1805. Joseph Clark priced his groceries in dollars, but Harvey and Worth's bill for hardware and saddlery had to be converted into dollars from British pounds. *Courtesy of the Ohio Historical Society.*

Amount brot over — $ 1470.49

Amt bot of J Clark brot up — 281.60

,12½ 6 lbs nutmegs @ 5ₐ 30. 0

½ barrel soft Shell'd Almonds 54

,50   14 lb nett 33 14.52

3 barrels Sugar & Coffee

     1.3.12 tare 0.0.17

     1.3.13 1 — 20

     1.3.10 1 — 24

     5.2.7 0.2.25

     0.2.25

,50   2.0.2 is 226 lbs up @ 32 72.32

,40 50 loaves Sugar 333 lb @ 23 — 76.75

3 bls coffee 1.3.4 — 17

     1.3.8 — 07

     1.3 — 17

     5.1.12 51

     1.23

,50   4.3.17 is 549 lb, 32 — 175.68

,42 1 box white Soap 5 2lbs @ 15 2 bxs 8.93

,19 1 box coofish 1.0.0 nett box — 6.75

3..   1 quarter cask Sherry wine 32 gl @ 150 48.—

3..   2 bbls 4th proof brandy 33½

     66 gls @ 145 — 96.42

     barrels — 3.0

,34 1 keg Spanish indigo 25 lbs @ 3. 58.50

,38 3 kegs twist tobacco 447 lb nett @ 15 69.50

8 bbls 2 kegs 60 cooterage 1.33 5.93

     Dolls 945.90 945.90

     Carried $ 1146.39

creditors. He occasionally sent his western produce and furs to others, but generally Clark took charge of selling his furs, ginseng, hemp, and pork. Woodbridge had a similar relationship with grocer William Wilson during the 1810s.[28]

In addition to mercantile houses, auctions began to show up in the Woodbridge invoice books as places to acquire goods in the 1810s. The War of 1812 sparked a significant change in the range of options open to westerners when they shopped in the East, as British merchants saw their cargoes seized and sold at auction for a high price in America's ports. After the conflict, British merchants began to send agents to the ports themselves to auction off goods, cutting out American commission merchants, especially in 1817 and the decade following.[29]

Relations between Woodbridge and his eastern suppliers did not always run smoothly. He often wrote to complain that their bills contained errors or that he had been charged for goods he never received. Woodbridge also responded angrily if the eastern merchants sent him inferior goods and once accused a supplier of palming off old, out-of-style dry goods to unsuspecting associates far away. But he did once write the firm of Cooke and Cresson that he had received a package of men's hose that did not appear on any of the bills, asking if it came from them.[30]

The work western merchants engaged in to link East and West required toil, risk, and worry. Joseph Hough, a merchant of Hamilton, Ohio, north of Cincinnati, left a chronicle of the work involved in running a business in the West. First, he wrote, "It was necessary for the merchant to buy pork and pack it; to buy wheat, buy barrels, and contract for the manufacture of the wheat into flour, and then build flat-bottomed boats and with great expense and risk of property, commit the whole to the dangers of the navigation of the Miami, Ohio, and Mississippi Rivers." Hough found that riding a horse from Cincinnati to Philadelphia, purchasing goods, and arranging for wagons to Pittsburgh, keelboats to Cincinnati, and wagons to Hamilton took three months each year as he shepherded his goods from East to West. Forced to travel over exceedingly poor roads and to brave all sorts of weather, Hough wrote that "those three months were months of toil and privation and of exposure of every kind." During the fall of 1816 the Ohio ran so low that Hough and his men often had to unload the goods, scrape out the channel, float the boat forward, and reload before continuing downstream. The trip from Pittsburgh to Cincinnati took thirty-nine days that year, longer than it took an average wagon full of goods to cross the mountains from Philadelphia to Pittsburgh—usually the most difficult part of the journey.[31]

III

What frame of reference might a Philadelphia merchant have had when Dudley Woodbridge Jr., Asa Runyon, or Joseph Hough walked into his or her establishment? For one Philadelphian's view, we can turn to the ledger of Samuel Meeker, an agent of the William P. Meeker Company of London. In addition to arrangements with large companies in New Orleans with whom he engaged in overseas ventures, Samuel Meeker supplied seventy-seven mercantile concerns with goods west of the Appalachian Mountains between 1807 and 1810. The ledger lists nearly five hundred fifty accounts, so westerners represented approximately 15 percent of his customers who bought on credit. Any westerner seeking credit needed a letter of introduction from someone the merchant knew and trusted. In the early 1800s eastern merchants sent agents to the West once or twice a year to collect debts.[32]

Seven of the firms Meeker supplied with goods did business at the Ohio's headwaters in Pittsburgh, thirteen merchants resided in Ohio, and one merchant lived in Indiana territory. Fifty-seven of the firms (nearly 75 percent) did business south of the river, including thirty-one in Kentucky and seventeen in Tennessee. Just over half of all the firms did business in the urban centers of Lexington, Nashville, Cincinnati, Pittsburgh, New Orleans, and Natchez, with just under half of them operating in smaller towns throughout the region. Clearly westerners south of the Ohio had ties to Philadelphia just as strong as those between their northern neighbors and the East. The dominance of entrepôts in the western landscape can also be discerned from the distribution of Meeker's customers.

Beginning in January 1807 one-third of Meeker's western accounts represented a balance brought forward from a previous ledger with no new purchases made in the three years that followed. Of those twenty-seven accounts, six with totals ranging from twenty-six to six hundred two dollars were never paid. Five others had some or all of their totals collected by John Dickinson, a Nashville attorney, with a hefty amount of interest and charges added. For all seventy-seven western merchants, one in five made no payment on their account during the three-year time period. Apparently extending credit to western merchants was a risky business. And like Woodbridge, though credit accounts represented part of a company's assets, Meeker found that gaining access to the capital often could not be accomplished without utilizing the services of lawyers.

Between 1807 and 1810 Meeker sold goods on credit to western merchants on sixty-nine occasions. Just over half of the transactions involved sums under five hundred dollars, just over one in five involved sums between five hundred and one thousand dollars, and nearly one in four involved sums over one thousand dollars.[33] Meeker's ledger does not make clear what sorts of goods he specialized in, but it seems most likely that a customer like Dudley Woodbridge Jr. would have been one of his larger customers, although a merchant in a subregional hub like Marietta could not have competed with the elite businessmen in Natchez and other entrepôts.

Seventeen of the western merchants paid their account in cash, though six of the totals were under one hundred dollars. Over half the accounts were paid with bills receivable, a mix of cash and bills receivable, or by third parties, including lawyers who collected debts. Nine of the seventy-seven firms settled their accounts through Samuel Meeker's other concerns and agents in New Orleans and Natchez. Most of the bills receivable were undoubtedly bills of exchange that Meeker's customers had drawn on merchants in Pittsburgh, Cincinnati, Natchez, or New Orleans that represented the money they received for the goods they shipped from the hinterland to the larger entrepôts. Meeker received goods as payment less than a handful of times in Philadelphia itself. The firms in the largest western cities, then, acted as middlemen between most western merchants and their counterparts in the East.

Though many eastern merchants like Meeker undoubtedly concentrated on simply supplying westerners, others took a more direct hand in fostering western business, making links between East and West even more firm. Intrigued by news of trade in St. Louis, Joseph Hertzog, a successful Philadelphia wholesaler and land speculator, decided to set up a branch of his business on the Mississippi. Hertzog went into partnership with a man named Zachary Mussina, the friend of a friend, in order to ship over thirteen thousand dollars worth of goods west and set up a store there in the spring of 1810. On the trip to St. Louis, Mussina was to act as an agent for the new firm in cities along the Ohio, especially Pittsburgh, Cincinnati, and Louisville. The Philadelphia merchant intended for his partner to leave some of the goods in these towns for others to sell on a commission basis. Accompanying Mussina was Hertzog's twenty-year-old nephew, Christian Wilt, who had been promised a partnership when he reached his majority if the business proved to be a success.[34]

However, events did not go as planned. Mussina sold the goods to an old business associate in the West, and although the sale produced a profit of over 30 percent, the money was tied up in notes that Hertzog had trouble collecting. Despite this initial disappointment, the Philadelphia merchant shipped a second supply of goods to Mussina and his nephew within a few months, and with that Wilt managed to establish a successful business. The young man did a good trade supplying exploring and trapping parties heading west toward the Pacific. The next year, as payment for past services and the sum of fifteen hundred dollars supplied by his father, Christopher Wilt gained a partnership in the firm, providing the easterner with a direct link to western produce and markets.

IV

After he had been in business but a decade, Dudley Woodbridge Jr.'s world began to fall apart. He would leave Marietta at the end of 1808, but return a short year and a half later after a brief sojourn in the upper valley's chief entrepôt—Pittsburgh, Pennsylvania. After his stay at the Ohio's headwaters, he would return to Marietta re-energized and ready to build a whole new set of connections that would encompass the Ohio Valley, from Pittsburgh to Louisville.

Tensions between settlers west of the Appalachians and eastern leaders and government officials were common in the years following the American Revolution. Westerners felt unprotected, hemmed in by Native Americans all around them, British to the north, and Spanish to the south. Trade and tax policies were sore points, and the Whiskey Rebellion provides one example of how far westerners would go to force the federal government to listen to their concerns. But the most powerful men in the West to oppose federal actions were speculators with unsettled land claims who clamored for government protection. One such man, James Wilkinson of Kentucky, first attempted to sever West from East in the late 1780s and later became Aaron Burr's partner in the conspiracy of 1806.[35]

Aaron Burr's duel with Alexander Hamilton in 1804 finished his career in the East—neither Federalists nor Republicans would support him again. But Burr's ambitions survived intact, and he looked west in order to do nothing less than create his own empire. Burr intended to take advantage of the chronic western unrest, first by fomenting rebellion in the New Orleans area among French settlers unhappy with American rule and then, in 1805, by descending the Ohio and Mississippi rivers to recruit men and financial backers for his plans to set up a new nation in the West. He dined with Margaret Blennerhassett on the island and charmed western senators such as Ohio's John Smith in Cincinnati. Burr opened a correspondence in December with Harman Blennerhassett, obviously attracted by his capital. Burr told different stories to different men to engage their support, and evidently his tale to Dudley Woodbridge Jr.'s partner included the takeover of Mexico, with Burr installed as emperor and Blennerhassett himself as a diplomat. Historians have speculated that the Irishman had grown bored with life in Ohio and was running out of money, leaving him vulnerable to Burr's blandishments. Blennerhassett invested significant portions of his remaining fortune in Burr's scheme, becoming a major financial backer.

Burr began putting his strategy into action in late 1806. But while his plans clearly represented a conspiracy, they were anything but secret. Rumors were rife in the West about a scheme to separate from the union during 1805 and 1806. Burr himself spoke indiscriminately to many men, and Blennerhassett did as well. The Irishman published four editorials in the *Ohio Gazette* to test public opinion on splitting the nation in two and constantly attempted to recruit men as he traveled. Men from Philadelphia to Cincinnati to New Orleans spoke of a conspiracy in the works. Dismayed at the amount of talk, Burr's partner, commander of the army and governor of the Territory of Louisiana, James Wilkinson, decided to turn Burr in to save himself. Jefferson had been receiving reports on the conspiracy for over a year, and Wilkinson's report sealed Burr's fate. When Burr finally moved in November of 1806, government agents shadowed him. Federal marshals seized the boats he had ordered built at Marietta on 9 December, a day before they were to set off down the Ohio River. Burr and Blennerhassett were in custody by the next summer and stood trial for treason against the United States in August of 1807.

Dudley Woodbridge Jr.'s role in all this is difficult to ascertain. He was never arrested as a conspirator, and standard accounts mention him only as the man who had the boats that Burr planned to use to carry a portion of his forces commissioned under the care of Joseph Barker. Yet Woodbridge must have known what his partner was about, for it was he who rode to warn Blennerhassett that the Ohio militia was coming to seize the boats on the night of 8 December. The two closed their partnership the next day, and Blennerhassett fled in the early hours of 10 December.[36]

What Woodbridge stood to gain by actively participating in the conspiracy is difficult to determine. Burr recruited military men from the ranks of Ohio's revolutionary veterans by telling them that the federal government stood behind his designs on Spanish territory, he recruited land speculators and state senators who opposed Jefferson, and he offered Blennerhassett power in exchange for money. Since Woodbridge belonged to none of these categories—he was neither a military officer, a large-scale land speculator, a politician, nor a wealthy man—Burr probably lavished on him nothing like the attention he gave to his partner. Woodbridge may simply have felt that Burr's plans would ensure that foreign powers could not cut off trade through New Orleans in the future. Or perhaps he simply took advantage of the business opportunities the conspiracy afforded a merchant capable of outfitting the expedition with supplies and boats.

Whatever his real role, it brought him under scrutiny. In June of 1807 William informed his uncle James Backus that "Dudley with several of our citizens had been forced to attend the trial of Burr as witnesses. But I believe they know nothing of importance." Woodbridge testified at Blennerhassett's trial as well, and thereafter the relationship between the two men cooled rapidly. Woodbridge let it be known that he thought Blennerhassett was something of an eccentric and perhaps a fool. Blennerhassett complained that Woodbridge had concealed his initial interest in Burr's plans and pulled away to save himself. The two men wrangled for years about money Woodbridge owed his old partner. Woodbridge agreed to pay Blennerhassett six thousand dollars as his half of what remained of their profits when the two ended their association. When Blennerhassett relocated to New Orleans after Burr's acquittal, Woodbridge procured Virginia slaves to pay part of the debt.[37]

Over the next two years, Woodbridge's fortunes declined. He began to have health trouble fairly early in life, especially pain in his hips. Woodbridge despaired making a good marriage because of his affliction and cautioned William not to let a rich girl get away following a quarrel. But Dudley could have done no better in Marietta than the match he finally made, marrying the eldest daughter of prominent land speculator Benjamin Ives Gilman in 1807. Unfortunately, Jane died bearing his first child less than a year later. Dudley set up a store in Chillicothe in partnership with his brother Jack, but the venture ran into difficulties. He so offended Jack in a series of letters that the younger man wrote William that their oldest brother had better change his tune or he would never speak to him again. In addition to such personal troubles, the embargo destroyed Woodbridge's boatbuilding schemes, creditors demanded payment, but those in debt to him did not pay. Woodbridge sued many of them, but to no avail. He finally decided to leave Marietta.[38]

Woodbridge planned to speculate in Kentucky tobacco, backed by his father-in-law and Philadelphia merchant Joseph S. Lewis, before continuing on to New Orleans and whatever future awaited him. On 18 December 1808 he left his infant daughter in the care of his parents and his sister, boarded the last ship in which he owned an interest, and left Marietta, he supposed, for good.[39] Family records do not reveal what the next year brought, but Woodbridge ended up across the mountains once more and came to know intimately one of the third order of western towns—Pittsburgh, Pennsylvania.

The principal entrepôt to the Ohio Valley in the early 1800s, Pittsburgh lay at the meeting point of the many streams of migration which headed west from all over the eastern seaboard. In early 1810, with capital provided by Benjamin Ives Gilman, Dudley Woodbridge Jr. established a new business there. By the time Woodbridge settled at the headwaters of the Ohio, Pittsburgh had become the largest city in the area, growing from a population of a little over fifteen hundred people in 1800 to eight thousand people fifteen years later. Pioneers sold the wagons they had used to cross the Appalachians and spent the proceeds on tools, furniture, clothing, and food before sailing down the Ohio. Tradesmen and merchants could make a good living supplying the wave of people, and investors began to organize iron and glass industries in the early 1800s. Pittsburgh merchants also supplied goods to traders farther west. As early as 1800, Pittsburgh was home to sixty-three business establishments, including twenty-three general stores.[40]

Visitors to Pittsburgh in 1802 and 1803 reported that the town encompassed 400 buildings, many of them brick. By 1807, however, Pittsburgh had grown so much that traveler Fortescue Cuming counted 236 brick houses, and 361 made of wood. Cuming added that over 20 percent of both sorts had been built within the last year. Residents heated their homes with coal, which was cheap and readily available. Cuming's complaints about how dirty the smoke made the city would be echoed by many others in the years to come.[41]

Western Pennsylvania had been settled before Ohio, and by 1810 residents exported significant amounts of flour. On a visit intended to gauge the success of his land speculations, an entrepreneur named Joshua Gilpin took careful note of the commercial possibilities. He wrote that a miller needed only a supply of six-months capital to make a start. Millers had to pay for wheat, grind it, then send it to New Orleans. All flour went down the Ohio when the river rose, meaning that gluts in the southern port were common, and flour often sat waiting to sell, going sour in the heat and humidity. They might sell the flour in New York instead, but either way, they would not see their profits for a half-year. Gilpin noted that some entrepreneurs engaged in the distilling business, but many farmers owned their own stills to turn rye into whiskey. He reported that farmers, millers, and manufacturers in western Pennsylvania who did not want to take the time and trouble to get their produce and goods to New Orleans themselves relied on Pittsburgh merchants to do the job for them.[42]

When Dudley Woodbridge Jr. settled in Pittsburgh, he used his old Philadelphia suppliers to import goods—Clark, Harvey and Worth, and Benjamin B. Howell and Company. But now, instead of speculating in furs and forming partnerships with country storekeepers, he aimed to become a wholesale merchant on a grander scale. In addition to groceries, Woodbridge sent Pittsburgh manufactured goods on to Ohio merchants, including iron goods, glassware, oil, nails, and paper. He wrote to a Lancaster merchant to tell him that he had all the plows, axes, sickles, and other iron goods the Ohioan could possibly want. In return, he would send Ohio goods east. Woodbridge wrote to Howell in Philadelphia that if anyone wanted to speculate "in the produce of our country," he could supply it. He also acted as a middleman for Kentucky entrepreneurs, speculating in hemp, yarn, and tobacco in Lexington, and shipping it east by river and land. Being established in Pittsburgh meant being able personally to make sure goods were outfitted properly for the long journey to Philadelphia. Dudley Woodbridge Jr. had begun the process of becoming a middleman between western manufacturers and merchants, instead of just supplying merchants and farmers with goods imported from the East.[43]

But Woodbridge only remained in Pittsburgh for six months. He did a good business, selling one thousand dollars worth of goods in one of his better months. Yet he was homesick. In fact, before he had even commenced business, he wrote home in late 1809 that he missed "the endearing chitchat of my little girl." He found Pittsburgh to be a "bleak place." In a letter to Jack in April of 1810, he wrote that while he liked the "bustle" of the city, he was not happy in his work. He wanted "to get into a kind of business that would please [him]." Woodbridge thought that "the retail business is very much overdone and without it being connected with some other branch cannot be made profitable." Thus, though business was brisk, he told Jack that he had arranged his life in such a way that he could pick up and leave at "any moment."[44]

Meanwhile, Woodbridge had been hearing good things about Ohio. His correspondence reveals knowledge of the growth of Springfield and Zanesville, north of Marietta on the Muskingum, as well as the establishment of manufacturing in both places. At that time, Zanesville residents expected the capital of Ohio to move to their city, and they were planning a building to house it—a furnace for casting opened, and a forge as well. In Marietta itself, William informed him that although he had been unsuccessful in collecting the firm's debts, Dudley's partner, Augustus Stone, was taking in twenty dollars a day at the store. Ohio seemed to be prospering, and Dudley decided to return. That fall, he indicated to his brother Jack that he was out of debt and had enough capital to begin anew. He had worked his way through his "embarrassments" and was ready to start again.[45]

No one knows why he chose to go back to Marietta instead of a larger, more important town such as Cincinnati. Woodbridge had made it plain in a handful of letters during his stay in Pittsburgh that he did not intend to go home to Marietta, but in the end, he did just that. Probably family ties played a significant role in his decision, as well as the wealth represented by his parents' land holdings. But when he returned, he did not go on with business as usual. His career would enter a new stage as he concentrated on linking his local business interests to that of others throughout the Ohio Valley, north and south of the river.

The tasks required of westerners like Hough, Woodbridge, and Runyon in linking together East and West could be difficult. They speculated in produce and furs, not always successfully, and made a trip to Philadelphia, New York, or Boston to buy goods and pay debts once or twice a year. The risks required of easterners like Meeker and Hertzog were just as real, but the strategies of both groups proved essential to the growth of the West's economy. The next stage in the process of economic development involved the emergence of a regional economy in the decade preceding the Panic of 1819.

5

The Dimensions of the Riverine Economy

As a visitor to the West, Fortescue Cuming kept a record of his trip as he descended the Ohio River in 1807. On a fine afternoon in July he wrote:

> we proceeded from Marietta, accompanied by a Mr. Fry, a genteel and well informed lawyer, from the vicinity of Boston in search of an establishment in some part of this new country. We had also as a passenger, a countryman, by trade a house carpenter, who resided in Virginia, about fifty miles lower down the river, and was returning home after a trip up and down the Muskingum as one of the crew of a keel boat.

Cuming reported on the afternoon meal thus:

> We landed on the right bank at Browning's tavern, a good house and pleasant situation, almost opposite the Little Kenhawa. Several travellers sat down with us to an excellent supper, amongst whom were a merchant from Lexington, a travelling speculator and well digger from French Grant, and a Mr. Smith from Cincinnati, who was deputed by the marshal of Virginia to collect evidence for the trial of Col. Burr, and his associates at Richmond.[1]

In less than a day of traveling on the Ohio, then, Cuming encountered a lawyer, a speculator, a merchant, a carpenter, and a federal law enforcement officer, among others, and the men came from states north and south of the river—Ohio, western Virginia, and Kentucky—as well as from the East. As the artery of trade and communication in the West, the Ohio River brought people together. During the first two decades of the nineteenth century, residents north and south of the river established a thriving commercial community centered on the Ohio and its tributaries, and so they called home "the Western Country."

A variety of factors fueled the regional economy's growth, including a wave of immigration, rampant land speculation, the War of 1812, and the tireless pursuit of profits by western merchants. Dudley Woodbridge Jr.'s business records reveal growing ties between himself and manufacturers of iron and glass in western Pennsylvania, producers of salt in western Virginia, growers of hemp and tobacco in Kentucky, as well as miners of saltpeter in Kentucky and lead in Missouri. New ties enabled him to establish a large wholesaling concern in Marietta, supplying other merchants as well as man- ufacturers in southeastern Ohio to a greater extent than he ever had before.

I

Americans swarmed down the Ohio River by the tens of thousands dur- ing the early nineteenth century. In Ohio they moved north, following the Muskingum, Scioto, and Miami valleys, and thus they remained tied to the commercial world of the Ohio along the river's tributaries. Following the War of 1812, western land speculation soared as settlers bought land on credit and counted on war-ravaged European markets to soak up all the agricultural goods they could produce. Pittsburgh, Lexington, and Cincin- nati served as entrepôts into the Ohio Valley.

In 1802 a traveler named François Michaux observed that inhabitants living along the banks of the Ohio River from Wheeling to Maysville usually lived within two or three miles of each other by water, and he could see set- tlements on the shores most of the time. A year later on a journey from Wheeling to Natchez, Thomas Rodney confirmed that view. While on the Ohio River, Rodney saw settlements nearly every day. Many seem to have been just a cabin or two, but others housed mills and saltworks, and some he labeled villages. On the shores from Maysville to Cincinnati, Rodney spot- ted two places with settlements located on both the Kentucky and Ohio shores with a ferry running between them.[2]

In addition to the growing number of settlements, travelers observed commercial life right on the river. They wrote of encountering floating stores in which traders lived and worked. Under their roofs, these establish- ments included display areas, shelves, and counters just like their shore- bound counterparts. Floating gristmills went up and down the Ohio, too. These were catamaran-like arrangements of two boats with a mill wheel be- tween, powered by the current, while the whole contraption rode at anchor. Millers typically charged one-sixth of the wheat or one-eighth of the corn ground for farmers. As late as 1821, one traveler reported, many "neighbor- hoods and even towns" obtained all their cornmeal in this manner. Traders with more bulky wares to sell also made their presence felt. In the early 1800s Dudley Woodbridge Jr. sometimes bought salt, iron, whiskey, and flour from boats that stopped at Marietta on their way downstream. Farm- ers living on the river's banks sold their produce to those same traders or to settlers descending the Ohio on their way to new homes.[3]

Floating mills provided those living on the Ohio's banks with their services in exchange for a portion of the flour during the first two decades of the nineteenth century. *From S. P. Hildreth,* Biographical and Historical Memoirs of the Early Pioneer Settlers of Ohio *(Cincinnati: H. W. Derby and Co., 1852), courtesy of the Ohio Historical Society.*

The number of United States citizens living west of the Appalachian Mountains grew tremendously between 1790 and 1820. Kentucky's population grew fastest in the 1790s (from a little over 73,000 to over 220,000 by the turn of the century) but slowed thereafter. The population of the first state west of the Appalachian Mountains nearly doubled to reach 406,000 by 1810 but grew to only 564,000 over the next decade. By contrast, Ohio's population grew more than tenfold between 1800 and 1820—from less than 50,000 to nearly 600,000 inhabitants. Uncertain land titles, a legacy of the 1780s, represent one reason Ohio's population grew faster than Kentucky's after the turn of the century. In 1802 a traveler remarked that "I did not stop at the house of one inhabitant who was persuaded of the validity of his own right but what seemed dubious of his neighbor's." Others made similar observations.[4]

Slavery clearly played a role as well. Richard Clough Anderson, a resident of Lexington, was one of many Kentuckians who speculated in lands north of the river. In 1815 he noted in his diary the following: "Money judiciously laid out in the purchase of land in the Indiana (new purchase) would be very prudent & safe. The land in that country populated by poor persons (divided into small tracks) & worked by freemen instead of slaves, will be highly cultivated & become more valuable than any Country settled by Virginians held in large parcels & cultivated by Slaves." When traveling through Lancaster, Ohio, a few years later, Anderson concluded that "the rapid improvement of this Country shews the good policy of excluding slaves & of the high benefits of dividing land into small parcels in the congress manner." Still, in 1820 the combined population of Kentucky and Tennessee just topped the population of the territories and states created by the Northwest Ordinance.[5]

Though the federal government offered for sale eleven million acres in Ohio at land offices in Cincinnati, Zanesville, Chillicothe, Steubenville, Marietta, and Canton, nearly half of the land sold had been bought on credit. Settlers overextended themselves because the government's system allowed them to speculate freely. The minimum size of a purchase had shrunk to just one hundred and sixty acres by 1804, and though the minimum price was two dollars an acre, a discount for cash decreased that figure. The federal government allowed purchasers five years to pay for their land: one-quarter was to be paid within forty days, but the next quarter of the purchase price was not due for two years, and the last half, two years after that; the buyers then had one year to pay off any outstanding debts due to late payments. During the 1810s the population grew so fast that rumors of land values rising to five or ten times their original value in a short time convinced many to take a chance. With only a quarter of the purchase price due within a little less than six weeks of signing, farmers claimed more than they needed, counting on selling a portion of their tract at a handsome profit before another quarter of the purchase price came due two years later. By 1821 the federal government had collected only about twenty-seven million of the forty-seven million dollars owed by Ohioans. Jefferson's embargo, the War of 1812, postwar inflation, and the Panic of 1819 all took their toll on farmers' ability to pay, and only a series of relief laws first passed in 1806 allowed the government to collect what it was owed.[6]

But private rather than government sales accounted for over half of the land sold in Ohio during the first two decades of the nineteenth century, and like the federal government, speculators offered easy credit. In 1809 nonresident landowners owned a substantial portion of the new state, but by 1815 much of it had passed into the hands of residents. Residents had also come to own most of the best-quality lands.[7]

To gain insight into the careers of large-scale land speculators as opposed to ambitious farmers, we can turn to the correspondence of Nahum Ward of Marietta. The son of a prominent Massachusetts family, Ward came to Ohio to scrutinize the old Ohio Company Purchase in 1809. He went home to Shrewsbury, took an appointment as deputy sheriff, and began to purchase unredeemed company shares from residents of the surrounding area. With five hundred dollars from his father, he bought enough to entitle him to five thousand acres in southeastern Ohio. He visited the West again in 1811, surveyed his tracts, looked at others, and returned once more to New England to buy more shares, but settled in Marietta soon thereafter. Ward's trips to and from New England continued until 1817, by which time he owned the rights to thirty-seven thousand acres of land in Washington, Athens, Morgan, Lawrence, and Meigs counties—all within the original boundaries of Washington County and the Ohio Company Purchase. He speculated in lands south of the river as well.[8]

Nahum Ward rented some of his land, letting a hundred-acre lot in western Virginia for three hundred bushels of corn a year. But he hoped to sell most of it, although the stability of western currency posed problems. In August 1815 he wrote his father to say he hoped to pay off his debts soon, but "New York money is at advance in this place of 7 per cent, Philadelphia is at 5 per cent." Still, he expressed great excitement to his family back east about the future of the West. He rejoiced that "upwards 600,000 souls are now in Ohio, and increasing daily," and speculated that Ohioans had come to outnumber Massachusetts residents. Ward predicted that within twenty years, Ohio would be the wealthiest state in the union. He continued to borrow, paying his creditors as infrequently as possible. In June 1817 Ward wrote his father that he hoped "our worthy friend Mr. Allen will let his money rest one year longer, when I hope to swim without assistance in my land concerns." But, he continued, "I am almost daily selling or purchasing [land]." In another missive he reported that "I have bought and sold a great many lands in this country, and had my expenses not been very great I should at this time have been free from debt."[9] Clearly, the life of a land speculator was anxious one.

Despite the efforts of Ward and others, Washington County's growth rate did not come close to matching the state's. Its population failed to double in the 1810s, growing from 5,991 in 1810 to 10,425 in 1820. Marietta township's population grew from 1,463 to only 2,028 over the same span. Richer lands beckoned in the Miami Valley at the other end of the state and on the upper Muskingum north of Zane's Trace. But when the booming land office business and sales in the military tract north of the Zanesville fueled that town's growth, Marietta's place in the region's economy would grow and change as well.

Thus the Ohio Valley beckoned settlers to come west, and both the federal government and land speculators strove to make it accessible to newcomers. But once immigrants made their decision, the trip to Ohio would prove to be quite an undertaking. In 1811 an English visitor named John

Melish estimated that a wagon drawn by a pair of horses could transport a family of seven west at a rate of twenty miles per day, six days a week, with the Sabbath serving as a day of rest. The northern route from Connecticut to the Western Reserve through New York was a six-hundred-mile trip, and Zanesville lay four hundred twenty-five miles from Philadelphia through southern Pennsylvania. The trip took between two and six weeks. Most travelers, Melish wrote, packed wagons with food and stopped along the way at homes and taverns to sleep.[10]

At least one young woman might have argued with Melish's promise of averaging twenty miles a day. Margaret Dwight had a difficult journey along the southern route in 1810. She wrote that wagons had to cross rivers and creeks daily. They might have to wait all day for a swollen stream to fall or detour along its banks looking for a place to cross. She heard wild stories of horses becoming mired in mud, wagons tipping over, and men drowning. Margaret wrote, "we have concluded the reason so few are willing to return from the Western country, is not that the country is so good, but because the journey is so bad." Still, she saw "waggons without number," and many passed her party daily with groups that consisted of twenty people or more.[11]

Once they reached Pittsburgh, settlers bought provisions and boats to descend the Ohio. The boats looked like crowded floating farms, with families living alongside their livestock and utilizing the tools, furniture, and home furnishings that would soon be put to use in a more conventional setting on land. Not surprisingly, these larger vessels were dubbed arks. Upon landing at whatever river town they intended to pass through on the way to their new homes, settlers sold the boats to merchants and farmers, who used them to ship produce to the market at New Orleans.[12]

The best time for settlers to descend the Ohio was during the time of high water in the spring. A young Englishman named Francis Baily attempted to sail down the Ohio in the late fall of 1796 before the river froze, but that winter proved to be an especially early and cold one. Baily found some spots with ice thick enough to allow a loaded wagon to cross. When he camped on shore one night, midway between Wheeling and Marietta, rains in New York and Pennsylvania caused the river to rise ten or twelve feet. The ice cracked, filling the dark with the Ohio's angry roars of protest. The next day, the riverbed was a moving body of ice with huge plates that grated together, crushing boats and killing men caught in the current. Ice overflowed the banks and downed stands of trees, but as the flood subsided, the river froze over and did not break up again until the late winter runoff of melting snow. As time passed, Baily took special notice of how the river changed from season to season. He wrote that the Ohio did not even fill its banks in the winter, giving it a desolate look. But with the spring freshet, the valley took on a much more inviting look as the river's banks turned green once more.[13]

For those heading to southeastern Ohio, Zane's Trace served as the most important route to the interior. In the late 1790s private individuals improved the path to accommodate wagons west of Wheeling and north of Maysville, but most of the trace remained open only to people on foot or horseback. The trace became a mail route immediately upon completion, and a Chillicothe merchant named John McDougal ran a pack train to Philadelphia through Wheeling a few times a year. When Ohio became a state in 1803, 5 percent of the monies from the sale of public land was designated for road construction and maintenance—3 percent under state and 2 percent under federal supervision. The state doled out money to the counties, and thus efforts to improve the trace went ahead in an unsystematic fashion. But improve the trail Ohioans did, and in the years following, Zane's Trace became a true wagon road.[14]

Even with improvements, though, travel proved to be anything but smooth. Bogs and swamps created hazards, and ruts appeared all along the route during heavy rains and in the spring when the countryside thawed out. Travelers stayed in the taverns that sprang up along the trace. Some establishments had been built to house customers, but many families simply welcomed travelers into their cabins in order to add a little extra cash to the larder.

Settlers heading for homes south of the Ohio took the sixty-mile road from Maysville to Lexington. Others arrived from Virginia and the Carolinas along the Wilderness Road blazed by Daniel Boone a generation earlier. Just as Pittsburgh's merchants had done for southeastern Ohio and western Virginia, Lexington merchants oversaw the settling of western Kentucky and Tennessee. They imported eastern goods and exported the farmers' surplus, shipping grain, tobacco, and hemp to New Orleans. Profits were high in the earliest days, but competition picked up by 1810 when at least thirty retail merchants did business in town. Lexington's population grew from over 4,300 in 1810 to nearly 7,000 just five years later.[15]

When François Michaux came to the Ohio Valley to study the region's botany and remark on life there, he was following in the footsteps of his father, André, who had visited the region a few years before. The elder Michaux had not seen fit to comment on Lexington in the mid-1790s, but by 1802 his son found much to note. He complained that Lexington's muddy streets were unpaved but approved of the fact that most of the houses were made of brick. Manufacturing had barely gotten off the ground because labor was in short supply. Lexington did have newspapers, ropewalks, tanneries, potteries, and powder mills, but most businessmen were traders. Farmers from all over Kentucky bartered there. Goods came from Baltimore and Philadelphia to Maysville in four to six weeks, and a fully loaded wagon could make the trip by road from there in two-and-a-half days. Michaux estimated that 70 percent of the goods on sale in central Kentucky's largest town were of English manufacture, including jewelry, cutlery, tinware, and iron goods. Coffee and sugar came from the Caribbean.[16]

Just five years later in 1807, Fortescue Cuming, the traveler who encountered men from so many different states and walks of life on the river below Marietta, found paved streets with sidewalks in Lexington, and the number of manufacturing concerns had grown tremendously. The town's culture seemed to be improving as well. Transylvania University, a day school for boys, and three boarding schools for girls all flourished there.[17]

The energy with which the Lexington elite attacked new commercial opportunities set them apart from their counterparts across the mountains in the Chesapeake. The planters of Virginia had been living an anxious life as the tobacco market declined for more than a generation. Kentuckians bred fine horses, imitated the clothing and homes of the Virginia gentry, and cultivated a sense of polite society, but they had learned not to overtax the land from the example of their ancestors' burned-out tobacco fields. Hemp prices were on the rise, and unlike the eastern elite, Kentucky merchants invested profits not only in displays of wealth, but in manufacturing concerns as well.[18]

To the north of Lexington, Cincinnati served as the entrepôt for settlers heading for southwestern Ohio. When Francis Baily visited the city in 1797, he remarked on the number of frame houses there. Most of the city's inhabitants, he wrote, were engaged in business. Supplies for western forts came to Cincinnati first before going on to their final destinations. Five years later, another visitor praised the large stone courthouse and wrote that city residents were busy building more homes. In 1808 a third traveler found all traces of the old army fort gone but wrote of the many brick dwelling places, some of them two stories or more. He wrote that the houses were "well built, well painted, and have . . . [an] air of neatness," attributing the city's appearance to the New England origins of its settlers.[19]

Cincinnati's population grew from 500 in 1795 to 2,540 in 1810, nearly double the size of Marietta. In 1814 the number of inhabitants swelled to 4,000, roughly twice Marietta's population six years later in 1820, though still only a little over half the size of Lexington. Still, by 1811 visitor John Melish found that the number of dry goods stores alone in Cincinnati numbered thirty. In 1815 physician and local historian Daniel Drake wrote that more than seventy merchants imported goods from Baltimore and Philadelphia, and many of them "engaged in a wholesale business with . . . the adjoining country in Kentucky, Indiana and Ohio."[20]

In 1813, when Dudley Woodbridge Jr. twice wrote to the partnership of Baum and Perry in Cincinnati seeking New Orleans sugar and cotton, he was contacting one of the first firms to introduce their own line of commercial barges to the Ohio and Mississippi rivers. The barges reached lengths of one hundred feet and were capable of carrying perhaps one hundred tons of freight. Westerners loaded them with whiskey, flour, and pork for the journey downstream, and they returned with sugar, dry goods, and coffee. Though men had to haul them upriver against the current, the freight rate compared favorably with that of hauling goods overland from Philadelphia to Pittsburgh. Still, the trip proved long, with many dangers along the way. In 1818 fewer than two dozen barges operated between Cincinnati and the southern port.[21]

The rising western population fanned the flames of commerce. And just as settler-speculators tended to overextend themselves, so, too, did would-be merchants. Two acquaintances of Philadelphia merchant Richard Ashhurst set up shop in Pittsburgh as partners in January of 1816. About Pittsburgh's mercantile community, they were far from sanguine: "there has been a great many sacrifices made here last month[,] we understand[,] in consequence of a great many tradesmen & c[raftsmen] beginning Business who knew nothing at all of Business[.] [I]t is the general apprehension a great many of them will be obliged to decline in the spring."[22]

The observations of a trio of English farmers who descended the Ohio River looking for a place to settle two years later provide striking descriptions of western commerce. Henry Fearon wrote:

> There is class of men throughout the western country called "merchants," who, in the summer and autumn months, collect flour, butter, cheese, pork, beef, whiskey, and every species of farming produce, which they send in flats and keelboats to the New Orleans market. The demand created by this trade, added to a large domestic consumption, insures the most remote farmer a certain market. Some of these speculators have made large fortunes.

The other two men, however, found western traders less praiseworthy. In Cincinnati, "business and politics engross the thoughts of the men," observed Elias Fordham. "They live in their Stores and Countinghouses, and associate with their wives as little as may be." Thomas Hulme echoed these sentiments. "I was sorry to see very little doing in this town," he complained during a layover in Indiana, "they cannot *all* keep stores and taverns! One of the shopkeepers told me he does not sell more than ten thousand dollars value per annum: he ought, then, to manufacture something and not spend nine tenths of his time lolling with a segar in his mouth." Later in his journey, Hulme wrote, "Nature is the agriculturalist here; speculation instead of cultivation, is the order of the day amongst men." Hulme was referring to land speculation, but his impression that profits dominated the minds of most men in the West is a telling one.[23]

II

For a decade, Dudley Woodbridge Jr. and other merchants had been cultivating the hinterlands of towns throughout the Ohio Valley and connecting them to the Atlantic trade world. As the population of the Ohio Valley burgeoned after 1810, these merchants would take their commercial schemes to another level, establishing connections between towns throughout the river's drainage from Pittsburgh to Louisville. Dudley Woodbridge Jr.'s business records reveal the extent of the riverine economy that emerged in the West.

Jefferson's trade embargo destroyed Marietta's ship-building business, but while working in Pittsburgh, Dudley Woodbridge Jr. liked what brother William had to report of southeastern Ohio's growth well enough to return home as war with Great Britain loomed on the horizon. During and after the war, Woodbridge would establish a new business, one whose connections would grow to encompass the entire Ohio Valley.[24]

The War of 1812 cut off farmers' access to foreign markets, but the growth of internal markets made up some of the loss. New settlers bought their neighbor's produce until they had their farms up and running, and that could take a year or more. The populations of Pittsburgh, Cincinnati, and Louisville also grew tremendously, providing urban markets for agricultural produce. As for merchants, they sold more and more western products within the region itself. Kentucky tobacco and saltpeter came up the Ohio, as did cotton from Tennessee and sugar from New Orleans. Lead came east from the upper Missouri. Like their eastern counterparts, western merchants began manufacturing cotton and woolen cloth in Cincinnati, Chillicothe, Lexington, and other towns when cut off from British textiles.[25]

Before his sojourn in Pittsburgh, most of the letters Dudley Woodbridge Jr. wrote to men outside of Marietta's hinterland went to Philadelphia suppliers, merchants in Pittsburgh or Wheeling who took care of storing and shipping goods, or to lawyers in Cincinnati, Chillicothe, and Louisville who collected debts for the firm. The occasional letter went to men seeking to buy or sell Ohio lands and to New Orleans, Natchez, or other towns, soliciting information or news of goods gone astray. Woodbridge acquired salt, whiskey, and flour from western Pennsylvania and Virginia, as well as his own Ohio hinterland, but the goods he sold farmers and supplied to other merchants came across the mountains.[26]

There were a few exceptions to this fairly simple set of relationships with more distant western merchants. Although he imported most of his more complicated hardware (such as penknives, hinges, and padlocks) from the East, Woodbridge ordered simple ironware (such as axes, kettles, and nail-rods for making nails) from the Oliphant furnace south of Pittsburgh as early as 1800. Brown, Hart, and Company of Lexington, Kentucky, wrote in the summer of 1805 seeking potash. Woodbridge answered that these by-products of land-clearing had gone to the Pittsburgh glassworks before the prices dropped, but now farmers failed to keep and store them. Still, he would see what he could do about rounding some up and shipping them to Maysville if the price was right. But regular business between Woodbridge and merchants in western Pennsylvania, western Virginia, western Ohio, Kentucky, and Tennessee did not begin to grow until after 1810.

When he returned to Marietta, Woodbridge's ties to Pittsburgh manufacturers and merchants flourished first. He ordered "upper" and "sole" leather from tanner William Hays to supply Marietta's shoemakers. The mercantile concern of Thomas and Jonathan Cromwell had replaced Ebenezer Denny as the handler of Woodbridge's hemp and skins heading east, and the Mariettan ordered nails, nailrods, glass pitchers and bottles, blistered steel, and wrapping paper from them as well. In addition, he asked the Cromwells to obtain goods from two Pittsburgh manufacturers—wool hats and "4 gro' smallcoat buttons at Suttons manufactory," and "1 doz Peebles nappd hats." Ledgers indicate that Woodbridge established his own accounts with Peebles and the firm of Sutton and McNickle in the years following. Woodbridge also bought iron in Pittsburgh from George Anshutz to sell to manufacturers in Zanesville. Others showing up in his ledgers include Bakewell, Page and Bakewell, R. Patterson, Robinson and Barber, McCullough and Poynts, William Robinson Jr., and Scudder and A. Hart. Woodbridge also bought shares in the Manufacturing Company of Pittsburgh.[27]

As early as 1802 Pittsburgh provided a home to over 160 artisans representing more than forty crafts, including shoemakers, bookbinders, cabinet makers, engravers, and wheelwrights. The growing town housed a brewery, two glass factories, a paper mill, a number of oil mills, as well as fulling mills, ironworks, sawmills, and gristmills. The manufacture of iron quickly came to represent Pittsburgh's most valuable line, followed by textiles and boatbuilding. Town residents also produced saddles, whiskey, hats, and brass and tin goods.[28]

Despite such variety, by 1815 iron products made up a quarter of all Pittsburgh's output. Entrepreneurs established six nail factories between 1799 and 1812, and Joseph McClurg opened an air foundry in 1804 that produced machine parts. In 1811 the first rolling mill went up—businessmen began importing raw iron and producing their own bars, taking over a function that had once taken place only in the countryside where iron was found. One reason Pittsburgh's early manufacturing sector eclipsed those of all other western cities was because land was poor at the Ohio's headwaters. Entrepreneurs there invested profits in manufacturing while men in Cincinnati and other places speculated in the lands of the fertile Miami Valley as well as the territories of Indiana and Illinois in hopes of making a quick and easy profit.[29]

As Pittsburgh grew, it added the role of market to its former functions of waystation for merchants and entrepôt for settlers. Farmers in the Connecticut Western Reserve made cheese for Pittsburgh customers; some sold substantial quantities there for twelve cents a pound. Other Ohioans sold cheese to the western Pennsylvanians as well, and city residents bought bacon from Kentucky pork producers. Dudley Woodbridge Jr. had associates sell salt, flour, pork, and lard in Pittsburgh for him in 1816.[30]

Commercial connections also grew between Woodbridge and westerners south of the Ohio River. The most important tie between the citizens of Ohio and western Virginia involved salt. Settlers and meat-packers needed the preservative for meat, and salt pork filled a critical niche in western diets. Initially, Woodbridge had done business with the Scioto Salt Works in Ohio's Virginia Military District. But after the War of 1812, he switched his allegiance to salt manufacturers to the south. In 1813 Woodbridge and Pierce of Zanesville offered to sell salt for William Steele of the Kanawha Valley for a 5 percent commission. In addition, Woodbridge supplied Donally, Steele and Company of Charleston, western Virginia, with goods. Among such costs as rent and bills for barrels and transport, Steele's company listed thirteen hundred dollars to rent eleven slaves in 1813.[31]

Fortescue Cuming is but one visitor who provided his readers with a description of a western salt plant. The site was divided between two entrepreneurs who ran seven furnaces between them. He observed that "Each furnace contains fifty cast iron pans, of about twenty gallons each. . . . A furnace requires eight men to do its work. . . . The water is wound up by hand by a windlass, in buckets, and emptied into wooden troughs, which lead to the furnaces." Sixty pounds of water yielded one pound of salt. At this particular spot in Kentucky, Cuming reported that each furnace could produce between sixty and one hundred bushels of salt per week, and the proprietors paid their landlords between three hundred and five hundred bushels per year as rent.[32]

Saline springs could be found at many sites in western Pennsylvania, Ohio, Kentucky, and Illinois, but by 1850 two-thirds of the salt used in the West came from the Kanawha Valley of western Virginia. The forests provided all the timber manufacturers needed to stoke the furnaces they used to boil off the water, leaving salt behind. One trade publication listed fifty-two furnaces there in 1815. Each utilized between forty and sixty thirty-six gallon kettles, and together they could produce between twenty-five hundred and thirty-five hundred bushels each day—a production rate nearly five times greater than the one estimated by Cuming a few years earlier at a site in Kentucky. With access to the Ohio and its tributaries, Kanawha salt became a staple throughout the Ohio Valley.[33]

For connections in Lexington, Kentucky, Dudley Woodbridge Jr. relied on the firms of Trotter, Scott and Company, Samuel and George Trotter, and J. and D. Maceoun. For his main concern and its various branches, Woodbridge bought gunpowder from these companies and sold powder for them on a commission basis to other merchants in Zanesville, Pittsburgh, and other towns.[34]

Kentuckians manufactured gunpowder from niter found in the state's cave systems. Plateaus covered with hardwood forests had the proper conditions for the concentration of nitrates, and most saltpeter came from sites near the Great Saltpetre Cave south of Lexington and the Mammoth Caves to the west. Kentucky contained nearly four thousand caves, but residents mined fewer than one hundred fifty of them: to be profitable, a mining site had to be dry and situated close to a road. Most gunpowder manufacturing took place in Lexington, with the raw materials brought in by wagon.[35]

The Trotters serve as a one example of western merchants who sank their profits into manufacturing. The family began its mercantile career supplying traders in southern Ohio, Kentucky, and northern Tennessee with eastern manufactured goods, as well as distributing local cotton and tobacco. Samuel and George Trotter built one of Lexington's largest wholesale businesses during the first decade of the nineteenth century. The brothers soon added an extensive trade in gunpowder obtained from a variety of mills in town before branching into manufacturing themselves. Their uncle, another George Trotter, became involved in mining saltpeter and manufacturing gunpowder in the early 1800s, and his nephews followed soon thereafter.[36]

Samuel Trotter purchased land and built a powder mill in 1810. Prior to the War of 1812, most of the powder manufactured in Lexington was consumed regionally in Kentucky, Ohio, and Pennsylvania, but because Kentuckians produced more saltpeter than the Lexington mills could use, much of the raw material went to New Orleans. During the war, however, powder went east as well when the Trotters received two large contracts from the Ordinance Department in Washington. Like Steele's saltworks, the Trotter mills depended at least in part on slave labor. The Trotters owned some of the slaves but rented experienced mill workers as well.

The powder industry flourished between 1800 and 1815 but declined thereafter, when easterners found it cheaper to import saltpeter from the Caribbean and powder from Great Britain. The Trotter mills continued to operate, however, and did a good business within the Ohio Valley itself.[37]

Other Lexington entrepreneurs turned to hemp manufacturing. The cotton boom stimulated demand for hemp products—rope for cotton bales and hemp for bagging material. Business had slowed for the Hunts in Lexington by the turn of the century. By 1798 Abijah had left Cincinnati and followed the army, always his best customer, to Natchez. John closed the branch stores in neighboring towns, and when business dipped further in 1801, he retired from retailing with a tidy nest egg that he began to invest in manufacturing concerns. Hunt's establishment produced hemp between 1803 and 1814, and he shipped his products to all the port cities on the Atlantic coast, north and south, as well as to New Orleans, Natchez, St. Louis, and Nashville. He was not alone—by 1809 Lexington boasted thirteen ropewalks and five bagging factories. The Bluegrass region exported more hemp and hemp products than any other in the United States until the mid-nineteenth century.[38]

In addition to his southern links to western Virginia and Lexington, Dudley Woodbridge Jr. also established contacts in Nashville, Tennessee, during the War of 1812. His association with the firm of Cantrell and Read began with a deal to provide the partners with Kanawha Valley salt and quickly progressed to the sale of cotton. Woodbridge sold bales in both Zanesville and Pittsburgh, receiving a commission of 5 percent.[39]

Selling cotton upriver as far as Pittsburgh had actually begun well before Woodbridge became involved. Chronicler François Michaux wrote of Nashville entrepreneurs sending it north as early 1802 and reported that he had seen barges full of it at Marietta. Michaux wrote, "Thus are the remotest parts of the western states united by commercial interests, of which cotton is the basis, and the Ohio the tie of communication."[40]

Woodbridge's contacts with Louisville merchants involved buying sugar and coffee imported from New Orleans and selling tobacco on 5 percent commission for a man named James H. Overstreet. He made similar arrangements with Cincinnati merchants. The economies of both towns were more dependent on trade, commerce, and wholesaling than manufacturing prior to the steamboat era. Louisville residents capitalized on their location at the falls of the Ohio, and Cincinnati residents capitalized on the tremendous growth of southwestern Ohio's population.[41]

Selling on commission could be a cumbersome business, however. The owners of the goods set the prices, and if items didn't sell, Woodbridge had to write for permission to lower the rates. He also complained frequently that others sent him inferior products and expected him to sell them for top dollar. Woodbridge informed one Cincinnati supplier in 1818 that shopkeepers in and about Marietta would not buy the poor cotton he had sent. Mobile traders sold cotton and other goods from boats on the river as well, providing even more competition.[42]

Contacts between western merchants and manufacturers extended to the banks of the Mississippi River. Deposits at Ste. Genevieve in Missouri had been the earliest source of salt before closer ones in Ohio, Kentucky, and western Virginia became dominant, but exports of lead from Missouri grew as the nineteenth century progressed. Although Woodbridge imported white and red lead from the Trotters in Lexington, many others imported minerals from the Mississippi Valley. Craftsmen used red lead in the manufacture of glass and pottery in Pittsburgh, Zanesville, and other Ohio Valley cities. St. Louis merchant Christopher Wilt traded lead for glass in Pittsburgh in 1812. Others used white lead in the manufacture of paint.[43]

III

During the 1810s, then, Dudley Woodbridge Jr. gained access to a wide variety of manufactured goods, as well as cotton, tobacco, salt, and other materials from entrepreneurs in western Pennsylvania, western Virginia, Kentucky, Tennessee, western Ohio, and Missouri. In order to distribute these products, Woodbridge built a warehouse soon after his return to Marietta and began wholesaling in earnest. He supplied local merchants as well as traders in a variety of other towns, but his greatest concentration of customers came from the communities of Springfield (later called Putnam) and Zanesville, sixty miles upriver on the Muskingum. Indeed it was Zanesville's growth that helped Woodbridge revive his mercantile career.

Ebenezer Zane had established a "ferry" at his tract of land on the Muskingum in 1797 to fulfill his obligation to the federal government; it consisted of a couple of canoes lashed together, covered with planks, and could do no more than move one person and a horse at a time from shore to shore. Zane gave the land to his brother and son-in-law as compensation for their help in blazing the trace. When the two men arrived and found squatters at the site, they hired Marietta attorney Paul Fearing to evict them and refused to pay them for their improvements. When Zane's brother platted the town in 1800, he improved ferry service by providing a flatboat. When the state of Ohio organized Muskingum County in 1804, the legislature designated Zanesville as the county seat. Mariettans Rufus Putnam, Levi Whipple, and Increase Matthews owned the land across the Muskingum from Zanesville, and there they founded the town of Springfield.[44]

Woodbridge's most important contact to the north would prove to be one Ebenezer Buckingham. The two had been born the same year—1778. Buckingham came to Marietta in 1797 and went to work surveying for Rufus Putnam, later marrying the general's youngest daughter. Buckingham and the Woodbridge brothers seem to have known each other well. Like many surveyors, he ended up owning a prime bit of land. In 1802 Lucy Woodbridge wrote her son William that land was not selling in Marietta, for people bypassed the town and headed for the military lands farther up the Muskingum. Buckingham moved to Springfield and "adventured his prospects in that country," Lucy wrote. Probably his relationship with Putnam helped determine his choice of hometown. Over the next decade, Buckingham established stores in Zanesville and surrounding towns, went into partnership with Ohio Company cofounder General Benjamin Tupper, among others, and speculated further in land.[45]

The United States military district Lucy wrote of encompassed two million acres of land to the west of the Seven Ranges (lands surveyed under the authority of the land ordinance of 1785 north and east of the Ohio Company Purchase). Established in 1796, the district was set aside by Congress as military lands to be claimed with warrants by soldiers. But eastern policy makers established a minimum purchase of a quarter-township or four thousand acres, putting the lands well beyond the means of any veteran entitled to a hundred-acre tract. Speculators bought up the warrants, and just one hundred fifteen men came to claim over two-thirds of the territory. In 1800 Congress ruled that there should be hundred-acre tracts designated for the original holders of warrants, but such action proved to be too little, too late.[46] Springfield and Zanesville lay at the southern edge of the district on the Muskingum River (with public land for sale as well, to the south between Zanesville and Washington County), ensuring that together the towns would play a key role in the commercialization of the upper valley.

In 1807 one traveler reported that Buckingham's town thrived. Springfield consisted of about fifty houses in addition to taverns, stores, gristmills, and sawmills. By contrast, upon taking the ferry across the Muskingum to Zanesville, he encountered a dull place. But political wangling in Ohio found the state capital located in Zanesville from 1810 to 1812, and that proved to be all the impetus the town needed to grow. A later traveler reported that its population had doubled from six hundred to twelve hundred residents between 1809 and 1811. Zanesville became a large, thriving town made up of many brick buildings and nearly two dozen taverns and stores, with a complement of artisans that included stone cutters, brick makers, carpenters, cabinet makers, smiths, tanners, and printers.[47]

The town's commercial sector was large and varied. Ebenezer Buckingham invested in Zanesville's first glass-making establishment and owned one-third of the stock in the Putnam Manufacturing Company, established in 1815 to process cotton. Rudolph and Abraham Pitcher opened a paper mill in 1810, and a merchant named Ebenezer Meriam processed pot and pearl ashes. Meriam advertised in the local paper for farmers to bring in ashes as they cleared their land of trees, and he bought kitchen grease to use in the manufacture of candles. The mills of John Wartinbee and Isaac Dillon and the Putnam Manufacturing Company imported machines to card wool in 1816 and 1817, competing for the business of local farmers. The partnership of Dillon and Newport advertised a new "factory" on Licking Creek in the fall of 1816—it consisted of a fulling mill and a loom with a flying shuttle to turn yarn into cloth. A man named Moses Dillon built and operated a forge and iron foundry, in addition to sawmills and gristmills, and paid local men to cut the wood he used as fuel.[48]

Dudley Woodbridge Jr. established a branch store in Zanesville in partnership with a man named Thomas L. Pierce, and he also supplied the growing commercial and manufacturing community with eastern goods, New Orleans sugar, Pittsburgh glass and iron, west Virginian salt, Tennessee cotton, and Kentucky powder, hemp, and tobacco. In addition to Buckingham, his customers included Samuel Frazer, Kirker and Fulton, Alexander McLaughlin, Andrew Miller, Horace Nye, James Taylor, Samuel Thompson, and old partners Joseph Munro and Daniel Converse. From the foundries he ordered kettles, ovens, lids, and other castings.[49]

As with managing branch stores, dealing with his Zanesville customers required skills in handling people. In the spring of 1813 a situation developed in which goods for one merchant went on ahead up the Muskingum in a boat while the goods for others remained back in Marietta for a time. With too few boats available for the transport of goods, Woodbridge had to soothe his customers a bit to avoid jealousy and to assure them that he would take proper care of everyone.[50]

As his wholesaling network grew, Dudley Woodbridge's business at Marietta changed as well. A ledger covering the years from 1811 to 1816 contains the accounts of 323 customers in Ohio and western Virginia.[51] Comparing this ledger to that of a decade earlier makes it clear that Mariettans were doing more than just scraping by. Although the number of customers using more than one method of payment only dropped from 50 to 40 percent, the number of all credit customers paying entirely with cash rose from 21 to 49 percent. The number of customers using cash at least once rose from 57 to 77 percent. Those paying with work dropped somewhat, but the number of artisans grew while the number of those doing generic work and hauling fell sharply. Hemp all but disappeared, although a few still used it as barter, and others traded bed cords, lines, cordage, and rope. The proportion of customers bartering with agricultural goods, including pork, beef, oats, hay, potatoes, corn, apples, and flour, rose somewhat but still did not represent a significant source of income. Trade in finished goods rose from 5 to 9 percent, including sugar, butter, cheese, cider, leather, tallow, candles, and soap. The fall of men's generic work and the rising volume of trade in finished goods that often represented women's work indicates that Washington County had become more settled. A number of women traded linen and socks, and a few paid their account by weaving cloth.

The number of customers paying with orders from third parties dropped precipitously, but it must be noted that most of the orders from a decade ago had come from just two men—boatbuilder Joseph Barker and Woodbridge's extravagant partner, Harman Blennerhassett. Many of the new orders came from plantation and slave owner Alexander Henderson of western Virginia. His overseer and managers were Woodbridge customers, as was Henderson himself.

The ledger of James Weir of Greenville, Kentucky, provides a comparison to the Woodbridge records from south of the Ohio.[52] Between 1813 and 1815, the merchant sold goods on credit to 328 customers. Only 126 (38 percent) used more than one method of payment, a ratio nearly the same as that of Woodbridge customers. But the number of Weir's credit customers paying entirely with cash was 95, or 29 percent, compared to half of the Woodbridge customers. Two hundred five Weir customers used cash at least once, making the ratio 62 percent, compared to 77 percent of Woodbridge customers. Still, the majority of customers of both merchants had access to cash at one time or another.

Most of Weir's customers used barter to pay part or all of their account, and the most common items came under the category of linen, yarn socks, and the making of shirts and clothing. Some of the cloth is labeled cotton but most was "tow"—cloth made from hemp fibers. Fifty-three customers, or 16 percent, paid their account in this way. Some of them were women with accounts under their own names, whether they were related to a male customer with his own account or not. Together, the Woodbridge and Weir ledgers indicate that the labor of local women was not an inconsequential part of western trade.

When country linen and related work are added to the number of customers bartering butter, whiskey, sugar, and salt, the 20 percent of Weir customers that utilized finished products was double the ratio of Woodbridge customers. A little less than 10 percent of Weir's customers paid with corn, oats, chickens, hogs, pork, lard, bacon, ham, and beef. Weir's customers included six artisans—two smiths, a cooper, a builder, a shoemaker, and a hatter. Twenty-five men performed generic work and hauling. Miscellaneous items included boats, deerskins, a watch key, bricks, feathers, and razor straps. One customer paid with the hire of a "negro." The payment of 64 accounts (20 percent) involved third-party notes, cash, and assumptions, and Weir utilized a lawyer named Charles Wing to collect money from 89 (27 percent) of his customers.

The ledger of Edelin Benedict, a hatter and merchant in Bardstown, Kentucky, provides a view of the West's economy from one artisan's point of view.[53] From 1816 to 1819 Benedict sold mostly hats to 151 customers. Eighty-two of them, or 54 percent, used cash to pay Benedict, and 72 of that number used cash only. Eight customers bartered wool that he used in his craft, and one provided carding services. Other artisans in town exchanged axes, saddles, bridles, shoes, and cupboards with Benedict, which he presumably sold in his store. Eleven customers paid their accounts with whiskey.

As with the first decade of the nineteenth century, though, ledgers alone that detail the activities of customers who used credit do not reveal the full scope of the western economy. During the War of 1812 the army pumped a large volume of specie into the West, and as banks proliferated in the postwar years, customers had access to more paper money than ever before. In the flush times that followed the conflict, cash business far exceeded the credit transactions to be found in Woodbridge blotters and daybooks. A new store appeared in Marietta in the fall of 1816—John Mills and Co., a partnership that consisted of Mills and Dudley Woodbridge Jr. That October Mills sold $893 worth of goods for cash, and just $163.44 worth on credit. In November cash transactions came to $858, while credit transactions totaled only $278.94, and Mills took in just $12.94 worth of "country produce" as barter. Cash sales peaked at $1,100 in December but then dropped sharply during the winter months to a low of just $236 in February, while credit sales totaled $161.75 during the same month. Country produce equaled only 5 percent of the store's cash take in December, but barter increased to between 10 and 15 percent of the cash total during the cold winter months. Still, it is obvious that the store did a cash business in 1816 and 1817.[54] Easier access to cash, however, was not a sign of a strong economy. Instead it would prove to be a warning of bad times to come.

It is important to note that barter with local farmers for their surplus crops never made up a significant portion of Woodbridge's accounts (although in 1803 there may have been very little surplus available). Unlike some other western merchants, Dudley Woodbridge Jr. looked beyond local exchange throughout his career. In his first decade of business, he invested in such large-scale projects as the brig *Dominic,* purchasing flour in Steubenville and pork in Cincinnati to make up the load. During the war he speculated in cotton. Over the years Woodbridge sank money into loads of furs, hemp, and ginseng. In the 1810s he extended his wealth and power through wholesaling. The storekeepers he supplied and the men who ran his branch stores undoubtedly dealt with local farmers on a much more regular basis than he did himself. Yet it was the fast-growing population of farmers that made his far-flung commercial network possible. In the 1820s John Mills operated a partnership with a merchant named Waterman Palmer in Parkersburg, western Virginia, and Palmer did engage in the practice of contracting with local farmers for large volumes of flour.[55]

During the first decade of the nineteenth century, Dudley Woodbridge Jr. had helped establish Marietta's hinterland and forge commercial connections between that hinterland and eastern markets through New Orleans and Pittsburgh. At the same time, his western counterparts engaged in similar activities in other towns north and south of the Ohio River. The War of 1812 brought specie across the mountains, but it also disrupted trade as the Atlantic became embroiled in conflict, and westerners began to explore markets within the region itself. With nationalism soaring at war's end, Americans descended the Ohio in larger numbers than ever before. They speculated in land and planted crops.

As both the western population and the western economy surged, merchants facilitated the flow of agricultural goods and raw materials not only to markets outside the region, but to markets along the Ohio and its tributaries as well. In addition, while continuing to import eastern manufactured goods, merchants began promoting the trade of goods manufactured in Pittsburgh and Lexington. Thus while the commercial connections Dudley Woodbridge had first established between East and West in the 1790s remained strong, his son took an important part in the process of developing a new regional economy in the West itself in the two decades that followed.

6

The Western Country

In 1813 a New York merchant named Isaac H. Jackson decided to move to the Ohio Valley. He planned to visit a variety of places before choosing his new home, and with him he carried a handful of introductions from fellow merchants in New York, Baltimore, and Philadelphia to their counterparts across the mountains. Each letter to a merchant in Pittsburgh, Pennsylvania, Marietta, Ohio, and Russellville and Lexington, Kentucky, made the same pronouncement—Mr. Jackson would be a worthy addition to "the western country."[1]

Mr. Jackson and his colleagues in the East clearly understood that "the western country" referred to the broad expanse of territory west of the Appalachian Mountains, be it the lands north or south of the Ohio River. Indeed it was the recipients of Jackson's letters—western merchants—who helped create such a region. Ordinary settlers, though often more concerned about their own independence and local neighborhood networks, also recognized such a place, even if they occasionally complained about the character of westerners living on the opposite bank. But though a Western Country existed, getting goods from that place to Atlantic markets often frustrated Ohio Valley residents. It would be in calling for the breaking down of barriers to trade—their demand for banks, their response to the Panic of 1819, and the way they embraced the transportation revolution—that the denizens of the Western Country proclaimed a common identity.

I

Merchants had the widest-ranging connections among westerners, and relationships between them went beyond simply transacting business. In June of 1812 Dudley Woodbridge Jr. got word that a boat had been caught on a snag and sunk about ten miles below Marietta. He rode out to look at the damage and to make sure the packages had been brought ashore and attempts to dry them were underway. He then wrote to fellow merchants up and down the river so they could see to the recovery of their goods. In addition to informing Thomas Boal of Cincinnati, Samuel January of Limestone (Maysville), and the firm of Scudder and A. Hart of Pittsburgh about what had occurred, Woodbridge listed the names of others in their towns and hinterlands whose names appeared on the boxes and bales.[2]

Merchants also looked after each other's business on a more regular basis. Woodbridge often wrote others to request help in locating missing boxes and trunks, and western merchants always stood ready to help each other find shipments and packages gone astray. Woodbridge exchanged money from local banks for other currency when his Pittsburgh counterparts made such requests, and western merchants also helped pass along mail and instructions. Dudley Woodbridge Jr. forwarded letters to men he knew in other towns to give to clerks and agents heading in their direction.[3]

Merchants also called on one another to settle disagreements. When a dispute arose over an arrangement to find salt for Ebenezer Buckingham, Woodbridge consulted with three merchants in Marietta, and they agreed with his point of view. But, he wrote Buckingham, if "you still differ in opinion with me, I shall insist . . . upon abiding the decision of Mr. McLaughlin & one or more respectable merchants of Zanesville."[4]

Partnerships between merchants in the West could be spread out over long distances. One trio of men combined to run the firms of Duncan, Dobbin and Co. in Louisville, Forsyth, Dobbin and Co. in Wheeling, and Duncan, Forsyth and Co. in Pittsburgh. Many, though, were of a fairly short duration. Dudley Woodbridge Jr. went into business with a variety of men throughout his career, and others did the same. The career of Thomas Kelsey offers one example. He lived in Hamilton, Ohio, twenty-five miles north of Cincinnati on the Miami River. Kelsey and a partner established the firm of Kelsey, Smith and Company in 1810. Five years later, Kelsey bought out Smith's share, although both men remained in town doing business on their own. Kelsey next opened a distillery with a man named Ramsey, and other ventures and partners followed in the years to come. The partnerships of the Trotter family in Lexington followed a similar path. In the newspaper of any western town, one can easily trace the organization and dissolution of the place's mercantile establishments as firms advertised the end of partnerships in order to collect all debts due before splitting up for good—perhaps this was one reason for ending a partnership.[5]

The connections of Dudley Woodbridge Jr.'s Marietta neighbors with those living south of the Ohio River mirrored the merchant's, although their networks were not as far-reaching. Marietta's newspapers routinely published the election results of Wood County, (West) Virginia; Wood County

THE GREAT HINCKLEY HUNT, DEC. 24, 1818.

Ties between western farmers north and south of the Ohio: a "Great Circus Hunt" united men from Washington County, Ohio, and Wood County in western Virginia. An advertisement in Marietta's *American Friend* on 23 March 1821 read, "We have now only to request the attendance of every man and boy who has any grudge or ill-will against the wolves, bears, and panthers." "The Great Hinckley Hunt" depicts a similar event. *Courtesy of the* American Field *and the Ohio Historical Society.*

and Washington County residents staged large-scale hunts together to rid the woods of wolves and other predators; and Marietta leaders endeavored to establish an agricultural society which was to include farmers north and south of the river. In addition, westerners frequently married into families on the opposite bank. When one of the Putnams, David's son Charles, commented on the health of area residents, he noted the death of Isaac Williams across the river in Virginia, a man who had been instrumental in helping the New Englanders establish their town three decades before.[6]

Perhaps because merchants relied so heavily on each other, they ignored the sectional origins of their neighbors across the river for the most part, but ordinary settlers were not always so polite. In 1813 Isaac Baker of Lexington, Kentucky, wrote the following to a friend who attended school back east: "as you have gone to New England to acquire a few of those tricks I suppose which Yankees practice with so much success in the western country, I have determined to remember you in your wanderings." A decade later Felix Rennick, an Ohioan with Virginia roots, wrote an associate that he did not intend to try driving cattle to market in the winter, though of his competitors he wrote, "for a Yanky, I had like to have said nothing is impossible." A few weeks later Rennick wrote that the rains were so bad that only a Yankee would try to get goods to market down the Ohio that March. Still, he admitted to being impressed with the "vigilance & enterprise" of the northern settlers as they faced obstacles to their plans. Some westerners, however, adopted a different tone. When Mariettan Luther Dana Barker passed through Louisville in 1820, he wrote home that he was pleased that Kentucky slaveholders had been so hard hit by the financial panic that had swept through the nation the year before.[7]

During the early nineteenth century, some Kentuckians referred to Ohio as the Yankee State and grumbled about northerners' sly dealings, while some Ohio Yankees contended that their southern neighbors were both stubbornly independent and lazy. But the letter of Baker, who refers to "the western country," and a letter of Felix Rennick's brother George, who refers to "our western commerce," make it clear that their world was one in which Kentuckians and Ohioans interacted regularly as residents of the same region.[8]

References to the Western Country can be found in the correspondence of many Ohio, western Virginia, and Kentucky families. They are common in the accounts of travelers as well. When William Coolidge of Baltimore descended the Ohio River, he found the region to be an unattractive place where most people lived wretched lives, although he wrote of encountering "enlightn'd" people while traveling on steamboats. A few years later, another visitor from Baltimore, John Sharkey, came to a different conclusion—he described "bustling" western communities and people brimming with "spirit." Though one expects the occasional reference to white indolence because of the presence of slavery south of the river, Thomas Green of Virginia came west to check on his tenants and concluded that it was the westerners north of the Ohio who were lazy because fertile soil meant an easy living. Some visitors wrote about differences between the northern and southern banks, and others felt that all westerners were alike. Residents themselves wrote of the Western Country when referring to markets, opportunities, religious matters, politics, sickness, land, and, of course, home.[9]

Merchants like Dudley Woodbridge Jr. were not the only people to write of coming to the Western Country to make a profit or grow rich. For ordinary settlers, too, the West represented opportunity. The fertile soil produced fine crops, though in 1806 a settler named Gabriel Lewis informed family back in Virginia that getting flour to market was difficult, and thus he considered the possibility of raising stock instead. John Loving, another Virginian who moved to Kentucky and decided to "make some money" raising cattle and hogs, wrote to family six years later that more people were on "the road to wealth" in the West than back east. Isaac Baker, a Kentuckian visiting Nashville in 1814, wrote that "the people are all so assiduously engaged in making money that no one appears to have any time to give to society."[10]

Caleb Thorniley came all the way from England with his family and two others to settle on Ohio Company lands in the 1790s. According to him, there were many English families in the area with dozens to come by the summer of 1807 when he sent a letter praising his new home to a brother who remained on the other side of the ocean. He wrote of a friend who had become a merchant and made profitable trips to New Orleans. Thorniley's son was the farmer, he reported, and Caleb himself ran a tavern. He sent news of another man who was busy building bridges throughout the area to facilitate transportation and also reported on a market house in Marietta. "We are rising fast in riches," Thorniley wrote, "as in all the neighborhood of our Country and State." "We enjoy the fruits of our industry," he concluded, and added that "we possess greatness as a Nation and freedom as individuals."[11]

Just as references to markets abound in the letters and accounts of early settlers, so do references to the importance of the Ohio and its tributaries. A settler who claimed thousands of acres of land in and about Harrodsburg, Kentucky, in 1780 wrote of its proximity to rivers and easy navigation that would make his tracts more valuable. Lexington resident Richard Clough Anderson, who speculated in Indiana in 1817, wrote approvingly of fertile land "not more than 40 miles from the Ohio." The river also meant contact with others in the West. Moving closer to the Ohio meant a lessening of loneliness for one Kentucky family traveler François André Michaux spoke with. Many years later resident James Drake wrote, "I at one time almost came to the conclusion to locate on the Ohio River where a man is not very remote from any part of the Western Country." Drake did not move to the banks of the Ohio, however, and he provides an example of a westerner who, though he wrote of profits and land speculation, in the end chose the chance to obtain competency—a landed inheritance for his children—over access to markets. Drake left his family home in Kentucky to work in a land office in Indiana. Later he moved to Missouri, planning to own land himself and to speculate also. Like many others, Drake wrote of illness along the Ohio, including outbreaks of cholera—thus a healthy environment provided an added inducement to move farther west, even if his new home proved to be more isolated than the last.[12]

Indeed, competency proved to be very important to westerners of all kinds. In 1807 traveler Fortescue Cuming met a family from Massachusetts who had settled near Cambridge, Ohio, four years before. The man had cleared land and run a store, a distillery, and a sawmill but felt cut off from civilization. Other settlers who did not live on the banks of the Ohio or one of its tributaries also complained of loneliness. The man told Cuming he was going to sell out for a tidy profit and move to a more settled area of New York State. But the time spent in Ohio had not been wasted; attaining the status of landowner had made the man feel "independent."[13]

Achieving competency was not always easy. There is evidence of people in northern Ohio and southern Kentucky without access to a navigable river, living in less-than-ideal situations. Even those with access to merchants and markets could not always capitalize on the fertile soil. Western farmers, like the merchants, found that the uncertainty of navigating the Ohio and the glut of goods arriving on the high tide at New Orleans frequently yielded disappointment. As Gabriel Lewis wrote, "very few except merchants purchase produce, [and] they seldom give more than 1/2 cash the other in goods." The merchants had to use specie to pay eastern suppliers.[14]

Many westerners wore multiple hats in their quest to make a life for themselves. One settler in south-central Ohio's Virginia Military District rented land and worked for others part of the time for cash and barter—he could only clear his own land a bit at a time. A tavern keeper living near Frankfort, Kentucky, rented a farm to a tenant and planned to erect a carding machine. A Kentuckian who moved north of the Ohio to live near Chillicothe hoped to find better access to land in a state free of slavery but found himself mixing teaching duties, farm work, and tavern-keeping to get by.[15]

Differences existed between those living north and south of the Ohio River, but most residents called home "the Western Country." They had a similar sense of place and understood that the phrase referred to the Ohio Valley.

II

One problem that all residents living west of the Appalachian Mountains had to contend with was a lack of specie. As troubles grew, westerners would unite against the East, demanding just economic policies from both eastern creditors and the federal government in the form of the Bank of the United States.

Westerners needed banks badly in the early nineteenth century. Merchants sold western produce in New Orleans but received goods and credit from the East. Creditors demanded payment in specie or notes that could be

redeemed for specie. Western merchants wanted local institutions respon-
sive to their needs that would allow them to borrow against their stock in
order to send drafts anywhere at any time. Farmers, too, seeking loans and
mortgages, desired the establishment of banks. The first institution to issue
paper west of the Appalachian Mountains was the Lexington Insurance
Company in 1802.[16]

Prior to 1863 the Ohio State Legislature organized banks by special acts.
In 1803 Cincinnati entrepreneurs received a charter and established the
Miami Exporting Company to facilitate the shipment of pork, flour, and
whiskey. In addition to sponsoring exports, the company could issue notes
payable to the bearer, assignable by delivery only. They issued bills which
they redeemed with notes from other banks, and by 1807 banking became
the company's only function. Between 1808 and 1814 the state authorized
seven more banks. Ohio chartered the Bank of Marietta as the state's first
regular bank in 1808, with Chillicothe and Steubenville following soon
thereafter.

Western banks nurtured ties to eastern counterparts. As early as 1804 a
Pittsburgh bank opened as a branch of the Bank of Pennsylvania and sold
drafts of its eastern parent institution at a premium of 1 percent. At some
point Marietta's bank apparently made a similar arrangement with the Bank
of the Potomac to funnel eastern notes west. The Zanesville and Steubenville
banks drew on banks in Philadelphia and Baltimore. Local bankers allowed
western merchants to obtain these banknotes for a premium of less than 2
percent in 1813. Dudley Woodbridge Jr. owned stock in more than one bank
in order to obtain drafts on his own notes rather than bills of exchange for
goods from merchants in distant entrepôts, meaning he could get cash
quickly and easily. He wrote his brother Jack (then a banker in Chillicothe)
that stockholders in Marietta's bank could obtain loans amounting to seven-
eighths of their stock after giving the cashier a power of attorney to sell the
stock if the investor failed to make good on the note or renew it. Eastern
notes went east to pay suppliers, and western notes were used to pay transport bills from Pittsburgh and the accounts of merchants who consigned
goods to Woodbridge from Lexington, Louisville, and other western towns.
Western merchants sent bank notes by mail or messenger cut in half, with
the second shipment following the first by a few days or a week.[17]

The charter of the Bank of the United States ran out in 1811, and Ohio
chartered four more state banks during the War of 1812. Ohio banks were
sound during the conflict itself because specie came west through federal
military contracts. In November of 1812 a Pittsburgh paper reported that
"eight waggons loaded with specie for the western army arrived here on
Saturday evening last, under an escort of lieutenant's guard." Dudley

Woodbridge Jr. had little trouble obtaining cash to send east in 1812 and 1813, and he attributed the state of affairs to the war itself. The ledger covering the years from 1811 to 1816 reveal that Woodbridge remitted payments to eastern and western suppliers almost exclusively in cash, only occasionally sending "sundries" or drafts east. In addition, the Zanesville merchants he supplied paid him in cash as well. It cannot be determined if farmers to the north paid the merchants in cash, or if those Woodbridge supplied found a ready market in the West themselves for the farmers' surpluses during the War of 1812. But James Weir's 1813–1816 ledger reveals a similar pattern between his main concern and its branches in southwestern Kentucky.[18]

Thus it might seem that the West had enough specie for all to benefit, but such was not the case. Westerners had built economic prosperity on paper foundations—literally. During the chaotic times of 1814, eastern banks suspended the payment of specie for notes, and western banks followed suit soon after. Many opposed this move (including Dudley Woodbridge Sr. and his namesake), fearing it would lead to abuses and inflation—and they would be proved right.[19]

When banks stopped redeeming their notes with specie, unauthorized banking grew. In order to turn a profit men set up banks, even if they had no capital to back their notes, as banking turned into a speculative activity. Boards of directors encouraged others to borrow, charged them interest when they paid the money back, and paid good dividends to shareholders. Such "bankers" could not redeem their notes with specie they did not possess, but they got away with such practices for awhile. But even authorized banks made attractive investment opportunities. During the flush days of speculation following the War of 1812, men borrowed money, paid back some of the loan, and then gave the bank a note for the rest that was to be redeemed later with dividends that averaged a 10 percent return. The number of banks chartered skyrocketed in the West. In 1818 alone, state legislatures authorized twenty banks in Ohio, forty-six in Kentucky, twelve in Tennessee, three in Indiana, and two in Illinois.[20]

Farmers and merchants demanded money and bankers were happy to supply it, and so paper money inundated the West. Prices rose and speculation inflated land values. But all the while, western paper lost its value in the East. In Philadelphia, western notes were discounted between 4 and 5 percent in late 1814, between 8 and 10 percent in late 1815, and between 12 and 15 percent in early 1817. An increasing number of counterfeit notes made a bad situation worse.[21]

Woodbridge's letter book for 1816 is filled with correspondence about currency. When he attempted to redeem notes at a Parkersburg bank across from Belpre in western Virginia, his agent objected to the paper money he received in return. But the cashier replied, "take such as I choose to give you or take the money you brought away." In August Woodbridge wrote the Trotters in Lexington that he could sell powder that fall, "but the trash we are obliged to receive in payment for goods is such that it would cost too much to convert it into good paper." Less than a month later, he reported that some customers preferred to buy their powder in Pittsburgh because merchants there accepted unchartered Ohio and Virginia currency, using it to pay wagon drivers. To Overstreet in Louisville, Woodbridge wrote that he could find no Kentucky paper to remit, only unchartered notes from Ohio and Virginia. That November he informed a Philadelphia supplier that seven-eighths of the notes currently in circulation were unchartered.[22]

To give easterners their due, Philadelphia merchants suffered as much or more than their western counterparts because of the lack of specie. Western merchants made up twenty-three of Philadelphia merchant Jonathan J. Robinson's one hundred and twelve customers who bought goods on credit in the years following the War of 1812. One resided in Pittsburgh, one in a small Ohio town, and one in western Virginia. The others all did business in Kentucky and Tennessee. In July of 1816 Robinson wrote Andrew Hynes that he had forwarded his goods to the care of a merchant in Nashville. Robinson stated that he wished the order had been larger and hoped that it signaled the beginning of "a more extensive & permanent trade betwixt us, which I feel a pleasure, as well as an interest, in cultivating."[23]

However, Robinson began experiencing problems that fall. He wrote one creditor that his capital had run low and trade had declined since the end of the war. To the firm of Wormald, Gott, and Wormald he reported the following: "The scarcity of money here & the great inequality in the currency of the states by which the merchants in the interior are disabled from meeting their engagements with their former punctuality without losing from 12 to 15 prcent in the exchange which they will not do." The same letter went to a dozen other suppliers. To another creditor he complained that westerners put off paying because they hoped for better exchange rates in the future.[24]

Within a year Robinson was all but bankrupt. He wrote his creditors that although his stock of goods equaled his debts, auctioning them off meant receiving a fraction of their value. Western merchants could not or would not pay. He pleaded for more time, and most seem to have given him extensions of a year or two. Apparently Robinson owed money to twenty different firms, many of them in England. Robinson did auction off some of his goods, and he borrowed money from a bank in Philadelphia as well. In the spring of 1819 he wrote one associate that he had surrendered all his property and could do no more. Though most of the business had been done by 1820, scattered letters over the next decade indicate the amount of time it took to wind up his affairs. The experience did not break him, however, for he retired to a farm in the country where he lived in peace for years to come.[25]

The 1810s had been a decade of tremendous growth in the West. The population exploded as a wave of immigration swept down the Ohio, and merchants established and nurtured growing commercial networks upon the high tide. Banks proliferated and land speculators, both large and small, flourished. But Americans were deeply in debt and overextended. Europe's economy soon stabilized, dropping demand for American grains, and a London economic crisis in 1818 led to English banks calling in loans. The Bank of the United States had been heavily involved in Ohio's expansion after 1816, and when the bank called in its loans to cover its overseas debts and other obligations, no one could pay. Farmers suddenly found themselves without a market and merchants were without money, and so the whole system collapsed.[26]

The relationship between the national bank and the banks of the West began in a promising enough fashion. The federal government chartered the second Bank of the United States in 1816, and it opened for business on 1 January 1817. Cincinnati and Chillicothe leaders successfully lobbied for branch offices, and leading men in the two towns bought stock with personal notes. Eastern banks resumed specie payment, and Ohio banks agreed to do the same if the Bank of United States would aid them and give them time to redeem their paper. The Bank of the United States loaned western banks the money to gain a sound footing, and discounts on western notes in Philadelphia fell to 6 percent once more.[27]

Western branches of the Bank of the United States loaned money to state banks, and, in turn, they loaned the money to entrepreneurs and farmers. But western merchants used the loans to pay off eastern creditors. Because the balance of trade strongly favored the East, the East sapped money from the West at an alarming rate. However, when the flood of notes issued by western branches of the Bank of the United States were redeemed in Philadelphia and New York, easterners found their banks depleted of specie. When an economic crisis in London forced British banks to recall loans, eastern banks found themselves in trouble.[28]

Because U.S. notes had gone east to pay creditors, local banknotes from farmers used to cover loans to buy land represented a large share of the paper money residing in western vaults. When the crisis began, the Bank of the United States insisted that state banks repay their loans in specie or in notes that could be redeemed for specie. The state banks could not comply, and a wave of bank failures followed. As money depreciated, prices fell; no one could sell their crops or their land, and customers could not pay store-keepers. The western economy came to a crashing halt, and a wave of fore-closures followed.[29]

East and West blamed each other for the Panic of 1819. Westerners claimed eastern bankers designed policies to bankrupt them, but easterners countered by accusing westerners of being "extravagant." On a trip to Philadelphia in July, Louisville merchant Daniel Southard wrote his partner back home that Kentucky and Tennessee merchants were being jailed for nonpayment of debts. The mood in the city was such that some were calling for the prosecution of "everyone from the west."[30]

Dudley wrote his brother in mid-July that Marietta's men of commerce were having financial difficulties. By November he was investing, utilizing any money he could lay his hands on to buy the property of men desperate for cash. It seems that Woodbridge was making the most of a bad situation because he and his family could not leave Marietta. Woodbridge owned over twenty thousand dollars worth of land he had inherited from his mother and could not sell during hard times.[31]

That same summer, Woodbridge sent Luther Edgerton on a trip to attempt to redeem over nineteen hundred dollars in cash for paper that meant something. Woodbridge instructed the clerk to go first to Chillicothe where his brother would take some of the Ohio cash and exchange it for Marietta banknotes. He hoped Jack would also take the Kentucky paper off his hands for either Marietta or U.S. notes, but if not, Edgerton was to head for the bank at Maysville to exchange the money. If that bank declined, the bank at Frankfort, Kentucky, might pay U.S. paper for the cash from Tennessee and Indiana as well. Hoping that the cash would retain at least three-quarters of its value, he wrote, "from Frankfort go to Cincinnati & there convert the balance of money you have on hand to US on the best terms you can not exceeding 25 percent premium."[32]

Many Ohio Valley residents north and south of the river found their western identity in confronting eastern politicians and bankers. Westerners struggled with the lack of specie and resented the East's stranglehold on banking policy. Bankers from Ohio, western Pennsylvania, and western Virginia met in Steubenville in 1816, and bankers from Ohio, Kentucky, and Indiana met in Cincinnati in 1817 to discuss how they might work together to resolve their problems. In 1817 and 1818 the Bank of the United States declared that only specie, or banknotes that could be redeemed for specie, could be used to pay off loans. Many western notes did not qualify, and residents north and south of the river were in an uproar. The Ohio legislature attempted to tax the bank in 1819. A Steubenville paper characterized the actions of eastern bankers as "oppression."[33] Westerners demanded that the federal government come up with some plan to provide for debt relief. An article in the *Kentucky Reporter* warned that the West was "well situated for the formation of a separate government," and if easterners failed to respect their property rights, "a dissolution of the union" was possible.[34]

The Panic of 1819 devastated western cities. Pittsburgh's manufacturing sector had actually found itself in trouble well before. With the end of the War of 1812, imported manufactured goods provided heavy competition for local wares. But in 1819 more businesses failed and unemployment rose, as did imprisonment for debt. A similar process took place in Lexington. Speculators and entrepreneurs failed in Cincinnati, and unemployment rose there as well. Martin Baum, one of the richest men in the region, had to liquidate over two hundred thousand dollars of his holdings to pay back the Bank of the United States. Louisville, perhaps the most commercially oriented of all the cities, was less hard hit and recovered the fastest when steamboats began to ply western waters in the early 1820s. Because so many loans had been issued to finance land speculation, the Bank of the United States ended up owning significant portions of western real estate.[35]

Before the chaos broke, Dudley Woodbridge Jr. had begun winding up the most active portion of his career. He helped set up his clerk, John Mills, in his own business in August of 1816, and soon thereafter he was renting Mills the warehouse, although Woodbridge continued to engage in other mercantile activities. He turned forty in 1818, he and his second wife were the parents of a growing brood of children, and he had long been plagued with stiffness and pain in his hips and legs as well as migraine headaches. Woodbridge remained a very active commercial presence in Marietta for another three decades, but clearly his days of cheerfully surviving immersions in ice-cold rivers were at an end.[36]

As to the fate of land speculator Nahum Ward, he may or may not have intended to settle in Marietta permanently in his youth, but thirty thousand acres of unsold land kept him there for the rest of his life. In October of 1827 Ward wrote to his brother that "I have plenty of the comforts of life but little money—Lands have fallen down, down to nothing." A year later he reported that "I am doing very little business as land selling is a gloomy trade"; and the following year complained that he could "not sell land for money." Ward had gone deeply into debt in the 1810s, and he did not climb out of it for decades. His debts hung heavily on his mind. Ward often apologized to his father for his inability to pay what he owed him; at times he could not sleep because of worry. Once he wrote, "the continued failure and disappointment for want of funds is distracting—I shall take a leap out of my present situation the first opportunity that I can afford anything for your relief." However, for every statement that he was "as poor as the poorest," or "as poor as a church mouse," one followed indicating that he was not in personal distress, and his farm and garden kept his family well fed.[37]

As for western farmers, society north and south of the Ohio River shared important similarities during the first two decades of the nineteenth century. In Kentucky settlers had long proclaimed a homestead ethic, believing that their labors gave them a right to own the land. But they always wanted more land. The settlers may have speculated for slightly different reasons than those of the wealthy and powerful (competency versus profit), but speculate they did, and thus they did not struggle harder to overturn the prevailing political and economic system. In Ohio's case, although settlers may have envied and resented those with more land or money, they did not band together to protest the distribution of wealth either. Ohio's settlers, like Kentucky's, believed that success lay just over the horizon. Westerners counted themselves free men, even if in debt, and they believed they could always move on to better opportunities farther west.[38] Their demands that the opportunity to get ahead be available equally to all free, white, native-born men would fuel the rise of the second party system in the decades to come, and they would especially clash with entrepreneurs over banking issues, but for the most part, they would not call for the dismantling of the expanding market economy, for that is where they believed opportunity lay.

In 1819 and the half-decade that followed, however, the outlook seemed bleak. The local prices western farmers could get for their crops in the boom times of the postwar years included 50¢ a bushel for corn, between $1.00 and $1.50 a bushel for wheat, between $6.50 and $12.00 dollars a barrel for flour, between $3.50 and $7.00 per hundredweight for beef and pork, and 60¢ a gallon for whiskey. In 1819 those prices dropped between 50 and 80 percent: 12¢ a bushel for corn, between 20¢ and 75¢ a bushel for wheat, between $2.50 and $3.00 a barrel for flour, between $1.00 and $3.00 per hundredweight for beef and pork, and 12.5¢ cents for a gallon of whiskey. In the depression that followed the panic, prices remained so low that merchants and farmers could not recoup the cost of transport, and trade stagnated.[39]

III

Many in the West believed that the solution to their problems lay in improving transportation between East and West to provide better access to markets. The transportation revolution began before the Panic of 1819 but flowered in the decades that followed, helping the West recover from economic collapse.

English inventors began to develop steam engines that could power watercraft in the mid-eighteenth century, and Americans began their own experiments in the 1790s. Although Americans carried out their work in the East, their goal was improving transportation on western rivers. In 1815 a Lexington newspaper quoted the Cincinnati *Gazette* as follows: "The invention of the steamboat was intended for US." Inventors Robert Fulton and Robert Livingston tried to persuade western states north and south of the Ohio to give them exclusive rights to navigating the Mississippi and Ohio rivers, arguing that only then could they be sure to recoup the costs of development. But residents in Kentucky and Ohio took great exception to this idea, protesting that steamboats were absolutely essential to the growth of their region. As with banking policies, they thought they scented an eastern plot to dominate them. One Cincinnati newspaper wrote that rivers are "the *common highway* of the West," and any attempt to monopolize travel would limit westerners' freedom.[40]

Men moving west in the decades following the Revolution had not necessarily left the Atlantic seaboard to escape the influence of developing markets. They had come to the Ohio Valley seeking competency, attracted by cheap, fertile land that boosters told them would yield many more bushels of corn and wheat per acre than they could hope for in the places of their birth. Beginning in the late eighteenth century, farmers became speculators in the Ohio Valley, both north and south of the river, hoping to profit from rising land values as the western population grew. Steamboats would improve their access to the wider world of trade, and as the volume of trade expanded, land values would rise even more. They did not fill newspapers with letters to the editor asking if the development of steamboats would be good for the West—they knew it would be. Rather they protested that through agreements that amounted to a monopoly over trade, those who developed the steamboats were seeking to deny them equal access to the benefits improved transportation technology could bring. Thus westerners concerned themselves with a perceived threat to equality of opportunity.

Fulton and Livingston did gain the right to navigate the lower Mississippi free from competition, but entrepreneurs in and about Pittsburgh soon entered the fray. A handful of steamboats departed from the headwaters of the Ohio between 1811 and 1815. Two years later a large craft made the voyage from New Orleans to Louisville in twenty-five days. Westerners broke Fulton's monopoly at will as rumors circulated freely of money to be made in the new industry. They crowed about emancipation from the East, and merchants in the Atlantic ports worried that New Orleans entrepreneurs would supplant them as suppliers of manufactured goods. In 1818 boatbuilding on a large scale began in earnest in the Ohio Valley.[41]

Steamboats made an immediate impact on the cost and speed of transportation. In the early nineteenth century, it took the crew of a barge or keelboat between three and four months to make a trip upstream from New Orleans to Louisville. These craft could do no better than ten or twenty miles a day. By contrast the first steamboats could travel fifty miles a day, and by the mid-1820s the fastest could do one hundred. The length of a trip upstream to Louisville fell to a little over a month by the late 1810s, to under three weeks in the 1820s, and to a little under a week by the early 1840s. As for freight rates, shipping a hundredweight of goods upriver from New Orleans dropped from five dollars for keelboats in the early nineteenth century to under one dollar for steamboats by the 1820s. Later that decade a thousand steamboats arrived at Louisville in a year, they docked at Cincinnati on a daily basis, and arrivals in Pittsburgh averaged one a week.[42]

With the rich timber resources available and its early development of iron and machine manufacturing sectors, Pittsburgh would lead all other cities in the production of steamboats until the Civil War, and together, Pittsburgh, Cincinnati, and Louisville launched nearly 90 percent of all such craft constructed in the West. Of the nearly thirty-six hundred steamboats produced before 1862, Pittsburgh manufacturers turned out over fifteen hundred, Cincinnati just under one thousand, and Louisville nearly seven hundred fifty. Steamboats and their repairs also sparked lucrative industries in the manufacturing of machinery and engines.[43]

Steamboats quickly replaced keelboats as the carriers of traffic upstream, although many people continued to use the older craft in the decades to come on smaller streams and on the Ohio's shallower tributaries. But steamboats did not replace flatboats. In some ways the arrival of steamboats stimulated the flatboat trade, complementing it rather than displacing it. Flatboats carried a large volume of bulky raw materials from various points within the Ohio's drainage above Louisville to the factories and mills of Pittsburgh and Cincinnati, where entrepreneurs constructed the machinery and affected the repairs made necessary by the rise of new industries tied to the transportation revolution.[44]

Flatboats also remained a cheap method for farmers who wanted to take goods to market themselves. During the 1820s thousands of flatboats continued to arrive in New Orleans every year, the majority of them from above the falls at Louisville. In the 1830s a man named John Irwin who attempted to run a furnace in Boston, Kentucky, south of Louisville, found himself inconvenienced by just this fact. He complained that he had a hard time feeding his white laborers and black slaves because Kentucky farmers had become too independent. Farmers got good prices for their surplus crops in Natchez, Vicksburg, and New Orleans, Irwin wrote, so he had to buy early before they took their yearly trip and to pay what they demanded for meat and flour.[45]

Steamboats also had an impact on urban development. The history of the town of Madison, Indiana, serves as one example of a river town that flourished when steamboats revolutionized travel and commerce. When settlers bought land at the newly established federal land office in Jefferson-ville in 1808, one group founded the town of Madison midway between Cincinnati and Louisville. After surveying the site, landowners laid out the town using the grid pattern so typical of western cities. The new settlement grew slowly at first. In 1811 Madison's population consisted of only a dozen families who supported two taverns and two stores, as well as a small group of artisans—blacksmiths, hatters, a brick maker, and a stonemason.[46]

But after the War of 1812, more people came to settle in Indiana, passing through Madison on their way to lands in the interior of the state. By 1825 the town's population had grown to one thousand, and the town's commer-cial sector included fourteen dry goods stores, ten groceries, two taverns, and a market house, in addition to a variety of mills. During the late 1820s, as the agricultural surplus of Madison's hinterland grew, so did its process-ing and export market. In the 1830s citizens began to build wharves to lure steamboats, and the range of the town's processing industries included meat packing, brewing, and tanning, as well as the production of soap, brushes, lard, and candles. Its population totaled two thousand by 1840, and during the two decades that followed, Madison manufacturers began producing steamboats and steam engines.[47]

Louisville, Kentucky, on the Ohio's southern shore, prospered to an even greater degree. The town recovered more quickly from the Panic of 1819 than either Pittsburgh or Lexington as the transportation revolution greatly enhanced its role in Ohio River trade. With the tremendous growth of up-stream traffic during the 1820s, the city became the center of steamboat op-erations. Merchants found themselves busier than ever, handling tons of goods moving out of and coming in to the region until Louisville became a city of warehouses. The city financed the building of a canal around the falls of the Ohio in the late 1820s, but as the size and shape of steamboats grew, the too-small locks became all but obsolete within a decade. Thus during the 1820s and 1830s two-thirds or more of the steamboats arriving in Pitts-burgh came from Louisville. One group of boats brought goods from New Orleans and St. Louis to the city at the falls, and another group took the goods on to Cincinnati and Pittsburgh. During the 1810s and 1820s the city's population grew at a pace more than ten times that of Kentucky as a whole. Still, in 1840 Louisville's population was less than half the size of Cincinnati's.[48]

But steamboats did not bring prosperity to everyone. With the rise of Louisville and the tremendous growth of Cincinnati, Lexington found its preeminent role in the region's economic development usurped by others. Lexington's population topped fifty-two hundred in 1820 but failed to reach six thousand by the next census. In contrast, during the same decade, Louisville's population doubled, and then doubled again by 1840. Lexington boosters fought their town's decline by attempting to sponsor turnpikes and railroads. They also attempted to take the lead in cultural matters. Transylvania University flowered in the 1820s, gaining a national reputation for its training in the fields of law and medicine, and many future western leaders were educated there. But by the 1830s Cincinnati would emerge as the leader of cultural as well as economic development in the West.[49]

Residents of the Ohio Valley, north and south of the river, referred to their home as "the Western Country," and easterners used the phrase as well. Merchants established the strongest ties that helped bind the region together as one economic unit, but farmers established ties, too, although most were not as complex or far-reaching. Though differences existed between the two banks of the river, westerners understood their region to be a place of opportunity where all could hope to achieve competency. Many of the settlers also shared a market orientation and speculated in lands as vigorously as those with access to more capital. Perhaps land speculators and speculative farmers had different goals—profit versus competency—but the fact remains that most wanted to improve their economic status, and they saw improved access to markets as one avenue toward that goal. Ohio Valley residents, north and south, traded with each other, married each other, and followed each others' politics. All welcomed the coming of steamboats, and when currency troubles began to foreshadow a panic to come, westerners banded together to castigate eastern bankers and policy makers in such a manner that one Kentucky newspaper editor threatened disunion. But what he could not know was that the solidarity between those living on both banks of the Ohio River had reached its peak in the early 1820s and would never be as strong again.

PART III THE BUCKEYE STATE

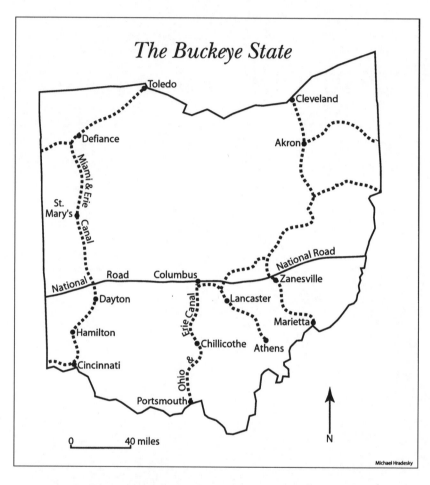

The Buckeye State

Toledo

Cleveland

Defiance

Akron

Miami & Erie Canal

St.
Mary's

National Road

National Road

Road

Columbus

Zanesville

Dayton

Lancaster

Erie Canal

Marietta

Hamilton

Chillicothe

Athens

Ohio &

Cincinnati

Portsmouth

0   40 miles

N

Michael Hradesky

The Buckeye State. As Ohioans shifted their attention from the commercial world of the Ohio and Mississippi valleys to the growth of industry and new routes east through the Great Lakes, the National Road and Ohio's canals challenged the Ohio River's central role in determining settlement patterns within the state.

During the early republic, the sense of place that grew up in the West had a twofold aspect. On the one hand, merchants had tied East and West together along lines of capital and credit from the first days of settlement. As Americans, Dudley Woodbridge Sr. and others who went west had claimed space for a new empire. On the other hand, during the first two decades of the nineteenth century, the riverine commercial economy of the Ohio Valley bound together those of Dudley Woodbridge Jr.'s generation living on the Ohio's northern and southern banks as westerners. They believed that theirs was the land of opportunity, and eastern policy makers too often meddled in western affairs. People, goods, and news traveled slowly across the mountains, and so the regional aspect of Ohio Valley residents' sense of place sometimes overshadowed national ties. Ohioans, western Virginians, and Kentuckians called home "the Western Country."

Then a financial panic swept through the entire nation in 1819. Afterward, Ohioans attempted to rebuild their economy by improving transportation between the Ohio Valley and the eastern seaboard. They decided to construct a canal, and that canal would both solidify and symbolize the state's ties to the East.[1] As Ohioans turned their attention to the development of a statewide economy, their old feelings of connection and fellowship with westerners south of the Ohio River would fade. The canals would also bring in a flood of New England immigrants to northern and central Ohio—men and women who felt no connection to westerners south of the Ohio at all.

7

Ohio's Economy Transformed

In the summer of 1822 a Philadelphia wholesaler wrote Dudley Woodbridge Jr., seeking a market for his goods in Ohio. Woodbridge replied:

> I received your favor of this date—The quantity of shoes & axes I cou'd retail in a year would be so limited, that it would not be an object to your acquaintance to send them so far—Our shoemakers & blacksmiths supply the market with mens shoes & axes—purchasers prefer buying of them—For 2 or 3 years I obtained nails of a superior quality from Phila[delphia] but those of a good quality can now be obtained so much lower from Pitt[sburgh] than the Phila[delphia] price adding carriage, that I presume no nails manufactured east of the mountains could be brought into competition as to the price with those obtained at Pittsburgh.

Artisans were firmly established in Washington County by that time, and iron manufacturers in Pittsburgh supplied the Ohio Valley with tools and other goods. But this state of affairs was not to last long. The transportation revolution would bring new people and more manufactured goods west, and with access to more labor and the growth of urban markets, western entrepreneurs would take up manufacturing on a large scale to compete with eastern goods, crowding out local craftsmen in places such as Marietta. And as for Pittsburgh, although its population of 7,249 only trailed Cincinnati's by 2,400 in 1820, by 1850 the latter had grown at such a pace that its residents outnumbered those living at the Ohio's headwaters by more than 2 to 1.[1]

Cincinnati had long been the most sizeable town in the Ohio Valley, but during the 1820s and 1830s it grew to be so large that with a population of just over 46,000 in 1840, the city was larger than all others in the United States, save only the ports of New York, Philadelphia, Baltimore, New Orleans, and Boston. And indeed Cincinnati served as the port of the Ohio River's basin. In 1820 Cincinnati's population of 9,642 had put it right in the middle of a dozen other towns with populations ranging from 6,500 to

13,500. Twenty years later, though the population of the top five American cities outnumbered Cincinnati's by as little as two to one (with the others much higher), the western city's three closest competitors ranged from only 60 percent to 75 percent of Cincinnati's size. Lagging further behind, no other American urban area topped 24,000 (only a little over half Cincinnati's size), including Pittsburgh and Louisville. The city opposite the mouth of the Licking had truly become a central place in the trans-Appalachian West, and it easily dominated the Ohio Valley to a greater degree than it ever had before.[2]

But the rise of Cincinnati was not the only change in Ohio's urban landscape. As the economy changed, older subregional hubs such as Marietta declined while new ones grew. Marietta's economy evolved along with the rest of the state's towns and cities, but as the Ohio River lost its dominance over the state's economy, so too would Marietta lose its role in the economy of southeastern Ohio.

I

Westerners may have hoped that steamboats would emancipate them from economic dependency on eastern bankers, merchants, and policy makers, but another element of the transportation revolution would bind the states north of the Ohio River more firmly and directly to the eastern economy and culture than ever before—canals. The state of New York authorized the building of the Erie Canal in 1817. Completed in 1825, it spanned over 360 miles between Buffalo and Albany, making it more than five times longer than any other American canal at that time. A decade later, traffic proved to be so heavy that the state had to initiate a series of projects to widen it. Eighteenth-century leaders such as George Washington had dreamed of artificial waterways that would unite East and West, and with the opening of the Erie Canal, such plans finally came to fruition.[3]

The combination of steamboats and canals cemented old ties between regions. Exports from Philadelphia to the Ohio Valley more than quadrupled between 1816 and 1826, and then tripled between 1826 and 1834. At the end of the War of 1812, western markets absorbed less than 5 percent of Philadelphia's manufactured goods, but by 1837 that share had risen to over 30 percent. From Ohio, Kentucky, and other western states, Philadelphians absorbed flour, pork, lard, tobacco, hemp, cattle, and horses; indeed the volume of western products arriving in Philadelphia quadrupled between 1816 and 1837. Still, the volume of the eastern city's exports had grown so fast that the balance of trade favored Philadelphia to a greater extent than before. The value of Philadelphia exports was four times higher than that of imports from the West in 1816, and seven times higher in 1837.[4]

The effects of the transportation revolution in the West are most evident in Ohio. In terms of canal mileage, the state stood second only to New York in 1830 and gained the top spot ten years later. After the Panic of 1819 Ohioans embarked on a course of internal improvements that they hoped would ameliorate the high transportation costs and long, hazardous trips down the Ohio and Mississippi rivers that had always hampered western commerce. Rebuilding their economy meant gaining easier access to eastern markets, and that meant utilizing the Great Lakes and the Erie Canal. Most Ohio residents would focus on state rather than regional economic concerns after 1820.[5]

Those who first advocated constructing canals as public works argued that internal improvements would further the course of democratization within the state because everyone would benefit—farmers, merchants, and manufacturers. Canals would bring about a more equitable distribution of wealth as commerce expanded and all gained better access to markets. But the route chosen for the Ohio and Erie Canal provoked instant controversy: it was to run from Portsmouth, in the middle of the state's southern border on the Ohio, north along the Scioto Valley, with a turn east to follow the upper Muskingum River toward a terminus at Cleveland on Lake Erie. A promise of canal construction from Cincinnati north through the Miami's valley would be necessary to gain the backing of the heavily populated southwestern corner of the state. The State of Ohio oversaw the building of the Ohio and Erie Canal between 1825 and 1832, and with the help of New York investors, engineers, and laborers fresh from the construction of the Erie Canal, the Ohio and Erie Canal went into operation without incurring serious cost overruns.[6]

But trouble developed soon thereafter. Those who had been bypassed by the canal lobbied for projects of their own, pushing the "equal benefits for all" rhetoric as far as they could. In the southeast, Zanesville residents demanded a side cut from the main line to their city, and Marietta residents insisted that the state improve the Muskingum River to give them access. Neither Democratic nor Whig leaders were willing to risk public disapproval by opposing state support of internal improvements, so the Ohio legislature approved five new projects, including access for Zanesville and Marietta, between 1832 and 1836. Engineering and construction errors, coupled with the Panic of 1837 and the depression that followed, nearly drove the state to bankruptcy, but Ohio did not abandon projects as some states did (probably because so much construction was already underway), and a wide variety of projects were complete by 1845. The state's troubles had disillusioned Ohio-ans, however, and many would oppose state intervention in the economy thereafter, making internal improvements a partisan issue between political parties in the future.

The Ohio and Erie Canal changed the composition and distribution of the state's population as settlers flooded in by way of the Erie Canal and the Great Lakes. Yankee farmers who settled in northern and central Ohio cre-ated a wheat belt from which grain flowed north on the canal to Cleveland, and from there directly to the East. In addition, unskilled Irish and German workers who came to work on the internal improvement projects settled in the cities to labor in growing manufacturing sectors. One English immigrant who came west looking for work wrote home, "come by way of New York for it is mutch cheaper on the cannall and better." Before 1820 few Ohioans lived far from the Ohio or the navigable portions of its tributaries—that changed with the coming of canals.[7]

Despite the wave of immigration, Ohio's population growth slowed substantially. It had multiplied tenfold between 1800 and 1820, but it took three decades for the state's population to do little more than double from just under 1 million in 1830 to just over 2.3 million in 1860. Even as new-comers poured in, a wave of residents poured out with the opening of the prairies of Illinois and beyond, and with the discovery of gold in California. It was the influence of the Ohio and Erie Canal that made the growth of the northeastern corner of the state an exception. Cleveland's population grew from 6,071 in 1840 to just over 43,000 by 1860.[8]

Still, even though the volume of trade flowing from West to East through the Great Lakes grew rapidly, the canals did not destroy trade south to New Orleans or Cincinnati's place in the region's economy. Prior to the coming of steamboats on western rivers, nearly all goods shipped from the interior of the continent to the East Coast had gone down the Ohio. Although the trans-portation revolution had been underway for nearly two decades by the end of the 1830s, that ratio of goods had only fallen to 83 percent and did not drop below 50 percent until the 1840s and 1850s. Thus the flow of western produce south continued unabated—the flow north simply began to match it, before finally exceeding it after mid-century. Corn, pork, and whiskey from Cincinnati continued along its old path, while wheat from the newly developed north and central regions of Ohio went the northerly route. Within the region itself, barges distributed coal from Pennsylvania, Ken-tucky, and Ohio throughout the Ohio's valley until the end of the antebellum era. But New York salt brought in by canal did begin to undermine western Virginia's hegemony.[9]

Cincinnati's population swelled as people from the countryside moved there, looking for opportunity. Others came from the region's smaller towns—places like Marietta. In 1837 twenty-four-year-old William Emerson, a Mariettan born and bred, first saw Cincinnati when he took to the road, traveling and teaching school in western Ohio, northern Kentucky, and eastern Indiana. The city seemed so large, crowded, and busy that he felt like a "country villager." Cincinnati, he wrote, was "nothing but a 'heap' of businesses." He noticed a high degree of specialization as well. "It is not as it is in country towns," he observed, "where the merchants are universal geniuses, and dabble in every thing from watch seals and silk shawls down to crockery ware and codfish."[10] A decade later Emerson moved there for good. In April of 1847 he wrote his father that "being blest with some portion of time, and the day being decent, I'll write you in rhyme."

> Marietta it seems is all coming down here,
> New Emigrants every new morning appear,
> Some coming to stay and some coming to go,
> The way they flock to the citys not slow.
> More Washington County have I seen here
> In a month than I have when at home, in a year.[11]

The rise of Cincinnati is indicative of the transformation taking place in the Ohio Valley during the middle years of the nineteenth century.

Cincinnati's early growth came from expanding commercial opportunities as the western population grew. A wide variety of artisans practiced crafts there, but they manufactured most of their goods for customers in Cincinnati and the Miami Valley. In the 1810s and 1820s the city grew at a pace three times faster than Ohio's as a whole, reaching nearly twenty-five thousand by 1830. As Pittsburgh and Lexington floundered following the Panic of 1819, Cincinnati rose to a preeminent position in the Ohio Valley, but as late as 1830 it remained a city devoted to trade. Half of the goods imported were eastern dry goods that still came overland to Pittsburgh before descending the Ohio. But the other half came from the western sources—iron and ironware from Pittsburgh, timber from western Pennsylvania, and sugar, coffee, tea, and china from New Orleans.[12]

The coming of steamboats and canals actually enhanced Cincinnati's role in the region—partly by spurring the rise of manufacturing. Entrepreneurs began building steamboats and engines, and then expanded to the production of sugar mills and cotton gins. As the transportation revolution speeded up shipping times, the processing of hogs and meatpacking increased as well. The Ohio canal itself had a significant impact. The new

Marietta in 1833 (top) and Cincinnati in 1841 (bottom). Despite Marietta's busy role as a hub of settlement between 1790 and 1820, when Marietta-born William Emerson visited Cincinnati in 1837, he wrote that the burgeoning city made him feel like a country villager. Though Marietta and Cincinnati were both settled in the late 1780s, by 1840 Cincinnati had become the Queen City of the West, and its population far outstripped that of Marietta. *Both courtesy of the Ohio Historical Society.*

wheat belt created a market for Ohio manufacturers, stimulating industry. When Ohioans built canals in the western part of the state in the 1840s, Cincinnati's manufacturing sector grew tremendously by way of markets in northwestern Ohio and northeastern Indiana. Eventually competition from canals in Indiana and Pennsylvania drove freight rates so low that eastern manufacturers flooded the West with goods, and so Cincinnati entrepreneurs responded by manufacturing goods on a larger, more efficient scale than ever before to compete. They sent stoves, machinery, textiles, and wood products to markets in the interior of the state, and self-employed craftsmen such as those Woodbridge had referred to in 1822 could not compete.[13]

Manufacturing in the West had always been hindered by labor shortages, but that, too, changed with the coming of canals. For over sixty years the Ohio Valley had lured families from the East with the promise of land. But in the 1830s European immigrants from industrial and urban areas found the labor market in Ohio to be one of the region's chief attractions. In addition to Cincinnati, they settled in Wheeling and Louisville, but the presence of slavery there kept most from western Virginia and Kentucky. Englishman Richard Mighill wrote home to his parents in 1834 that Cincinnati and the surrounding area was "fine cuntry for a labring or trad[e] man.... Thare are a grate many canal and turnpikes agoing on." He and his brothers found jobs in Ohio's growing cities, as well as in St. Louis and New Orleans. They reported that groceries and provisions could be had for low prices.[14]

Foreign immigration had a decided impact on Cincinnati. In 1825 nearly 80 percent of the city's adult white male population had been born in the United States. Of the foreign-born, most were English or Scots-Irish. But by 1840 the proportion of foreign-born had more than doubled to 46 percent. Over half of them were Germans, and by 1850 the number of Catholics from Ireland had grown as well. As the city expanded, poorer sections of town developed, and the more prosperous residents began to build homes in neighborhoods removed from the seamier side of life. Tensions between Protestants and Catholics manifested themselves in the temperance movement, as old-time residents blamed German brewers and Irish drinkers for the city's ills.[15]

As its population burgeoned, Cincinnati became "the Queen City" of the West. Newcomers flooding in did not only include canal workers from the East, farmers from the countryside, and immigrants from Europe; Cincinnati also attracted professional men, including doctors, lawyers, ministers, teachers, and newspaper editors. The city's cultural supremacy rested on its museums, libraries, and colleges, including a medical school, and residents blazed the trail in calling for a public school system in Ohio. Although wealth became more concentrated over time in the hands of an elite few, all classes of society strove to harness the rise of the second party system to create a government that would serve the needs of the people through a system of relief for the poor and the construction of waterworks and hospitals.[16]

II

In addition to Cincinnati, Ohio's canals had a tremendous impact on the roles other towns and cities played within the state's economy. New subregional hubs waxed while others waned. Steubenville had been the second-largest city in Ohio in 1820, but its growth slowed dramatically thereafter, and its rank fell to seventh by 1850. The town of Miltonville, south of Toledo, had served as the hub for Wood County, but when the state of Ohio built the Wabash and Erie Canal along the opposite bank of the Wabash River, one of the towns downriver usurped its role, and Miltonville eventually disappeared altogether. On the other hand, Zanesville and Chillicothe grew tremendously between 1830 and 1850, while Columbus's population nearly tripled during the 1840s.[17]

The role new subregional hubs played in Ohio's economy proved very different from that of early leaders such as Marietta and Steubenville. During the first two decades of the nineteenth century, the first subregional hubs had emerged as merchants such as Dudley Woodbridge Jr. imported and distributed eastern goods while gathering and exporting farmers' surpluses. But canal boats and steamboats could carry much more grain to market at a much quicker pace, and Ohio farmers began to concentrate on growing wheat and corn in greater quantities as staple crops. The canals enhanced the use of waterpower along their courses, and the economic foundation of the new subregional hubs consisted of mills that processed large volumes of flour, as well as meatpacking industries and distilleries that turned corn into whiskey. These concerns were of a larger scale than similar businesses of the past—the processing of agricultural goods before the transportation revolution had been as much for local and regional consumption as for export. Thus the new subregional hubs were larger than the older towns of prominence had been. In turn, larger populations supported the growth of manufacturing, and the new hubs tended to specialize in a particular sector in addition to processing agricultural goods; entrepreneurs in river ports built steam engines, and their interior counterparts concentrated on consumer goods made of paper, leather, and iron.[18]

At another level of economic development, the canals fostered new relationships between different sections within the state itself as each area specialized in and traded a variety of foodstuffs with others. Farmers of the Western Reserve produced meat and dairy products, selling their butter to

Deep Cut. Home to a busy mercantile establishment on the Miami and Erie Canal in the 1830s, Deep Cut faded from sight when railroads replaced canals as the most important transporters of Ohio's produce and manufactured goods. In contrast to Deep Cut and Marietta, Cincinnati, with its role as both entrepôt and central place in the Ohio Valley, grew progressively larger with each step forward in the transportation revolution: keelboats on western rivers, barges on Ohio's canals, and railroads through the countryside. *Courtesy of the Ohio Historical Society.*

Ohio's growing urban markets. At the same time, their imports of grain and pork from the southern sections of the state tripled between 1840 and 1860. In turn, wheat and corn producers in southeastern Ohio imported beef from points north and west. The marketing of raw materials within the state grew as well. Canals brought Youngstown coal to Cleveland, making that city an important fueling stop for traffic on the Great Lakes, and coal deposits near Athens became available to manufacturers throughout the state. Athens had once been within Marietta's hinterland (Woodbridge supplied a family of merchants named Shipman there), but over time it became tied increasingly to the burgeoning city of Columbus.[19]

Such developments had an impact on southeastern Ohio. The Ohio Canal followed the Muskingum's channel north of Zanesville, bypassing both it and Marietta. In addition, large steamboats could not make the trip between the two towns, and few smaller ones tried. Residents clamored for access to the canal, however, and in 1836 the state approved the improvement of the Muskingum River from the Ohio north to the canal's locks. It went into operation in 1841, and finally Mariettans interested in manufacturing had a clear path to markets in the central and the northern portions of the state and could ship goods back east by way of the Great Lakes as well.[20] The Nyes and the Putnams represent two families who took advantage of this shift.

Ichabod Nye, a contemporary of Dudley Woodbridge Jr., had come to Marietta with his father-in-law in 1789. He opened the settlement's first tannery to service those in his immediate vicinity, and he operated a general store as well. In 1830 his son, Anselm Tupper Nye, purchased a foundry established by others the year before. The younger Nye's business flourished, producing stoves, plows, and hollowware items, such as dinner pots and stew kettles.[21]

David Putnam, a lawyer and land speculator, was also a contemporary of Dudley Woodbridge Jr. His fourth son, Douglas, helped his father manage the family's real estate holdings for twenty years before the elder Putnam retired in 1845. With David out of the way, Douglas began investing the proceeds of land sales in manufacturing. In the 1850s he bought a recently established bucket factory, and by 1860 Putnam and two partners ran a factory that produced woodenware as well.[22]

The Woodbridges did not weather the transition so well. In 1814 an associate wrote Dudley Woodbridge Jr. to ask if he cared to invest in a canal company. Woodbridge declined and wrote, "I think it may be productive property but individuals usually manage property to better advantage than large companys." As his career unfolded, Woodbridge did invest in bank stock and the stock of manufacturing concerns in nearby towns, but he continued to focus most of his capital and energy on the branch stores of his central firm.[23]

In many ways the business tradition to which Woodbridge belonged had not changed in hundreds of years.[24] Merchants imported and exported goods, took charge of transportation through the carrying trade, and extended credit to farmers and artisans. Primitive communication and transportation networks meant manufacturers had to rely on merchants to market their goods. Merchants' lives were ones of risk and speculation, and they ran their affairs in a very hands-on way, with perhaps a partner or two to act in their place when necessary. Merchants took charge of the preindustrial economy by facilitating the movement of a fairly low volume of unspecialized goods between city and country.

Because the rate of communication equaled the rate of human travel during the first decades of the nineteenth century, businessmen continued to put their trust in the reputations of people they knew, and though the volume of trade flowing through their hands grew, firms continued to operate with a minimal staff. Most were composed of just two or three partners.

Dudley Woodbridge Jr. established many partnerships over the course of his career, but each represented a small, separate concern in which he had a great deal of control.

Westward expansion and long-distance trade sparked the major change that took place in the American business world during the years of the early republic—the rise to prominence of wholesalers. As American textile and iron manufacturing grew, wholesalers began to specialize. They further stimulated manufacturing by extending credit to entrepreneurs and pressed for the development of better methods of transport. Wholesalers required insurance agencies and banks, and as their business expertise grew, they began to muscle in on the manufacturing sector themselves. Western wholesalers did not specialize as quickly, but instead worked in tandem with easterners, allowing them to extend their reach into the interior. As the United States expanded, information continued to be the most valued commodity of all, and westerners served eastern wholesalers and manufacturers with their knowledge of local markets at the same time they served their neighbors with access to credit.

Dudley Woodbridge Jr. had been a wholesaler of much skill, but unlike many of his contemporaries, he failed to make the transition to manufacturing. When Jack wrote his older brother, asking for advice on the purchase of a furnace and forge in 1824, Dudley advised against it, stating that the iron business was too risky. He wrote, "It is a very desirable thing to have a competence, but the difference between having a moderate property & a large one would very rarely if ever I think justify a middle aged man in resigning the loss of all his property for the prospect of gaining what is not absolutely necessary for either his familys comfort or happiness." A quarter-century earlier Woodbridge had written to his uncle of plans to become rich, but now he referred to the goals of competency espoused by farmers. His newfound aversion to risk came at a time when his letters to family members became filled with exhortations to be born again. Like many Americans in the 1820s, at some point Woodbridge experienced a very emotional religious conversion, and he spent a great deal of energy as time went on trying to ensure that his brothers, wife, and children did the same. During the economic expansion that began with the construction of the Ohio and Erie Canal, Dudley Woodbridge Jr. spent his time managing the family store in Marietta, buying and selling land, and renting lots and buildings to other merchants.[25]

Dudley Woodbridge Jr. lived out the rest of his life quietly. He seems never to have sought public office, although he did serve as the treasurer of Marietta's volunteer fire company in the 1820s. In the decades that followed,

Dudley Woodbridge Jr.
(1778–1853).
J. D. Cadwallader,
Cadwallader and Tappen,
Photographists, courtesy of the
Local History and Genealogy
Department, Washington
County Public Library,
Marietta, Ohio.

one representative from the credit reporting agency of R. G. Dun and Company characterized Dudley Woodbridge Jr. as the "oldest trader of the place," and another wrote that he was the "best off in the co[unty]." During the last decade of his life, Woodbridge was apparently free from debt and considered to be a very good credit risk. He began to suffer from increasingly severe migraine headaches as he grew older and made notes of their comings and goings. They became so bad by 1841 that Dudley wrote his brother the following: "from frequent, continued & severe pains in my head[,] my mind, memory & eyesight are much impaired." But, he assured William, when he felt well, he could "still supervise [his] store." He died in 1853 at age seventy-four.[26]

Unlike the third generation of the Tupper, Nye, and Putnam families, Dudley Woodbridge's grandchildren did not take up where their father left off. The eldest son, Dudley Morgan Woodbridge, served as an itinerant Methodist preacher for a time before dying of an illness at an early age. By his father's own report, during the 1830s second son George Morgan Woodbridge "was unfortunate in his mercantile career." Woodbridge blamed part of his son's failure on the commercial climate of the time, writing his brother that "in the present day it is much more unpleasant & less profitable than 30 years ago." But he also lay some of the blame at his son's door, reporting that George did not "love the details of a retail establishment." Washington County voters sent him to the state legislature from 1842 to 1844, but George Morgan Woodbridge did not run again, instead choosing to attempt a business career once more—"for want of some other pursuit," in his father's words.[27]

The R. G. Dun and Company reports on the young man in the years that followed were far from encouraging. Agents found him to be a poor businessman and not a safe credit risk in 1849. George sold dry goods in 1850, began acting as a land agent in 1852, and attempted to form a coal-oil manufacturing firm in 1854. By the middle of the decade, George was deeply in debt, and one agent reported that he would break if his creditors started making demands. But he seemed to have stayed out of serious trouble because of the Woodbridge family name and his own reputation for honesty. However, another agent considered George Morgan Woodbridge "dead broke" in 1860. Still, he lived a long, full life in Marietta, administering army pensions for Civil War veterans, working as a tax assessor, buying and selling land, and writing soothing prose about the natural wonders of southeastern Ohio for the local paper.[28]

During the 1840s the third son, William Morgan Woodbridge, managed the family store with his father's help. When Dudley Woodbridge Jr. died, he left William enough capital to continue. One R. G. Dun and Company agent reported that he was not an active person and lacked energy. His business was small and safe and improved a bit over time, but he had been favored with little business capacity. By 1861 William was out of business. The reports on youngest son John were even less flattering. The most intriguing R. G. Dun and Company report of all concerned John's daughter, Lucy. Company records reveal that she was her father's heir, and after his death she was "regarded as of sufficient bus[iness] capac[ity] to manage [the] est[ate]." Unfortunately, the third Lucy Woodbridge of Marietta disappeared from view the next year when she married and moved away.[29]

The real successor to Dudley Woodbridge Jr.'s role as aggressive commercial leader in Marietta proved to be a man he trained in the business, John Mills. His father, William Mills, left Massachusetts to settle on Ohio Company land in 1792, and John was born in Marietta three years later when Dudley Woodbridge Jr. was seventeen. When John reached his eighteenth birthday, he entered Woodbridge's employ as a clerk when the elder man's first two sons were toddlers. A few months before his twenty-first birthday, Mills entered into a partnership with Woodbridge. Dudley helped his former clerk establish John Mills and Company by furnishing him with a capital outlay of five thousand dollars. Mills ran his own store, and the two men shared the profits. Two years later, a new agreement expanded Woodbridge's capital investment to twenty thousand dollars (almost exclusively made up of merchandise and goods), and his share of the profits rose to two-thirds. The two remained partners until 1821, at which time Mills began renting Woodbridge's warehouse and doing most of the wholesaling in Marietta himself.[30]

In some ways Mills's business resembled Woodbridge's before it. He extended his influence within the area by taking as a partner a man named Waterman Palmer in Parkersburg, which was across the river in western Virginia, a few miles below Marietta. Palmer engaged in flatboat trips down the Ohio to trade with people living near the river's banks, and he made contracts with local farmers for wheat. When he eventually moved to Pittsburgh, Palmer provided Mills with a contact in that city. But unlike Dudley Woodbridge Jr., Mills made the transition to manufacturer. Over the next four decades and more, John Mills would be Marietta's most important businessman. He directed the Marietta Bank, lobbied for the Muskingum Improvement, helped lure a railroad to the town, and presided over the Marietta Chair Company, a concern that employed seventy-five workmen. Mills also provided leadership to the local temperance moment and Marietta College.[31]

The efforts of Marietta's boosters yielded some benefits, although southeastern Ohio's economic growth could not match that of other parts of the state. Retail establishments grew more specialized as jewelers, druggists, dry goods merchants, and hardware dealers opened up shop. In addition to the manufacturing concerns of Mills, Nye, and Putnam, other entrepreneurs began to build steamboats in Marietta. The Muskingum Improvement proved successful because many who made the trip between the Ohio River and Cleveland preferred going up the Muskingum to intercept the canal at Zanesville rather than traveling the canal's entire length from Portsmouth downstream.[32]

Washington County farmers attempted to expand their enterprise as well. The volume of tobacco grown as a cash crop increased yearly until the Civil War, apples always found markets along the Ohio, and some of Marietta's most prosperous farmers began to specialize in raising sheep for wool while others adopted new haying machines and revolving rakes. But they fought an uphill battle in the steep, rocky hills of southeastern Ohio, and the farmers of Marietta's hinterland could not compete with other sections of the state in terms of agricultural output.[33]

Perhaps what kept Marietta afloat during hard times was the arrival of a new wave of immigrants from Europe. After the Panic of 1819 Nahum Ward found himself stranded in Marietta, tied to southeastern Ohio by tens of thousands of acres of unsold land. In 1822 he published a pamphlet in Scotland that brought over 150 people to the United States. Unfortunately, they arrived in 1823 during one of the worst epidemics in Marietta's history—probably yellow fever that found fertile ground during a rainy June and July. Many of the immigrants perished along with a larger number of town residents, including patriarch Dudley Woodbridge Sr. The surviving Scots settled on Ward's lands in Barlow and Wesley townships, and Ward's pamphlet continued to bring Scottish settlers to Marietta a decade later. According to Ward, one man who settled on his land sent for his family and encouraged others to come, "for Mr. Ward can supply us all with farms."[34]

In addition to settlers from Scotland, Washington County received a new flood of German immigrants during the 1830s. Among the first were two brothers named Peters. Although most Germans who came to Ohio traveled by way of the Erie Canal, Charles and Jacob arrived on the shores of America at Baltimore and followed the National Road to Wheeling. Charles left Jacob and their families there and descended the Ohio, looking for a place to settle. When he arrived in Cincinnati, Charles found a city caught in the grip of a heat wave and still recovering from the great cholera epidemic of the year before. Cincinnati would be a prime target of European migrants in the decades to come, but Peters saw it at its worst that summer, and so the brothers decided to settle in Washington County. Before they acquired a home of their own, they boarded with a family named Brophy because (according to family legend) Mrs. Brophy was the only person they could find who spoke German along the banks of the Ohio. Such would not be a problem in years to come.[35]

Other Germans followed. In 1836 Nahum Ward reported that Washington County was "filling up with good society and our state with thousands of Emigrants from Europe." The settlement of Germantown increased the population of Liberty township from nothing to 500. Two other townships surpassed the county's growth rate as well—the settlement of Bonn reinvigorated Salem, and Elba did the same for Aurelius. Nahum Ward owned a good bit of the land, and he had much of it cleared, seeing that his tracts had houses and barns to attract settlers. Bonn "on the whole," he reported in 1842, "is, for these hard times, a flourishing little place."[36]

Marietta itself did not flourish, however, and even as newcomers came to stay, William Emerson and others left. The town's population stood at 5,254 in 1850, one-twentieth the size of Cincinnati.

Thus did the economy of both Cincinnati and Ohio mature as the commercial economy built by men like Dudley Woodbridge Jr. began to give way to the emerging industrial economy of his successor, John Mills. The rise of Cincinnati did not mean the fall of all other towns, but the impact of artificial waterways created new subregional hubs, while those that had gained their prominence because of the Ohio River declined. And as canals rather than the Ohio itself became the main provider of access to lands north of the river, the region would change in other ways as well.

8

A New Sense of Place

When Nahum Ward first crossed the Appalachian Mountains in 1811 and 1812 to speculate in the lands of the Ohio Valley, he wrote letters to his father back in Shrewsbury, Massachusetts, praising "the western country," for he believed he could make his fortune there. While raising a family in Marietta, Ward continued to refer to himself as a resident of the "western woods" and wrote about strong anti-Mason sentiment "in this section." More news of politics followed, and he reported that "Antimasonry will rise throughout the West" in November of 1832. In the aftermath of the Panic of 1837, Nahum Ward's letters were full of news of the Whig Party. In the fall of 1840 he spoke confidently of majorities in many states: "Virginia, Tennessee, Georgia, Mississippi, Missouri, and Illinois will all go for Harrison or we are greatly disappointed." "Should Martin Van be selected," Ward continued, ". . . distress will continue to pervade the South & West. . . . But if we can elect Harrison—confidence will be restored [and] business will be active."

By 1843, though, his political opinions had undergone a transformation. Nahum Ward wrote of abolition, free states, slave states, and politicians that "do the bidding of the slave holders." During the summer of 1846 he took his family on a trip to what he called the "*far West*" (his emphasis). He visited the plains at the foot of the Rocky Mountains and described forts and Indians. The following winter Ward visited Charleston, South Carolina, declared himself repelled by both the city and the people, and proclaimed that slavery was a sin. In 1849 the transplanted New Englander lamented that Marietta's "young gentlemen of standing" were traveling through Missouri (a place Ward called "the border of the Indian Country") and on to California.[1] After his trip across the Mississippi River in 1846, Nahum seemed to stop thinking of his family in Marietta as the "western" branch of the Wards, for references to the Western Country, so prevalent before that date, all but disappear from his correspondence thereafter.

Nahum Ward was not the only Ohioan to find his sense of place evolving in the wake of the transportation revolution, for the economic transformation unleashed by steamboats and canals represent but one aspect of change taking place in the trans-Appalachian West. When Ohioans began to focus on building internal improvements, they slowly turned away from concentrating on a regional, commercial economy that encompassed a wide area—the Ohio Valley, north and south, from Pittsburgh to Louisville—and began concentrating instead on intensifying the production of staple crops and manufacturing at home. As they did so, a new sense of place would supersede the old. The opening of new lands for settlement across the Mississippi River also played a part in this evolution. As time went on, fewer and fewer people would call Ohio "the West," and Ohioans began calling home "the Buckeye State." When the foundation of the connections between westerners north and south of the Ohio weakened, the swelling freshet of abolition would be able to sweep away ties that had once bridged the river, and those living to the north would begin to call their region "the Old Northwest." This new name served to remind Ohioans of the state's antislavery roots in the Northwest Ordinance of 1787 and also deliberately excluded their neighbors to the south in Kentucky and western Virginia. The notion would take hold that the Ohio River represented the barrier between North and South.

I

Initially, debate over the funding of internal improvements heightened the feeling among those living north of the Ohio River that they were westerners. Not wanting to alienate his southern constituency, President Andrew Jackson opposed federal intervention, declaring that canals were local improvements and thus represented special interests. Westerners countered that canals linking East and West would benefit the nation as a whole. But within the states on the northern bank, the politics of internal improvements would lead to disunity. In the 1830s residents of southern Illinois hoped new projects would bring the level of their economic opportunity on par with those who enjoyed access to the Great Lakes and the Erie Canal to the north. A similar situation developed in Indiana. Battles over proposed routes for canals, and later railroads, took shape quickly.[2]

This decline in western unity was not simply a result of economic competition, for though the residents of southern Illinois had simply crossed the Ohio from Kentucky to find new homes, the residents of northern Illinois came from another region altogether. The coming of canals changed the composition of the West's population as a wave of settlers from New England poured west along the Erie Canal, through the Great Lakes, and on to northern Ohio and Illinois, as well as southern Michigan. One scholar has characterized these late-arriving Yankees as imperialistic. Convinced that they and their way of life represented the civilized element of American society, they sought to remake the West. New Englanders wished to impose new religious sensibilities and moral discipline on people they considered crude. Yankees had long feared the rising political power of westerners as the region's population mushroomed, and now they intended to assert control over the area themselves. In 1863 one transplanted New Englander reminisced about waging "a thirty years war" for control of the region—a war they won to the north of the Ohio River.[3]

These new Yankees came to a world very different from the one members of the New England Ohio Company had vowed to tame four decades before. Canals, and later railroads, allowed them to retain much stronger "home ties" than the ones earlier immigrants had missed. During the early republic, northerners and southerners living on the banks of the Ohio had no choice but to pull together, even if they didn't always see eye to eye. But these new Yankees built farms and shipped their produce east by way of the Great Lakes rather than the Ohio River.

The newcomers concentrated their efforts on such cash crops as wheat, fruit, and dairy products in the north and central reaches of Ohio. They scoffed at the efforts of their neighbors to the south, calling them lazy. The southerners who crossed the Ohio River heading for southern Indiana and Illinois in the 1820s were, for the most part, poorer sorts. They came north hoping to find lands of their own, complaining that rich plantation owners controlled Kentucky and other points south. By 1850 land values in the southern sections of Ohio, Indiana, and Illinois were the lowest in their respective states. But in fact, the southerners had moved onto land that was less likely to produce a good crop than lands to the north. The southern sections of all three states (with the exception of the Miami Valley north of Cincinnati) were hilly, wet, and suffered the ruinous effects of erosion. Yankees arrived along the northern route, found better land for farming, and often came with some cash to begin their new life in the West. They may not have admitted it, but it was not their moral sensibilities that gave them an advantage.

II

Even as westerners in Ohio, western Virginia, and Kentucky joyously embraced the beginning of the transportation revolution as one and then banded together against eastern bankers during the Panic of 1819, the Missouri Compromise put slavery squarely onto the national political map. Opinion was divided over the question of Missouri's statehood in Indiana, Illinois, and Ohio, though in the end, Ohio's legislature instructed its national congressmen to vote against extending slavery westward. But as the corn belt grew along the Ohio River, many farmers on the northern shore supported the extension of slavery into their own states. In addition to southern-born westerners, some of these advocates hailed from the same New England states as those growing wheat to the north. Wheat grew best in the drier climate above the Ohio's drainage, while corn thrived in the wet valley itself. The amount of labor needed to grow corn as a staple crop lay somewhere between the labor demands of cotton and the ease with which a man controlling the labor of a large family could make a profit growing wheat. Americans moving westward did not want to work for others; they sought land of their own. Thus in the 1840s and 1850s slaves represented one source of labor that appealed to some westerners in the southern portions of the states created by the Northwest Ordinance. Because of the ordinance, controversy over the issue had plagued state politics since the territorial era but grew stronger as the nineteenth century progressed.[4]

Thus characterizing the general feeling of those living in the Ohio Valley about slavery is not as simple as it might first appear, for the sectional origins of residents do not tell the whole tale. It is instructive to compare attitudes toward slavery in Kentucky held by the wave of Englishmen who descended the Ohio to settle on the prairies of Illinois in the decade following the War of 1812 with that of Yankees flooding into the region by way of canals a decade later. Both groups held in contempt the southern-born poorer sorts who crossed the Ohio River in search of opportunity but admired southern gentlemen. English travelers abhorred the notion of slavery but remarked frequently on the orderliness planters imposed on Kentucky's landscape, as well as southern hospitality. One man, Elias Fordham, wrote that although he did not like slavery personally, he thought that allowing it to spread to Indiana would increase land values. "I would not have upon my conscience the moral guilt of extending Slavery over countries now free from it, for the whole North Western Territory," he wrote. "But," he continued: "if it should take place, I do not see why I should not make use of it. If I do not have servants I cannot farm; and there are *no* free labourers here, except a few so worthless, and yet so haughty, that an English Gentlemen can do nothing with them." Yankees, too, expressed admiration for Kentucky planters, whom they considered to be refined, while condemning those in the southern portions of their new states who were not.[5]

Certainly very few whites made African Americans feel welcome. The Ohio legislature passed a series of black laws starting soon after statehood. An 1804 statute required free blacks and mulattos to provide proof of freedom to enter the state, and three years later, a law required them to post a five-hundred-dollar bond to guarantee good behavior. In 1831 the state of

Ohio declared that only whites could serve on juries, and black children were barred from public schools in Ohio throughout the antebellum era. African Americans were no more welcome in Indiana, Illinois, Michigan, and Wisconsin.[6]

Prior to 1820 most African American residents of the Ohio Valley lived south of the river. Both Lexington and Louisville had large slave populations where women worked as domestics, and men built roads and handled cargo. Both Denmark Vesey's plot in 1822 and Nat Turner's rebellion in 1831 spurred southerners to evict free blacks, however, and many of them moved north of the Ohio. Others left southern states of their own accord as racial tension grew. The growth of Pittsburgh's African American population kept pace with the growth of the town's white population, but Cincinnati's black population grew at a faster pace, though the two cities' African American populations originated in different regions. By mid-century over 70 percent of the Queen City's free black population had been born in Virginia, Kentucky, and other southern states. By contrast, more than 70 percent of Pittsburgh's came from Pennsylvania itself. But visitors remarked that free blacks in both cities were not treated much better than slaves to the south.[7]

The growth of a "Little Africa" in their city worried other Cincinnati residents. By 1828 more than twenty-two hundred free blacks lived there, representing 10 percent of the population. In the summer of 1829 city trustees announced that they would enforce Ohio's old black laws. African Americans were to register, to prove their free status, and to post a bond within a month, or they would be evicted. Leaders in the free black community asked for more time, and some whites in the city sympathized with their point of view. But members of Cincinnati's economic elite allied with city's poorer sorts who disliked losing jobs to blacks. Late in the summer, whites went on forays into black neighborhoods, attacking people and destroying property. By summer's end, half of the black residents had left town. Cincinnati's commercial leaders opposed abolitionists because they did not want to alienate southern customers and associates; thus "gentlemen of property and standing" helped lay the groundwork for another wave of riots against blacks in 1836.[8]

In the 1820s several African American families moved into Marietta's Washington County, followed by others a decade later. In 1835 the Barnett family arrived in Barlow township from Virginia. A relatively prosperous black man named Parker Lewis posted their bond, while another black family—the Holberts—provided room and board until the Barnetts acquired land of their own. Thus free blacks who had taken a chance in southeastern Ohio in the early 1800s helped others settle there later. Like other African

Americans, a man named Harry Bartlett shows up in a Woodbridge and Morgan ledger dated 1828–1831 with "(Black Man)" after his name. But even though the firm carefully noted his race, he bought sugar, coffee, and dry goods on credit, paying with a mixture of cash, a note, work, corn, and apples, just as his white neighbors did.[9]

Dudley Woodbridge Jr.'s attitudes toward African Americans proved to be as rife with contradictions as those of most whites at that time. In the early 1800s his black indentured servants were probably slaves in all but name, and Woodbridge funded the Washington County Colonization Society in the early 1830s—an association dedicated to sending free blacks to Africa. Yet in 1834 he indicated that he had given a woman called Nanny "forty dollars to assist in obtaining the freedom of her children." A decade later, like many of Yankee descent, Woodbridge strongly opposed the Mexican-American War because it would allow for the expansion of slavery. Paternalistically, he wished that "the poor blacks" be given religious instruction and an education. "I once thought," he continued, "that God was raising up the great nation to diffuse the principles of civil liberty & the Christian religion to the 'end of the earth'—but that hope can now hardly be indulged."[10] He seemed not to remember that in his youth he had once procured slaves to pay off a debt.

Some white residents took a more active interest in establishing black families in Washington County. David Putnam Jr., born in 1808, lived in Harmar, just across the Muskingum from Marietta, all his life. In the 1850s David and his elder brother Douglas helped a black man named George Harrison, his wife, and their children establish themselves in town. The younger Putnam sold Harrison land, and Douglas encouraged him to send one of his sons to Marietta College.[11]

Men like the Putnams were the exceptions in the West, however, and, indeed, in the nation as a whole. The rising tide of sectional division involved the race by southern planters and northern farmers to seize lands west of the Mississippi for themselves, and a battle for control in Congress as the North's population rose to challenge the advantage southerners had enjoyed since the enactment of the Constitution's Three-Fifths Compromise, to a much greater extent than any concern over the welfare of African Americans. As the North's economy evolved, there arose a free-labor ideology to stand alongside rural values of competency aimed at improving the lot of whites.[12]

In the trans-Appalachian West the economic development of Ohio and Kentucky began to diverge in the 1820s. The growth of Ohio's urban working class developed at the same time Kentucky's slave population grew. The transportation revolution elevated the role Louisville played in the region's economy, and Lexington found its preeminent place gone. The Bluegrass elite who had begun investing their commercial profits in manufacturing in the early 1800s concentrated more and more energy on hemp production, utilizing slave labor to supply the baling and bagging needs of King Cotton. Artisans fell on hard times, and farmers having difficulty finding land of their own moved north of the Ohio. In the Green River country to the southwest, Kentuckians specialized in slaves and tobacco production, while those who could not compete moved on, looking for land elsewhere.[13]

III

As the abolition movement gained strength in the 1830s, some writers began referring to the states created under the Northwest Ordinance of 1787 as "the Old Northwest." Referring to Ohio as "the West" would never disappear entirely, and indeed applying the term "Middle West" to Ohio would not begin until the late nineteenth century. But the Dakotas fast became the "new" northwest, and as abolition sentiment spread, the ordinance that outlawed slavery north of the Ohio River began to assume greater symbolic significance in how Ohioans defined their place—they began to deliberately exclude Kentucky and western Virginia.[14]

Not all westerners agreed, of course. Some regional boosters continued to define the Ohio Valley north and south of the river as one economic system. But while these boosters lobbied for internal improvements and railroads, others wrote that the state of Ohio had grown faster than western states south of the river because slavery had been excluded.[15]

The observations of outsiders serve to confirm this late development of a belief within the West itself that the region could be divided into northern and southern sections. Among visitors to the Ohio Valley between 1740 and 1860, the tendency to see differences between the two banks of the river was not uniform; it increased as the nineteenth century wore on, particularly after 1830. There were early exceptions to this rule, but generally those who credited Marietta's civilized appearance to the town's New England origins had their own regional axes to grind and often did not visit Lexington to see the strides southerners had made there.[16]

In addition to new, state-oriented economic loyalties and the spread of the abolition movement, the course of westward expansion itself influenced the changing sense of place in the Ohio Valley. Mary Emerson, born in Marietta in 1811, traveled south of the river into western Virginia to teach school. In the fall of 1840 she wrote her father that she wished to move farther west. Great things were planned for the prairies beyond Indiana, she wrote, and she believed that she could find work in the new settlements.

Two years earlier her brother William had offered some revealing advice to their brother Charles. He urged the younger man to study civil engineering rather than medicine, pointing out that the number of public improvements ensured steady work and good pay. William declared, "If you want to travel—come to the West—if you want to see strange sights, come to Illinois—if you want money, come to the West." The gold rush of 1849 would lure even more young Ohioans to a new West, a West beyond the Mississippi River.[17]

In a similar vein Harriet, a young New England bride, wrote to friends back home in 1842, begging them not to exaggerate the distance between her old home and new, stating that Ohio was not nearly as far away as the Rocky Mountains. Her husband, Dudley Woodbridge Jr.'s youngest son, John, referred to home as "the Buckeye State."[18] The Buckeye trees referred to were so named because their inedible nuts have a dark center, visible to the naked eye, rimmed with a lighter colored shell—thus they resemble the eye of a deer. Ohioans began calling themselves Buckeyes well before the 1840s, but the name does not appear in Woodbridge family correspondence until the third generation, the first to be born and raised in Ohio.

An examination of such state nicknames reveals that sectional identity in the Ohio Valley changed slowly, for many of them contained two levels of meaning—East versus West and North versus South. While traveling on the Ohio River, visitors heard such appellations as Ohio "Buckeyes," Michigan "Wolverines," Virginia "Tuckahoes," and Illinois "Suckers." Ohio's came into widespread use because the early settlers had used buckeye wood to make furniture. To some, the term "Sucker" referred to a kind of fish. For the most part, westerners used nicknames to indicate local pride. Cincinnati provides a case in point. By 1840 New England migrants made up approximately 10 percent of the city's population as a whole and 20 percent of its American-born population. Rivalry between long-time residents and newcomers who looked down their noses at westerners led to a division among "Yankees" and "Buckeyes"—the Buckeyes included the earliest settlers from New York and New Jersey, people born in Ohio, and people from Pennsylvania, as well as Kentucky and other points south.[19]

But despite such East-West associations, some of the state nicknames also had North-South connotations, and these were far from complimentary. For many, the use of "Suckers" to describe residents of southern Illinois referred not to fish, but to the parasites that infested and ruined tobacco in the fields—they used the term to imply that the Old Northwest would be better off without the poorer sorts who had moved across the river. The widespread use of the term "Hoosier" in Indiana had similar origins in southern lingo for the lowly. Kentuckians were called "Corncrackers."[20]

As the use of the phrase "Buckeye State" came into being, its spread can be detected in the names of Ohio's newspapers. In 1799 a Cincinnati entrepreneur initiated the use of the designation "Western" in paper titles with the *Western Spy,* a publication that ran under that name, with some variations, for over twenty years. One shy of four dozen other newspapers followed suit in the decades to come. By 1840, however, nearly two-thirds of them had ceased to exist, and in 1844 the *Western Herald and Steubenville Gazette* dropped the first part of its title to become simply the *Steubenville Gazette.* Papers in Dayton, Hamilton, Somerset, and Urbana underwent a similar transformation shortly thereafter. By 1860 only Mt. Vernon's *Western Episcopalian* carried on the tradition. On the other hand, seven antebellum Ohio newspapers utilized "Buckeye" in their titles beginning in 1834, and others followed suit after the Civil War. Most were short-lived, although Marion's *Buckeye Journal* flourished between the mid-1840s and mid-1850s, while Lisbon's *Buckeye State* ran from 1852 until the eve of the Civil War.[21]

Ohioans' sense of place was in flux, then, during the 1830s and 1840s. Although many continued to refer to Ohio as the West, others were convinced that "the West" really lay beyond the Mississippi River. They began to call home "the Old Northwest" and "the Buckeye State." The Ohio River had created the Western Country, but with the advent of the canal and railroad eras, it ceased to be the prime means of entrance into the interior of the continent. As their dependence on the Ohio waned, so too did their relationships with those across the river. As William Emerson of Marietta traveled, looking for work, in the fall of 1837, he wrote home that he had "crossed the River Ohio" and was "alive in a slave state, Kentucky." By that date, the fifty-nine-year-old Dudley Woodbridge Jr. had crossed the Ohio countless times but had never found the fact worthy of comment: to cross the river was more like crossing a street than a boundary. The younger man, however, regarded the Ohio River as symbolic of the separation between free and slave America. Yet, Emerson continued, "I find the people very agreeable as far as I have seen, I have as yet seen none of the *horrors* of Slavery. It is a . . . farming settlement, [and my] engagement [is to teach] for one quarter only." The people of Ohio still had much in common with those in Kentucky, but enough had changed in the region that such a simple fact seemed to surprise the young man.[22]

But Emerson's initial reaction foreshadowed trouble to come, and Marietta's community would not be immune to the effects of sectional tension. A member of one of the town's most prominent families, David Putnam Jr., became an ardent abolitionist and operator on the Underground Railroad. He made no secret of his activities, and while on a visit to Parkersburg, (West) Virginia, he was attacked by a mob. Putnam's experience gave him tangible proof that the Ohio River had indeed become the dividing line between North and South.[23] During the summer of 1845 a new controversy had Mariettans proudly proclaiming themselves "Buckeyes" and declaring in a very definite manner that the Ohio River should serve as a boundary.

The beginning of this controversy over slavery and abolition in southeastern Ohio and northwestern Virginia can be traced through the pages of the *Marietta Intelligencer,* a newspaper owned by two Whigs and edited by a man named Beman Gates. Gates had been born in Massachusetts in 1818 and had come west among the wave of New Englanders sweeping into Ohio following the construction of the New York and Ohio canals. In 1837 he and a companion set out for Tennessee but stopped in Marietta when Gates's bother-in-law became too ill to travel. After a time, the New Englander decided to make Marietta his permanent home.[24]

Under the editorship of Gates, the *Marietta Intelligencer* ran many stories detailing the cruelty of slavery. In February of 1844 the paper reprinted a newspaper account from Pittsburgh about a man sentenced to death for aiding an escaped slave. Gates wrote that while he knew his readers did not want to engage in discussions about abolition, he did not think they would want to ignore "legal murder." Over the next year and a half, Gates ran stories that recounted "expert" views of slavery, the growth of abolition in Kentucky, and the annexation of Texas. Apparently some residents just across the Ohio in Wood County, Virginia, complained that the transplanted Yankee ran an abolitionist press. But worse was yet to come.[25]

In mid-July of 1845 six slaves escaped across the Ohio River a few miles below Marietta. They belonged to the son of Alexander Henderson, the man whose running account kept to pay his overseers and take care of other plantation expenses appeared in the Woodbridge ledgers of the 1810s. A number of white Ohioans met them on the northern bank, but a group of Virginians following the runaways captured five of the slaves, as well as three white men. They took the Ohioans back across the river and put them in the Parkersburg jail. Nahum Ward, Anselm T. Nye, and others attempted to get them bailed out but were denied access to the prisoners. Lawyers from Marietta volunteered to assist the men, but the Virginians would not allow it.[26]

Citizens in both Marietta and Cincinnati held public meetings to denounce "the invasion of Ohio." The *Intelligencer* ran letters expressing outrage—one was signed by "Buckeyes" and another by "Many a Buckeye." A third reader wrote an allegory about "The Buckeye State and Her Sisters" that praised Ohio and criticized the actions of the "southern sisters."[27]

Mariettans and other Ohioans wanted to define the boundary between Ohio and Virginia in order to assert their jurisdiction over the "abduction" of Ohio citizens. During a boundary dispute a quarter-century before, the

"Invasion of Ohio," *The Buckeye Newspaper*, 21 August 1845. Outraged over the capture of escaped slaves and the arrest of white Ohioans who tried to help them on the Ohio's north bank downriver from Marietta, town residents declared themselves to be Buckeyes rather than westerners and demanded that the Virginians respect the river as the boundary between North and South. *Courtesy of the Ohio Historical Society.*

Supreme Court had ruled that because Virginia had ceded the lands north of the river to the Confederation, Virginia retained ownership of the river, and Ohio's land began at the river's edge. Ohioans argued that the men involved in the current dispute had been above the river's low water mark, but the Virginians maintained that their jurisdiction extended to the Ohio's high water mark, and the Ohio citizens had been captured within that line. An *Intelligencer* item from "Many a Buckeye to the Good People of Virginia" stated that neighbors should be friends, but Virginians ought to respect the dividing line. "The possession of the shore, therefore, which Virginia allows that we of the Northwest may rightfully claim," the Mariettans wrote, "gives us the entire control of our side of the River, at all stages of water, and for all intents and purposes."[28] The Ohio Buckeyes, like a famous New England poet of the future, had come to believe that good fences make good neighbors.

The Wood County Court found the three white men guilty of assisting runaway slaves in September, but just after the first of the year, the Virginians released them on their own recognizance. Lawyers from the two states argued about the case for more than a decade, but it was never settled, and the three men went their separate ways, living out their lives in anonymity in Ohio.[29]

Furor over "the invasion of Ohio" was indicative of the feelings stirred up by the rise of abolition sentiment. Still, many residents of the Western Country resisted splitting their region north and south along the river. Louisville, Kentucky, owed its tremendous growth after 1820 to steamboat traffic, and it would strive to hold on to its western identity as merchants and city leaders promoted it as the finest city in the West, destined to be the hub of the Ohio Valley's economy. Men engaged in commerce, manufacturing, and banking in Cincinnati did the same, fearing the loss of lucrative trade downstream. In Illinois and Indiana, southerners decried efforts by northerners to use sectionalism as an excuse to reject "the unifying bonds of Westerness." And it would be a westerner—Kentucky Senator John J. Crittenden—who made the last appeal to stave off the destruction of the union through compromise as the Civil War loomed.[30]

IV

The last links in the economic chain that bound Ohio to the East directly came with the construction of railroads in the 1850s. The steamboat era had brought a golden age of prosperity to towns such as Madison, Indiana, but by themselves, steamboats could not solve the main obstacle to trade in the trans-Appalachian West: the seasonal character of navigation. For larger boats, the river was navigable only during the spring and fall floods. Spring was the most predictable because melting snow augmented rain, but poor rains later in the year often left boats grounded. The year 1819 proved particularly difficult—the river was closed to steamboats from

April to February of 1820. Travelers wrote of being stranded, and one described "western merchants . . . lounging discontentedly about the streets of Pittsburgh, or moping idly in its taverns, like the victims of an ague." During the winter that followed, much of the river system froze over completely. A similar situation occurred in 1838, 1854, and 1856. Canals had failed to provide the answer, for though they proved less susceptible to dry spells, they froze over in the winter longer than did the Ohio itself.[31]

Although canals brought capital and people to Ohio and the state thrived, that prosperity proved to be only the beginning of an even larger economic expansion to come. It would be railroads that truly integrated the state into the national economy at a level that merchants like Dudley Woodbridge Jr. had dreamed of but had never been able to achieve, despite their best efforts.[32]

Initially many in Ohio were skeptical of the wisdom of promoting railroads over canals. They feared entrepreneurs would monopolize transportation in ways they could not when most men could operate a craft of some kind on western waters. Steamboats were not cheap, but railroads would call for a much larger capital investment, placing control out of the reach of all but the wealthiest. Still, railroads had their promoters, and the state of Ohio chartered seventy-seven companies during the 1830s. As public discontent with the state-controlled canal system grew, legislators left construction of railroads to private investors. Indeed the state supported railroad companies by giving them tax breaks and the power to claim land through the law of eminent domain—individuals had to give up property for projects designed to serve the public good. Here, too, the railroads got a break, because the commission overseeing such transactions allowed the railroad companies to pay rock bottom prices to landowners.[33]

The Baltimore and Ohio Railroad, among others, connected southern Ohio cities directly to the Atlantic seaboard. Exports of corn, pork, and beef downriver from Cincinnati finally dropped as entrepreneurs began using the grain to fatten swine and cattle, and then shipped livestock east on the iron horse. Wheat prices fell, and many in eastern Ohio turned to the raising of sheep and cows, sending wool and cheese east by rail instead. Those who continued to grow wheat shipped it unprocessed in boxcars, though flour did continue to flow north to Cleveland.

By mid-century Ohio's cities began to grow faster than rural areas as manufacturing took hold. Railroads brought raw materials to entrepreneurs quickly on a year-round basis, no matter what the weather. Because eastern manufacturers could now ship finished goods west cheaply, Ohio manufacturers continued to push toward larger, more efficient factories in order to compete. Ohio dairy farmers and growers of vegetables and other specialty crops also found expanding markets in the state's urban areas. Railroads finally brought an end to the flatboat trade that had flourished for more than a half-century.[34]

The transportation revolution had created the river port of Madison, Indiana, but it would also be responsible for the town's decline. The steamboat era did not bring growth only. Along with increased business, steamboats brought cholera to the town in the 1830s, and boiler explosions and engine fires created additional hazards to human life. When the railroad reached Madison from Indianapolis in 1847, it looked like Madison's future was finally safe and secure. Grains and other goods flowed through the town's mills and were shipped north. Madison reached its peak in the early 1850s, but like steamboats, railroads proved to be a mixed blessing. As entrepreneurs constructed multiple lines that ran from east to west, they leeched away produce from the town's hinterland. Madison's growth stalled as two hundred businesses closed their doors between 1852 and 1860, the majority of them before the Panic of 1857.[35]

As with Madison, a railroad link failed to bring back Marietta's old prominence. Farmers in the town's hinterland simply could not produce large enough crops to take advantage of new markets. The railroad link at Parkersburg proved more successful, and that city downriver in western Virginia began to usurp Marietta's former role in the area. Not until Marietta's petroleum deposits began to pay off after the Civil War would the city truly begin to thrive again, and even then, Parkersburg remained dominant.[36]

Railroads also brought deep, profound change for men of commerce as a new era of marketing appeared on the horizon. In the preindustrial economy, all goods and services had flowed through the hands of merchants. As the United States expanded westward, the merchants helped bring about the transportation revolution and facilitate the growth of manufacturing; many became manufacturers themselves. But the railroad industry required massive amounts of such raw materials as timber, steel, glass, and rubber. Soon the technology involved in the new industries became too specialized for everyone to master, and the capital investment needed exceeded the grasp of one man. In addition, the urbanization of America meant concentrated markets, but with faster, more efficient transportation and communication available, manufacturers no longer needed to rely on merchants to distribute their goods. Thus men of commerce ceased to provide the link between manufacturer and customer. The era of the wholesaler ended, and many businessmen found themselves reduced to the status of retailer.[37]

As travel by railroad supplanted the old river routes, people on the move ceased to mention the Ohio in their journals and travel diaries, and by the beginning of the Civil War, they no longer remarked on the growth and energy of Cincinnati and Louisville. Farther west, they crossed the Mississippi's course rather than moving between its banks, and so its length, like the Ohio's, disappeared from the view of many. As the hub of western rail lines, Chicago rose to become the center of an economic system that stretched north to Canada, east to Indiana and Ohio, and west to the plains beyond the Missouri and Mississippi Rivers. One train passenger in 1894 observed that the state of Ohio consisted of "very pretty cultivated country . . . but no large rivers."[38]

Thus by the middle of the nineteenth century, the Ohio River ceased to dominate and define the state of Ohio's growth patterns. Man-made transportation networks—canals and railroads—had usurped the river's central place. Rather than representing the lifeline of a region, the Ohio River became just one transportation route among many. As the state's economy became increasingly complex, the river became merely a tool in the state's industrial and commercial sector and has remained as such until the present day. Because the river has been objectified, people have striven to dominate, shape, and refine it—they have subdued the river and forced it do their bidding. In 1818, as the National Road threatened to preempt the Ohio as the West's highway, Pittsburgh's leaders made plans to rid the river of such obstacles to navigation as rocks and snags. The state of Pennsylvania first engaged special boats to clear the channel in the 1820s, and the federal government provided funds and engineers for the task soon after. In the 1870s federal engineers began to canalize the river, adding locks and dams to facilitate navigation by making the river's depth consistent and less subject to seasonal fluctuations. During the 1930s engineers built more dams to manage the river's floods. Residents came to the control the river in order to "meet the needs of the basin's ever increasing human population."[39] The first settlers of the Ohio Valley had been forced to adapt to the geography of the region, but their descendants utilized technological advances to impose their will upon the river and the landscape.

Daily economic life changed greatly for Ohioans after 1820, and their sense of place shifted with it. Rebuilding their economy after the collapse of 1819 meant taking part in the transportation revolution. The coming of steamboats and the construction of canals allowed agricultural output to increase dramatically, and the manufacturing sector grew as rural residents and European immigrants alike poured into Ohio's cities in search of jobs. But canals also brought New Englanders west, and thus many old residents turned their backs on the river just as newcomers streamed in who had no ties to westerners living on the Ohio's southern shore. As commercial connections within the Ohio Valley began to recede, as Americans began to move beyond the Mississippi, and as the abolition movement spread, the Old Northwest came to be viewed as a place set apart by a boundary between North and South—the Ohio River. What once united westerners now served as a barrier between them, and the publication of *Uncle Tom's Cabin* would only serve to solidify new perceptions.

But Kentucky Senator John J. Crittenden, along with southern-born residents of the Old Northwest who sided with the Union only when the firing upon Fort Sumter made a choice imperative, provide tangible proof that a region known as "the Western Country" had been based on very real ties during the first half of the nineteenth century. As Ohio's economic connection to the Northeast strengthened during the 1830s and 1840s, so, too, did Kentucky's ties to the South. Hemp production skyrocketed as cotton producers demanded baling and bagging materials, as well as the coarse hemp linen needed to clothe their slaves. Kentucky led the nation in hemp production during most of the antebellum period, and hemp-producing counties had the highest concentration of slave labor. Yet according to one scholar, only the harrowing experiences of the Civil War and Reconstruction finally convinced Kentuckians that they were southerners rather than westerners.[40] The ties that bound residents of the Ohio Valley together to form the Western Country had been so strong that they could only be severed completely by the most destructive of all human conflict—war.

Conclusion

For a long time, scholars relegated the history of the early republic to the final chapter of tomes about colonial history or the first chapter of studies focusing on Jacksonian America, while others concentrated on great thinkers, such as Thomas Jefferson and James Madison, who dominated the politics of post-Revolutionary America. This state of affairs has changed in recent years as historians reshape their periodization of early America in recognition of the changes taking place between 1750 and 1850. Expansion represents one important theme that unites new scholarship—the expansion of political rights to all free white men, the expansion of slavery, the expansion of America's population as families grew and immigrants arrived from Europe, geographical expansion as Americans moved west from the Atlantic seaboard, and the expansion of America's commercial economy. Though much of this growth took place at the expense of Native Americans and African Americans, and though it yielded both positive and negative outcomes for women, the rhetoric of revolution released strong currents of individualism, egalitarianism, and resistance to traditional authority that had begun during the first Great Awakening and continued to grow during the second wave of religious revivals that followed a century later.[1]

In such a climate, the conquest of the Ohio Valley represented westward movement of a different sort than that practiced by sixteenth- and early-seventeenth-century colonists. Entrepreneurs began planting towns to facilitate the settling of the interior of the continent, and Americans who crossed the Appalachian Mountains knew that new policies promised that territories would become states on an equal footing with the original thirteen. Farmers seeking to secure the family independence and merchants seeking to profit from the farmers' quest together created a market economy.

Most studies of the trans-Appalachian frontier focus on division. According to the generally accepted narratives, both northern and southern societies unfurled west of the Appalachian Mountains, but the Northwest Ordinance decreed that a slave society would develop to the south of the

Ohio River and a free society would develop to the north. During the 1790s Washington and the new federal government sent the army to exile Native Americans from the Northwest Territory, leaving those in the southwest to battle on alone, creating further disunity.[2] Other than as a boundary between slavery and freedom, the Ohio River itself did not truly seem important to most past historians until steamboats allowed Americans to harness its power. Thus the year 1815 acts as another divide, with pioneer history emphasizing the heroics of settlers isolated in the wilderness holding sway before that date, and the history of the transportation revolution emphasizing technological innovations reigning supreme after.

But looking at the Ohio Valley through the eyes of merchants such as the Woodbridges of Marietta, Ohio, gives us a glimpse of a different world, a world of connections that existed long before the transportation revolution: connections between East and West, between North and South, between merchants and farmers, and between one western town and all the others. One historian has labeled the trans-Appalachian frontier an agricultural world, while another insists that cities helped establish the new nation's foothold there. But the valley's true nature lies between, with two halves of one world acting in concert rather than in opposition as the promoters of each way of life realized that the success of their plans depended on the cooperation of the other. The farmers built local community and kin networks, while the merchants tied western communities to each other and to the outside world. Farmers sought competency and merchants sought profit, but all wanted to improve upon what they had known before.

An examination of the evolving role the Ohio River played in the lives of valley residents reveals a three-stage process of regional development. For ex-colonists bent on claiming the land for their new empire, the river represented a passageway to the continent. To those who followed and adapted to life in the West, the river acted as a unifying force that pulled westerners together, north and south of its banks. When Americans began to concentrate on internal improvements—using new technology to conquer time and distance—those north of the river began to focus their attention on state rather than regional economic concerns as the world of commerce began to give way to the world of manufacturing. As they turned their backs on the river, Ohioans allowed the spread of abolition to erect a barrier between North and South at the river that had once functioned as the lifeblood of all westerners.

Through the heart of this world flowed the Ohio River, the facet of western life that shines most clearly through the records of the Woodbridge family. The Ohio provided the foundation upon which westerners built their economy and their society. Allowing the political boundaries people used to carve the valley up into states rather than focusing on the key geographical feature that bound the people of the valley together obscures our view of the region's early development. Colonial backcountries had been relatively isolated places. It was the river itself that made the Ohio Valley frontier unique.[3] The Appalachian Mountains proved to be substantial obstacles to movement between East and West, but the Ohio and Mississippi rivers allowed westerners to export produce and goods south through the port of New Orleans. In addition, rivers allowed them to move through the region itself, creating connections between towns from Pittsburgh, Pennsylvania, to Louisville, Kentucky.

The Ohio's role as an artery that linked the nation together, North and South, East and West, ended just as the Civil War began. As Americans proceeded on to trains, automobiles, and planes, they remembered only that last image seared into the national consciousness by war—an image forged in the 1840s and 1850s of a river that stood as the divide between slavery and freedom. Native Americans expelled from the fertile valley and African Americans who crossed the river to freedom only to wait a century or more before gaining equality might tell another story—their treatment by whites was much the same on both shores.

In a different way, the people who live along the Ohio itself today know better, too. Many of Marietta's tourist attractions center around its steamboat-era past, and others advertised in the area include not only antique stores in town, but similar establishments in West Virginia, as well as tours of an old glass factory across the Ohio in Williamstown. Downstream, Covington, Kentucky, serves as a suburb of Cincinnati, and the Greater Cincinnati International Airport lies south of the Ohio. Radio announcers in Louisville refer to their region as "Kentuckiana" because local residents north and south of the river often feel they have more in common with each other than those in their respective states. In 1991 the Humanities Councils of Illinois, Indiana, Kentucky, Ohio, Pennsylvania, and West Virginia collaborated on a project entitled "Always a River: The Ohio River and the American Experience," a multifaceted public history program aimed at educating people about the river's role in American history.

And so the Ohio River flows on. It united Native Americans within its valley and beyond during the centuries before Europeans invaded the continent. By the time of the Revolutionary War, Euro-Americans and Native Americans made it a dividing line between white and Indian worlds as they battled over the valley's resources. Once the newly independent Euro-Americans established dominance over the region, the Ohio River once again served to draw together the peoples living on its northern and southern banks. But as civil war approached, Ohio residents came to believe that the river represented a boundary. The image dimmed for those who made their livelihood along the river's course, but it lingered in state and regional histories—and in the national imagination. Chances are good, though, that Dudley Woodbridge Jr. would understand perfectly why many current Louisville residents call home "Kentuckiana."

NOTES

Abbreviations

BWC	Backus-Woodbridge Collection, Ohio Historical Collection, Columbus
DML/CC	Dawes Memorial Library, Cutler Collection, Slack Research Collections, Marietta College, Marietta, Ohio
DML/MC	Dawes Memorial Library, Manuscripts Collection, Slack Research Collections, Marietta College, Marietta, Ohio
EWT	*Early Western Travels, 1748–1846,* 32 vols. (Cleveland: A. H. Clark Co., 1904–1907), edited by Reuben Gold Thwaites
FHS	Filson Historical Society, Louisville, Kentucky
WMCR	Woodbridge Mercantile Company Records, Regional History Collection, West Virginia University, Morgantown, West Virginia
WWP	William Woodbridge Papers, Burton Collection, Detroit Public Library

Introduction

1. John D. Barnhart, *Valley of Democracy: The Frontier versus the Plantation in the Ohio Valley, 1775–1818* (Bloomington, Ind.: Indiana University Press, 1953); Beverley W. Bond Jr., *The Civilization of the Old Northwest: A Study of Political, Social, and Economic Development, 1788–1812* (New York: Macmillan, 1934); R. Carlyle Buley, *The Old Northwest: Pioneer Period, 1815–1840,* 2 vols. (Bloomington, Ind.: Indiana University Press, 1950); Erik F. Haites, James Mak, and Gary M. Walton, *Western River Transportation: The Era of Early Internal Development, 1810–1860* (Baltimore: Johns Hopkins University Press, 1975); Louis C. Hunter, *Steamboats on the Western Rivers: An Economic and Technological History* (Cambridge: Harvard University Press, 1949); and George Rogers Taylor, *The Transportation Revolution, 1815–1860* (New York: Rinehart, 1951).

2. Stephen Aron, *How the West Was Lost: The Transformation of Kentucky from Daniel Boone to Henry Clay* (Baltimore: Johns Hopkins University Press, 1996); Andrew R. L. Cayton, *The Frontier Republic: Ideology and Politics in the Ohio Country, 1780–1825* (Kent, Ohio: Kent State University Press, 1986); Cayton and Peter S. Onuf, *The Midwest and the Nation: Rethinking the History of an American Region* (Bloomington, Ind.: Indiana University Press, 1990); Nicole Etcheson, *The Emerging Midwest: Upland Southerners and the Political Culture of the Old Northwest, 1787–1861* (Bloomington, Ind.: Indiana University Press, 1996); John Mack Faragher, *Daniel Boone: The Life and Legend of an American Pioneer* (New York: Holt, 1992);

Craig T. Friend, ed., *The Buzzel about Kentuck: Settling the Promised Land* (Lexington, Ky.: University Press of Kentucky, 1999); Peter S. Onuf, *Statehood and Union: A History of the Northwest Ordinance* (Bloomington, Ind.: Indiana University Press, 1987); *Pathways to the Old Northwest: An Observance of the Bicentennial of the Northwest Ordinance* (Indianapolis: Indiana Historical Society, 1988); Elizabeth A. Perkins, *Border Life: Experience and Memory in the Revolutionary Ohio Valley* (Chapel Hill, N.C.: University of North Carolina Press, 1998); Alan Taylor, *Liberty Men and Great Proprietors: The Revolutionary Settlement on the Maine Frontier, 1760–1820* (Chapel Hill, N.C.: University of North Carolina Press, 1990); Alan Taylor, *William Cooper's Town: Power and Persuasion on the Frontier of the Early American Republic* (New York: Alfred A. Knopf, 1995); Robert M. Taylor, ed., *The Northwest Ordinance, 1787: A Bicentennial Handbook* (Indianapolis: Indiana Historical Society, 1987); and Frederick D. Williams, ed., *The Northwest Ordinance: Essays on Its Formulation, Provisions, and Legacy* (East Lansing, Mich.: Michigan State University Press, 1989). Although ten years old, Gregory H. Nobles's "Breaking into the Backcountry: New Approaches to the Early American Frontier," *William and Mary Quarterly*, 3d ser., 46 (October 1989): 641–70, remains the best overview of backcountry studies to date. The authors of many of the articles and dissertations he discusses produced the most important monographs of the 1990s.

3. Gordon Morris Bakken and Brenda Farrington, introduction to the series, in *Where Is the West?* ed. Bakken and Farrington (New York: Garland Publishing, 2000); the editors bring together many important articles from this growing field, including Michael Steiner, "From Frontier to Region: Frederick Jackson Turner and the New Western History." See also John A. Jackle, *Images of the Ohio Valley: A Historical Geography of Travel, 1740–1860* (New York: Oxford University Press, 1977). There are a few older studies of the Ohio Valley: R. E. Banta, *The Ohio* (New York: Rinehart, 1949); Walter Havighurst, *River to the West: Three Centuries of the Ohio* (New York: G. P. Putnam's Sons, 1970); and Archer Butler Hulbert, *The Ohio River and the Course of Empire* (New York: G. P. Putnam's Sons, 1906). Recently the *Queen City Heritage* was rechristened *Ohio Valley History,* and in the first issue historian Andrew R. L. Cayton called for scholars to consider the valley as a "coherent whole"; see "Artery and Border: The Ambiguous Development of the Ohio Valley in the Early Republic," *Ohio Valley History* 1 (Winter 2001): 19.

4. Lewis E. Atherton's *The Frontier Merchant in Mid-America* (Columbia, Mo.: University of Missouri Press, 1971) is one exception, though he focuses primarily on the era of the transportation revolution and settlements from Cincinnati west. For overviews of the trans-Appalachian West, see Reginald Horsman, *The Frontier in the Formative Years, 1783–1815* (New York: Holt, Rinehart and Winston, 1970) and Malcolm J. Rohrbough, *The Trans-Appalachian Frontier: Peoples, Societies, and Institutions, 1775–1850* (New York: Oxford University Press, 1978), quotation on p. 9. For information regarding merchants see Jackson Turner Main, *Society and Economy in Colonial Connecticut* (Princeton, N.J.: Princeton University Press, 1985), 278–82; Edwin J. Perkins, *The Economy of Colonial America,* 2d ed. (New York: Columbia University Press, 1988), 122–38; and Glenn Porter and Harold C. Livesay, *Merchants*

and Manufacturers: Studies in the Changing Structure of Nineteenth-Century Marketing (Chicago: Elephant Paperbacks, 1989).

5. For an analysis of how early visitors described Marietta, see William Henry Hildreth, "Travel Literature of the Ohio River Valley (1794–1832)" (Ph.D. diss., Ohio State University, 1944), 154. For a new interpretation of Marietta's history, see the work of historian Andrew R. L. Cayton. For the clash between North and South north of the Ohio River, see Etcheson, *Emerging Midwest,* and Richard Lyle Power, *Planting Corn Belt Culture: The Impress of the Upland Southerner and Yankee in the Old Northwest* (Indianapolis: Indiana Historical Society, 1953).

6. For the history of the lower third of the Ohio, see Darrel E. Bigham, *Towns and Villages of the Lower Ohio* (Lexington, Ky.: University Press of Kentucky, 1998); Andrew R. L. Cayton, *Frontier Indiana* (Bloomington, Ind.: Indiana University Press, 1996); and James E. Davis, *Frontier Illinois* (Bloomington, Ind.: Indiana University Press, 1998).

7. Richard Wade, *The Urban Frontier: Pioneer Life in Early Pittsburgh, Cincinnati, Lexington, Louisville, and St. Louis* (Chicago: University of Chicago Press, 1964). See also Daniel Preston, "Market and Mill Town: Hamilton Ohio, 1795–1860" (Ph.D. diss., University of Maryland, 1987), 19–20; and Elizabeth A. Perkins, "The Consumer Frontier: Household Consumption in Early Kentucky," *Journal of American History* 78 (September 1991): 486–510.

Part I. Across the Mountains

1. A description of the Ohio's course can be found in R. E. Banta, *The Ohio* (New York: Rinehart, 1949), 7–17.

2. Chief of Engineers, United States Army, comp., *The Ohio River,* 5th ed. (Washington, D.C.: Government Printing Office, 1934), 1–2; Robert L. Reid, introduction, and Scott Russell Sanders, "The Force of Moving Water," in *Always a River: The Ohio River and the American Experience,* ed. Robert L. Reid (Bloomington, Ind.: Indiana University Press, 1991), xi–31, especially pp. xii, 14–15.

3. Robert Silverberg, *The Moundbuilders* (Athens, Ohio: University of Ohio Press, 1986); James B. Griffin, "Late Prehistory of the Ohio Valley," in *Handbook of North American Indians,* vol. 15, *Northeast,* ed. Bruce G. Trigger (Washington, D.C.: Smithsonian Institution, 1978), 547–59; Neal Salisbury, "The Indians' Old World: Native Americans and the Coming of Europeans," *William and Mary Quarterly,* 3d ser., 53 (July 1996): 435–58; Eric Hinderaker, *Elusive Empires: Constructing Colonialism in the Ohio Valley, 1673–1800* (New York: Cambridge University Press, 1997); Michael N. McConnell, *A Country Between: The Upper Ohio Valley and Its Peoples, 1724–1774* (Lincoln, Nebr.: University of Nebraska Press, 1992); Richard White, *The Middle Ground: Indians, Empires, and Republics in the Great Lakes Region, 1650–1815* (New York: Cambridge University Press, 1991); and Randolph C. Downes, *Council Fires on the Upper Ohio: A Narrative of Indian Affairs on the Upper Ohio Valley until 1795* (Pittsburgh: University of Pittsburgh Press, 1940). For the names of the Ohio's banks, see Elizabeth A. Perkins, *Border Life: Experience and Memory in the*

Revolutionary Ohio Valley (Chapel Hill, N.C.: University of North Carolina Press, 1998), 47.

4. Yi-Fu Tuan, *Space and Place: The Perspective of Experience* (Minneapolis: University of Minnesota Press, 1977), 54 (quotation). See also Perkins, *Border Life*, 10; and Daniel Blake Smith, "'This Idea in Heaven': Image and Reality on the Kentucky Frontier," in *The Buzzel about Kentuck: Settling the Promised Land*, ed. Craig T. Friend (Lexington, Ky.: University Press of Kentucky, 1999), 77–99.

5. Daniel Vickers, "Competency and Competition: Economic Culture in Early America," *William and Mary Quarterly*, 3d ser., 47 (January 1990): 3–29 (quotation on p. 3). See also Virginia DeJohn Anderson, *New England's Generation: The Great Migration and the Formation of Society and Culture in the Seventeenth Century* (New York: Cambridge University Press, 1991).

6. Vickers, "Competency and Competition," 12–19.

7. Ibid., 16–17, 20–29.

8. Of antebellum Americans, historian Michael Merrill writes, "The most effective opponents of capitalism did not imagine doing away with commerce, innovation, or capitalists. . . .They sought, rather, more equitable ways to share the benefits of expanded trade and increased innovation among the 'producing' classes of society. They did not ask whether there would be a market; they asked who would control it and which social class would reap the lion's share of its benefits." Merrill, "Putting 'Capitalism' in Its Place: A Review of Recent Literature," *William and Mary Quarterly*, 3d ser., 52 (April 1995): 323.

9. James R. Bentley, ed., "A Letter from Harrodsburg, 1780," *Filson Club Historical Quarterly* 50 (October 1976): 370–71. For a discussion of the search for independence in the southern backcountry by not only Anglo-Americans, but settlers from continental Europe as well, see Warren Hofstra, "The Virginia Backcountry in the Eighteenth Century: The Question of Origins and the Issue of Outcomes," *Virginia Magazine of History and Biography* 101 (October 1993): 485–508.

1. Claiming Space

1. Dudley Woodbridge to James Backus, 9 December 1788, BWC, box 1, folder 1.

2. Dudley Woodbridge to James Backus, 14 June and 12 November 1789, 8 February 1790, and 7 January 1791, BWC, box 1, folder 1. For a similar process farther west, see the observations of Francis Baily, *Journal of a Tour in Unsettled Parts of North America in 1796 and 1797*, ed. Jack D. L. Holmes (Carbondale and Edwardsville, Ill.: Southern Illinois University Press, 1969), 104–105.

3. Frances Manwaring Caulkins, *History of Norwich, Connecticut* (Hartford, Conn.: privately printed, 1866), 397, 511; Bruce C. Daniels, "Economic Development in Colonial and Revolutionary Connecticut: An Overview," *William and Mary Quarterly*, 3d ser., 37 (July 1980): 435–38, 448; and Richard Anson Wheeler, *History of the Town of Stonington, County of New London, Connecticut* (New London, Conn.: Press of the Day Publishing Co., 1900), 693.

4. Dudley Woodbridge to Thomas Mumford, 4 July 1780; to David Trumbell, 3 January 1782; to John Proctor, 10 April 1779; and to Thomas Blanchard, 18 December 1780; in "Dudley Woodbridge, Letters Sent," vol. 15, folder 2 and "Dudley Woodbridge Accounts, 1774–1796," vol. 3, folder 1; both volumes in the Woodbridge-Backus Collection, Baker Library, Harvard Business School, Boston.

5. Dudley Woodbridge to George Philips, 8 July 1786 and 21 October 1788; and to Captain Joseph Chapman, 3 January 1788, Woodbridge-Backus Collection, vol. 15, folder 2. Dudley Woodbridge, Schooner "Elizabeth" Papers, in the Backus-Woodbridge Records, Connecticut Historical Society, Hartford, Conn., folder 1.

6. Thomas M. Doerflinger, *A Vigorous Spirit of Enterprise: Merchants and Economic Development in Revolutionary Philadelphia* (New York: W. W. Norton, 1986), 293–96, 314–29; Arthur P. Whitaker, "Reed and Forde: Merchant Adventurers of Philadelphia," *Pennsylvania Magazine of History and Biography* 61 (July 1937): 237–62; Louis Tarascon Journal, 1799, original and typescript trans., FHS; and quotation from François André Michaux, "Travels, to the West of the Allegheny Mountains," in *EWT,* 3:159.

7. James Backus to Elijah Backus, 9 June and 15 June 1788, BWC, box 1, folder 1.

8. Petition of Army Officers; Rufus Putnam to George Washington, 16 June 1783; and Rufus Putnam to George Washington, 15 April 1784, in *The Memoirs of Rufus Putnam,* ed. Rowena Buell (Boston: Houghton, Mifflin and Co., 1903), 215–25; and Archer Butler Hulbert, "Introduction: The Ohio Company and 'Scioto Right,'" in *The Records of the Original Proceedings of the Ohio Company,* ed. Hulbert (Marietta, Ohio: Marietta Historical Commission, 1917), xx–xxx, xl–xlii.

9. Timothy J. Shannon, "The Ohio Company and the Meaning of Opportunity in the American West, 1786–1795," *New England Quarterly* 64 (September 1991): 396–97, 402.

10. Andrew R. L. Cayton, *The Frontier Republic: Ideology and Politics in the Ohio Country, 1780–1825* (Kent, Ohio: Kent State University Press, 1986), 24–26; Manasseh Cutler, *An Explanation of the Map Which Delineates That Part of the Federal Lands* (Salem, Mass.: Dabney and Cushing, 1787), quotation on pp. 20–21.

11. Peter S. Onuf, *Statehood and Union: A History of the Northwest Ordinance* (Bloomington, Ind.: Indiana University Press, 1987), 1–9, 21–33, 42–43. See also Cayton, *Frontier Republic,* 2–25; Benjamin Horace Hibbard, *A History of Public Land Policies* (Madison, Wis.: University of Wisconsin Press, 1965), 32–81; Eric Hinderaker, *Elusive Empires: Constructing Colonialism in the Ohio Valley, 1673–1800* (New York: Cambridge University Press, 1977), 260–67; Malcom J. Rohrbough, *The Land Office Business: The Settlement and Administration of Public Lands, 1789–1837* (New York: Oxford University Press, 1968), 10–11; and Paul Finkelman, "Slavery and Bondage in the 'Empire of Liberty,'" 66–70, Jack N. Rakove, "Ambiguous Achievement: The Northwest Ordinance," 2–12, and Gordon T. Stewart, "The Northwest Ordinance and the Balance of Power in North America," 21–31, all in *The Northwest Ordinance: Essays on Its Formulation, Provisions, and Legacy,* ed. Frederick D. Williams (East Lansing, Mich.: Michigan State University Press, 1988).

12. Andrew R. L. Cayton, "The Northwest Ordinance from the Perspective of the Frontier," in *The Northwest Ordinance, 1787: A Bicentennial Handbook,* ed. Robert M. Taylor Jr. (Indianapolis: Indiana Historical Society, 1987), 1–23; Paul Finkelman, "The Northwest Ordinance: A Constitution for an Empire of Liberty," in *Pathways to the Old Northwest: An Observance of the Bicentennial of the Northwest Ordinance* (Indianapolis: Indiana Historical Society, 1988), 4–11; Onuf, *Statehood and Union,* 28–39; and Rakove, "Ambiguous Achievement," 14–15, and Stewart, "Balance of Power," 30–34, both in Williams, ed., *The Northwest Ordinance.* In "Slavery and Bondage in the 'Empire of Liberty,'" Finkelman argues that the ordinance's antislavery provision was not considered particularly important or controversial to most northerners or southerners until the rise of the abolition movement decades after its passage.

13. Shannon, "The Ohio Company," 397–400; and Christopher Clark, *The Roots of Rural Capitalism: Western Massachusetts, 1780–1860* (Ithaca, N.Y.: Cornell University Press, 1990), 60–64. Important studies of the migration patterns of New Englanders include Virginia DeJohn Anderson, *New England's Generation: The Great Migration and the Formation of Society and Culture in the Seventeenth Century* (New York: Cambridge University Press, 1991) and Christopher M. Jedrey, *The World of John Cleaveland: Family and Community in Eighteenth-Century New England* (New York: W. W. Norton, 1979).

14. *A Family History in Letters and Documents, 1667–1837,* ed. Mrs. Charles P. Noyes (Saint Paul, Minn.: privately printed, 1919), 155; S. P. Hildreth, *Biographical and Historical Memoirs of the Early Pioneer Settlers of Ohio* (Cincinnati: H. W. Derby and Co., 1852), 302–303; and Shannon, "The Ohio Company," 400–401.

15. Buell, ed., *Memoirs of Rufus Putnam,* 9–59; Cayton, *Frontier Republic,* 16, 26, 34, 49; and Hildreth, *Biographical and Historical Memoirs,* 13–36.

16. Cayton, *Frontier Republic,* 21–31 (quotation on p. 21).

17. Israel Putnam to David Putnam, 11 January 1798, 1 July 1798, and 1 September 1798, Putnam Family Papers, Ohio Historical Society, Columbus, box 1, folder 1.

18. Benjamin Ives Gilman to Hannah Robbins, 16 August 1789, in Noyes, ed., *Family History,* 163.

19. Ibid., Benjamin Ives Gilman to Hon. Nicholas Gilman, 27 February 1790 and 27 December 1795; Benjamin Ives Gilman to Hannah Gilman, 25 April 1795, pp. 170–71, 206–11. See also Hildreth, *Biographical and Historical Memoirs,* 306–310.

20. Beverley W. Bond Jr., *The Foundations of Ohio* (Columbus: Ohio State Archaeological and Historical Society, 1941), 384; and Thomas J. Summers, *History of Marietta* (Marietta, Ohio: Leader Publishing Co., 1903), 46–62, 69.

21. Manasseh Cutler to Winthrop Sargent, 20 April 1786, and to Nathan Dare, 16 March 1787; Cutler Journal, August 1788, in *Life, Journals, and Correspondence of Rev. Manasseh Cutler, LL.D.,* ed. William Parker Cutler and Julia Perkins Cutler (Cincinnati: R. Clarke and Co., 1888), 1:189, 194, 412–13, 419. Andrew R. L. Cayton, "Marietta and the Ohio Company," in *Appalachian Frontiers: Settlement, Society,*

and Development in the Preindustrial Era, ed. Robert D. Mitchell (Lexington, Ky.: University Press of Kentucky, 1991), 187–200; S. P. Hildreth, *Pioneer History* (Cincinnati: H. W. Derby and Co., 1848), 352–59; and Reginald Horsman, *The Frontier in the Formative Years, 1783–1815* (New York: Holt, Rinehart and Winston, 1970), 116.

22. Hildreth, *Pioneer History,* 349–52, 419–22; and Summers, *History of Marietta,* 77–78.

23. This paragraph and those following are based on the Thomas Wallcut Journal in the Thomas Wallcut Papers, 1671–1876, Massachusetts Historical Society, Boston.

24. Dudley Woodbridge to James Backus, 11 November 1789, BWC, box 1, folder 1.

25. Thomas Wallcut Journal, entry of 27 January 1790.

26. Rufus Putnam to Manasseh Cutler, 16 May 1788, in Cutler and Cutler, eds., *Life, Journals, and Correspondence,* 1:377–79.

27. John Cleves Symmes to Jonathan Dayton, 18–20 May 1789, in *The Correspondence of John Cleves Symmes: Founder of the Miami Purchase,* ed. Beverley W. Bond Jr. (New York: Macmillan, 1926), 66. See also Bond, *Foundations,* 298–99, and Richard C. Wade, *The Urban Frontier: Pioneer Life in Early Pittsburgh, Cincinnati, Lexington, Louisville, and St. Louis* (Chicago: University of Chicago Press, 1964), 22–24.

28. Lucy's letter quoted in Louise Rau, "Lucy Backus Woodbridge, Pioneer Mother: January 31, 1757–October 6, 1817," *Ohio State Archaeological and Historical Quarterly* 44, no. 4 (1935): 413.

29. Dudley Woodbridge to James Backus, 14 June 1789 and 8 February 1790, box 1, folder 1, and to Elijah Backus, 8 May 1797, box 1, folder 3, all in BWC.

30. B. Cushing diary, BWC, box 4, folder 3. For women's roles as deputy husbands, see Laural Thatcher Ulrich, *Good Wives: Image and Reality in the Lives of Women in Northern New England, 1650–1750* (New York: Vintage Books, 1982), 35–50.

31. Dwight L. Smith, ed., *The Western Journals of John May: Ohio Company Agent and Business Adventurer* (Cincinnati: Historical and Philosophical Society of Ohio, 1961), 155; Dudley Woodbridge to Roger Griswold, 11 November 1789, typescript, Dudley Woodbridge–Roger Griswold Correspondence, Connecticut Historical Society, Hartford, Conn.

32. Quoted in Rau, "Lucy Backus Woodbridge," 416.

33. Peter C. Mancall, *Valley of Opportunity: Economic Culture along the Upper Susquehanna, 1700–1800* (Ithaca, N.Y.: Cornell University Press, 1991), 160–216. For other studies of backcountry commercial development, see James Weston Livingood, *The Philadelphia-Baltimore Trade Rivalry, 1780–1860* (Harrisburg, Pa.: Pennsylvania Historical and Museum Commission, 1947), 1–53; Charles J. Farmer, *In the Absence of Towns: Settlement and Country Trade in Southside Virginia, 1730–1800* (Lanham, Md.: Rowman and Littlefield, 1993); and Robert D. Mitchell,

Commercialism and Frontier: Perspectives on the Early Shenandoah Valley (Charlottesville, Va.: University Press of Virginia, 1977).

34. Catherine Elizabeth Reiser, *Pittsburgh's Commercial Development, 1800–1850* (Harrisburg, Pa.: Pennsylvania Historical and Museum Commission, 1951), 2–9; and Wade, *Urban Frontier*, 7–13.

35. R. Eugene Harper, *The Transformation of Western Pennsylvania, 1770–1800* (Pittsburgh: University of Pittsburgh Press, 1991).

36. Wade, *Urban Frontier*, 18–22.

37. Ibid., 13–18; see also François André Michaux, "Travels," in *EWT*, 3:240.

38. John Cleves Symmes to Jonathan Dayton, 18–20 May 1789, in Bond, ed., *Correspondence*, 65–66, 71–72, 82 (quotation on pp. 65–66).

39. Smith, ed., *Western Journals*, 131–56. An excellent overview of the evolution of American policy toward the Ohio Indians following the Seven Years' War can be found in Reginald Horsman, "The Collapse of the Ohio River Barrier: Conflict and Negotiation in the Old Northwest, 1763–1787," in *Pathways to the Old Northwest*, 33–46. The war between the United States and the Ohio Indians from the initial skirmishes through the 1795 Treaty of Greenville is examined in Eric Hinderaker, *Elusive Empires*, 236–44; Horsman, *The Frontier in the Formative Years*, 39–49; R. Douglas Hurt, *The Ohio Frontier: Crucible of the Old Northwest, 1720–1830* (Bloomington, Ind.: Indiana University Press, 1996), 95–142; and Richard White, *The Middle Ground: Indians, Empires, and Republics in the Great Lakes Region, 1650–1815* (New York: Cambridge University Press, 1991), 413–68. Rufus Putnam took part in negotiations between the United States and the Native Americans; his reports and observations can be found in Buell, ed., *Memoirs of Rufus Putnam*. See also Andrew R. L. Cayton, "'Noble Actors' upon 'the Theatre of Honour': Power and Civility in the Treaty of Greenville," in *Contact Points: American Frontiers from the Mohawk Valley to the Mississippi, 1750–1830*, ed. Cayton and Fredrika J. Teute (Chapel Hill, N.C.: University of North Carolina Press, 1998), 235–69.

40. John Cleves Symmes to Jonathan Dayton, 28 May 1790, in Bond, ed., *Correspondence*, 129.

41. Hildreth, *Pioneer History*, 274–304, 361–72; letter book, Dudley Woodbridge to Webster and Co., 21 April 1794, BWC, box 18.

42. Letter book, Dudley Woodbridge to Enoch Parsons, 3 April 1794; to Webster and Co., 28 June, 18 June, and 9 April 1793; and to James Backus, draft of letter not sent, 29 May 1794, BWC, box 18, folder 1. Dudley Woodbridge to Dunlevy, 10 May 1790; and to James Backus, 7 January 1790, 24 June 1792, and 26 October 1793, BWC, box 1, folder 1. Dudley Woodbridge to Roger Griswold, 7 January and 13 November 1792, Woodbridge-Griswold Correspondence.

43. John Cleves Symmes to Jonathan Dayton, 6 August 1795 and 20 January 1796, in Bond, ed., *Correspondence*, 172, 175–76.

44. Baily, *Journal of a Tour*, 51–58 (quotation on p. 52); André Michaux, "Journal of Travels into Kentucky, July 15, 1793–April 11, 1796," in *EWT*, 3:32; and Wade, *Urban Frontier*, 11.

45. Wade, *Urban Frontier*, 17, 20, 50.

2. Planting a Place

1. Benjamin Ives Gilman to Hon. Nicholas Gilman, 27 December 1795, 6 January 1808 and 6 December 1809, in *A Family History in Letters and Documents, 1667–1837,* ed. Mrs. Charles P. Noyes (Saint Paul, Minn.: privately printed, 1919), 210, 277–79, 296–98, 302–303; and Lee Soltow, "Inequality amidst Abundance: Land Ownership in Early Nineteenth Century Ohio," *Ohio History* 88 (Spring 1979): 136–37.

2. Thomas E. Ferguson and Thomas Aquinas Burke, *Ohio Lands: A Short History* (Columbus: Ohio Auditor of State, 1987), 3–8; and Soltow, "Inequality amidst Abundance," 138–39.

3. Jonathan J. Bean, "Marketing 'the great American commodity': Nathaniel Massie and Land Speculation on the Ohio Frontier, 1783–1813," *Ohio History* 103 (Summer–Autumn 1994): 152–69. See also R. Douglas Hurt, *The Ohio Frontier: Crucible of the Old Northwest, 1720–1830* (Bloomington, Ind.: Indiana University Press, 1996), 168–75; and Edward H. Rastatter, "Nineteenth Century Public Land Policy: The Case for the Speculator," in *Essays in Nineteenth Century Economic History: The Old Northwest,* ed. David C. Klingaman and Richard K. Vedder (Athens, Ohio: Ohio University Press, 1975), 118–37.

4. This and the three paragraphs that follow are informed by John Bernard Ray, "Zane's Trace, 1796–1812: A Study in Historical Geography" (Ph.D. diss., Indiana University, 1968), 32–55.

5. Shaw Livermore, *Early American Land Companies: Their Influence on Corporate Development* (New York: The Commonwealth Fund, 1939), 134–46.

6. Reginald Horsman, *The Frontier in the Formative Years, 1783–1815* (New York: Holt, Rinehart and Winston, 1970), 105–11; and Francis Baily, *Journal of a Tour in the Unsettled Parts of North America in 1796 and 1797,* ed. Jack D. L. Holmes (Carbondale and Edwardsville, Ill.: Southern Illinois University Press, 1969), 104–105.

7. Horsman, *The Frontier in the Formative Years,* 112–120.

8. Malcolm J. Rohrbough, *The Trans-Appalachian Frontier: People, Societies, and Institutions, 1775–1850* (New York: Oxford University Press, 1978), 32–42. In fact newcomers represented an important market throughout the first two decades of the nineteenth century. See Isaac Lippincott, *A History of the Manufactures in the Ohio Valley to the Year 1860* (New York: Arno Press, 1973), 63.

9. Martin R. Andrews, *History of Marietta and Washington County, Ohio and Representative Citizens* (Chicago: Biographical Publishing Co., 1902); Joseph Barker, *Recollections of the First Settlement of Ohio,* ed. George Jordan Blazier (Marietta, Ohio: Richardson Publishing Corporation, 1982); and S. P. Hildreth, *Biographical and Historical Memoirs of the Early Settlers of Ohio* (Cincinnati: H. W. Derby and Co., 1852).

For similar settlement patterns in early Kentucky, see Ellen Eslinger, "Migration and Kinship on the Trans-Appalachian Frontier: Strode's Station, Kentucky," *Filson Club Historical Quarterly* 62 (January 1988): 52–66; and Lee Shai Weissbach, "The

Peopling of Lexington, Kentucky: Growth and Mobility in a Frontier Town," *Register of the Kentucky Historical Society* 81 (Spring 1983): 118; for the Illinois frontier, see John Mack Faragher, *Sugar Creek: Life on the Illinois Prairie* (New Haven, Conn.: Yale University Press, 1986), 50–60.

10. Hurt, *Ohio Frontier*, 184.

11. Benjamin Dana Diary, typescript, Connecticut State Library, Hartford, Conn.

12. Account book, BWC, box 17, folder 1.

13. Elizabeth A. Perkins, "The Consumer Frontier: Household Consumption in Early Kentucky," *Journal of American History* 78 (September 1991): 486–510.

14. This and the following paragraphs are based on Dwight L. Smith, ed., *The Western Journals of John May: Ohio Company Agent and Business Adventurer* (Cincinnati: Historical and Philosophical Society of Ohio, 1961), 131–66, quotations on pp. 141, 133, and 155.

15. Jonathan Goldstein, *Philadelphia and the China Trade, 1682–1846: Commercial, Cultural, and Attitudinal Effects* (University Park, Pa.: Pennsylvania State University Press, 1978), 21–35. While on the trip down the Ohio in 1799, Frenchman Louis Tarascon reported to his associates that plenty of ginseng could be found in the West, especially in Kentucky; see Louis Tarascon journal, 1799, original and typescript trans., FHS.

16. Account book, BWC, box 17; daybook, 1796–1797, James Smith and Findlay Papers, Cincinnati Historical Society, Cincinnati, vol. 1; Account Book, 1797–1799, Mason County, Kentucky, and James Weir Ledger, 1813–1815, Greenville, Ky., FHS.

17. François André Michaux, "Travels to the West of the Allegheny Mountains, in the States of Ohio, Kentucky, Tennessee," in *EWT*, 3:156–59; and John Cleves Symmes to Jonathan Dayton, 21 August 1788, in *The Correspondence of John Cleves Symmes: Founder of the Miami Purchase*, ed. Beverley W. Bond Jr. (New York: Macmillan, 1926), 43.

18. Invoice books, 1783–89 and 1789–92, box 16, folder 1 and letter book, 1793–95, box 18, folder 1; all in BWC.

19. W. Wallace Carson, "Transportation and Traffic on the Ohio and Mississippi before the Steamboat," *Mississippi Valley Historical Review* 7 (June 1920): 34–37.

20. Letter book, Dudley Woodbridge to Webster and Co., 9 April 1793, 5 May 1793, 28 June 1793, 26 October 1793, and 26 May 1794, BWC, box 18, folder 1.

21. Letter book, Dudley Woodbridge to Webster and Co., 25 September 1794, BWC, box 18, folder 1 (quotation). See also letter book, Dudley Woodbridge to Webster and Co., 29 April 1793, 5 May 1793, 28 June 1793, and 26 October 1793, and 26 May 1794, BWC, box 18, folder 1.

22. Thomas J. Summers, *History of Marietta* (Marietta, Ohio: Leader Publishing Co., 1903), 245; letter book, Dudley Woodbridge to Webster and Co., 21 April and 14 July 1794, BWC, box 18, folder 1.

23. Ledgers, box 23, folder 1, and box 24, folder 1; both in BWC.

24. Ledgers, box 23, folder 3; box 24, folder 1; and box 27, folder 1, BWC. Daybook, James Smith and Findlay Papers, vol. 1.

25. Daybook, James Smith and Findlay Papers, vol. 1.

26. Ibid.; and Richard C. Wade, *The Urban Frontier: Pioneer Life in Early Pittsburgh, Cincinnati, Lexington, Louisville, and St. Louis* (Chicago: University of Chicago Press, 1964), 25–27.

27. Andrew R. L. Cayton, *The Frontier Republic: Ideology and Politics in the Ohio Country, 1780–1825* (Kent, Ohio: Kent State University Press, 1986), 49–77.

28. Andrew R. L. Cayton, "Land, Power, and Reputation: The Cultural Dimensions of Politics in the Ohio Country," *William and Mary Quarterly*, 3d ser., 47 (April 1990): 266–86. For Ohio's statehood movement, see also Cayton, *Frontier Republic*, 73–77; Nicole Etcheson, *The Emerging Midwest: Upland Southerners and the Political Culture of the Old Northwest, 1787–1861* (Bloomington, Ind.: Indiana University Press, 1996), 15–26; and Donald J. Ratcliffe, *Party Spirit in a Frontier Republic: Democratic Politics in Ohio, 1793–1821* (Columbus: Ohio State University Press, 1998), 13–100.

29. Cayton, *Frontier Republic*, 78–79.

30. Benjamin Ives Gilman to Hon. Nicholas Gilman, 6 January 1808 and 6 December 1809; Gilman to Benjamin Clark Gilman, 11 March 1811, in Noyes, ed., *Family History*, 277–79, 296–98, 302–303; Lucy Woodbridge to John Matthews, 26 July 1809, DML/MC; and Hildreth, *Biographical and Historical Memoirs*, 309–10.

31. John Cleves Symmes to Jonathan Dayton, 15 August 1791, in Bond, ed., *Correspondence*, 153. For an account of Symmes's troubles, see Hurt, *Ohio Frontier*, 160–64.

Part II. The Western Country

1. Yi-Fu Tuan, *Space and Place: The Perspective of Experience* (Minneapolis: University of Minnesota Press, 1977), 17, 88.

2. This model of urban relationships in frontier Ohio was developed by Edward K. Muller in "Selective Urban Growth in the Middle Ohio Valley, 1800–1860," *Geographical Review* 66 (April 1976): 178–99.

3. Creating a Subregional Hub

1. Dudley Woodbridge Jr. to Dudley Woodbridge, 2 February 1797, BWC, box 1, folder 3.

2. Dudley Woodbridge to Roger Griswold, 14 October 1789, typescript, Woodbridge-Griswold Correspondence, Connecticut Historical Society, Hartford, Conn. Letter book, Dudley Woodbridge to Webster, Adgate, and White, 9 January 1794; to James Backus 26 May 1794; second draft of letter to Backus, 26 May 1794, BWC, box 18, folder 1. Dudley Woodbridge to James Backus and to Dudley Woodbridge Jr., 9 January 1795; to Dudley Woodbridge Jr., 5 January 1796, BWC, box 1, folder 2.

3. Dudley Woodbridge to Dudley Woodbridge Jr., 5 January 1796, BWC, box 1, folder 2; Lucy Woodbridge quoted in Louise Rau, "Lucy Backus Woodbridge, Pioneer Mother: January 31, 1757–October 6, 1817," *Ohio Archaeological and Historical Quarterly* 44, no. 4 (1935): 434–35. Jack was a family nickname for youngest son, John.

4. Lucy Woodbridge to William Woodbridge, 11 and 25 July 1796 and 30 August 1803, WWP. Dudley Woodbridge to Dudley Woodbridge Jr., 4 February 1797, BWC, box 1, folder 3; Dudley Woodbridge Jr. to William Woodbridge, 8 June 1798, WWP.

5. Dudley Woodbridge to Dudley Woodbridge Jr., 21 October 1798, BWC, box 1, folder 3.

6. James A. Ramage, *John Wesley Hunt: Pioneer Merchant, Manufacturer, and Financier* (Lexington, Ky.: University Press of Kentucky, 1974), 21–40.

7. Nathaniel Hart to Uncle, 10 January 1791, Nathaniel Hart Miscellaneous Papers, FHS. Jonathan H. Hanna to George Wood Meriwether, 27 December 1809, 9 October 1811, 11 April 1813, 6 October 1816, and 17 March 1819; Meriwether to Hanna, 28 February 1817; invoice dated 1 May 1810; George Wood Meriwether Papers, FHS; Gary A. O'Dell, "The Trotter Family, Gunpowder, and Early Kentucky Entrepreneurship, 1784–1833," *Register of the Kentucky Historical Society* 88 (Autumn 1990): 394–96. See also Fortescue Cuming, "Sketches of a Tour of the Western Country," in *EWT*, 4:80, 212.

8. Edward Turner to Dudley Woodbridge, 31 July and 2 August 1797, BWC, box 3, folder 1; letter book, Dudley Woodbridge Jr. to Mordecai Lewis, 1 February 1799, BWC, box 3, folder 2; Raymond E. Fitch, "Introduction: 'The Fascination of This Serpent,'" in *Breaking with Burr: Harman Blennerhassett's Journal, 1807*, ed. Fitch (Athens, Ohio: Ohio University Press, 1988), xi.

9. Dudley Woodbridge to Joseph S. Lewis, 5 May 1799, BWC, box 3, folder 2; Dudley Woodbridge, undated, BWC, box 3, folder 6.

10. Dudley Woodbridge Jr. to James Backus, 15 February 1799, BWC, box 2, folder 1.

11. Of one thousand heads of household in Washington County in 1810, four hundred thirty-two owned land; see Gerald M. Petty, *Ohio 1810 Tax Duplicate, Arranged in a State-Wide Alphabetical List of Names of Taxpayers* (Columbus: privately printed, 1976), and Claire Prechtel-Kluskens, comp., *Third Census of the United States, 1810 [microform]: Population Schedules, Washington County, Ohio* (Washington, D.C.: National Archives, 1994). See also Beverley W. Bond Jr., *The Civilization of the Old Northwest: A Study of Political, Social, and Economic Development, 1788–1812* (New York: Macmillan, 1934), 334–41; Lee Soltow, "Inequality Amidst Abundance: Land Ownership in Early Nineteenth Century Ohio," *Ohio History* 88 (Spring 1979): 135–44; Lee Soltow, "Progress and Mobility Among Ohio Property-holders, 1810–1825," *Social Science History* 7 (Fall 1983): 405–406; and William T. Utter, *The Frontier State, 1803–1825* (Columbus: Ohio State Archaeological and Historical Society, 1942), 134–36. For contrasting views of the lives of tenants see Craig Thompson Friend, "'Work and Be Rich': Economy and Culture on the Bluegrass Farm," in *The Buzzel about Kentuck: Settling the Promised Land*, ed. Friend (Lexing-

ton, Ky.: University Press of Kentucky, 1999), 132–34, and Ellen Eslinger, *Citizens of Zion: The Social Origins of Camp Meeting Revivalism* (Knoxville, Tenn.: University of Tennessee Press, 1999), 76–77.

12. Prechtel-Kluskens, comp., *Third Census of the United States, 1810 [microform]*; S. R. Wilson to Dudley Woodbridge Jr., 2 October 1802 and 6 September 1807, WWP; and James L. Dennis, *Washington's Darker Brother: One Hundred Years of Black History in Washington County, Ohio, 1788–1888* (Parkersburg, W.Va.: privately printed, 1986), 7.

13. Utter, *Frontier State*, 148–61.

14. R. Douglas Hurt begins the most recent overview of Ohio farmers with the statement, "The Ohio settlers were a profit-minded people," see Hurt, *The Ohio Frontier: Crucible of the Old Northwest, 1720–1830* (Bloomington, Ind.: Indiana University Press, 1996), 211–48. See also Utter, *Frontier State*, 162–65.

15. Utter, *Frontier State*, 167–70; François André Michaux, "Travels to the West of the Allegheny Mountains," in *EWT*, 3:241–42; John Melish, *Travels through the United States of America, in the Years 1806 and 1807, and 1809, 1810, and 1811* (New York: Johnson Reprint Corp., 1970), 343.

16. Utter, *Frontier State*, 166; and François André Michaux, "Travels," in *EWT*, 3:240–41.

17. Paul Woehrmann, ed., "The Autobiography of Abraham Snethen, Frontier Preacher," *Filson Club Historical Quarterly* 51 (October 1977): 317 (quotations), 320; François André Michaux, "Travels," in *EWT*, 3:232–33; Elizabeth A. Perkins, *Border Life: Experience and Memory in the Revolutionary Ohio Valley* (Chapel Hill, N.C.: University of North Carolina Press, 1998), 215; and H. Tyler Blethen and Curtis W. Wood, "A Trader on the Western Carolina Frontier," 159, Tyrel G. Moore, "Economic Development in Appalachian Kentucky, 1800–1860," 215, and Paul Salstrom, "The Agricultural Origins of Economic Dependency, 1840–1880," 264, all in *Appalachian Frontiers: Settlement, Society, and Development in the Preindustrial Era*, ed. Robert D. Mitchell (Lexington, Ky.: University Press of Kentucky, 1991).

18. Ledger, BWC, box 30, folder 1. The five hundred accounts do not include the accounts of Philadelphia suppliers, traders Woodbridge supplied with goods, family members, or Woodbridge and Blennerhassett themselves.

19. Lewis E. Atherton, *The Frontier Merchant in Mid-America* (Columbia, Mo.: University of Missouri Press, 1971), 57, 142–46; Eslinger, *Citizens of Zion*, 35–36.

20. Letter book, Dudley Woodbridge Jr. to James Converse, 20 January 1801, and to Levi Allen, May 1801, BWC, box 24, folder 2. Letter book, Dudley Woodbridge Jr. to Michael Graham, June 1806, BWC, box 36, folder 1; letter book, Dudley Woodbridge Jr. to Michael Graham, December 1808, and to Caldwell, 18 December 1808, BWC, box 43, folder 1.

21. Mason County, Ky., Account Book, 1797–1799, FHS.

22. Daniel Halstead Papers, FHS.

23. For one scholar's analysis of the role of cash in the early West, see Craig T. Friend, "Merchants and Markethouses: Reflections on Moral Economy in Early Kentucky," *Journal of the Early Republic* 17 (Winter 1997): 553–74.

24. Blotter, WMCR, vol. 20.

25. Eslinger, *Citizens of Zion,* 31–78; and Malcolm J. Rohrbough, *The Trans-Appalachian Frontier: People, Societies, and Institutions, 1775–1850* (New York: Oxford University Press, 1978), 34–42, 93–95.

26. Letter book, Dudley Woodbridge Jr. to Harman Blennerhassett, 26 July 1802, and to James Converse, 6 May 1803, WMCR, vol. 1; letter book, Dudley Woodbridge Jr. to Joseph F. Munro, 21 February 1804, BWC, box 36, folder 1; Atherton, *The Frontier Merchant,* 143.

27. Muskingum Bridge, Western Reserve Historical Society, Cleveland, Ohio.

28. Stephen Aron, *How the West Was Lost: The Transformation of Kentucky from Daniel Boone to Henry Clay* (Baltimore: Johns Hopkins University Press, 1996), 116–21; and Eslinger, *Citizens of Zion,* 46–49. For an alternative interpretation, see Friend, "'Work and Be Rich,'" in Friend, ed., *The Buzzel about Kentuck,* 134–36. See also Elizabeth A. Perkins, "The Consumer Frontier: Household Consumption in Early Kentucky," *Journal of American History* 78 (September 1991): 486–510; and Christopher Waldrep, "Opportunity on the Frontier South of the Green," in Friend, ed., *The Buzzel about Kentuck,* 153–72.

29. Dudley Woodbridge Jr. did not lay out his views of what a merchant should be for historians to see, but his sister-in-law wrote to her son, who clerked for Woodbridge for a time, and makes clear Dudley's evaluation of the young man in a letter that does not survive; see Sarah Backus to William Backus, 24 August 1819, BWC, box 2, folder 3. See also Dudley Woodbridge Jr. to William Woodbridge, 5 July 1841, and William Petit to William Woodbridge, 3 December 1816; both in WWP.

30. Letter book, Dudley Woodbridge Jr. to John Woodbridge, 1 September 1808, BWC, box 43, folder 1. Dudley Woodbridge Jr. to William Woodbridge, 19 February 1807, WWP. Letter book, Dudley Woodbridge Jr. to William Rufus Putnam, 17 April 1832, WMCR, vol. 8.

31. Letter book, Dudley Woodbridge Jr. to Mr. Dyer, 9 May and 28 May 1800, and to Royal Converse, 5 May 1801, BWC, box 24, folder 2.

32. Letter book, memo to Henry Mills, 14 May 1804; see also Dudley Woodbridge Jr. to Asa Davis, 24 February 1804, BWC, box 36, folder 1.

33. Letter book, Dudley Woodbridge Jr. to John Harris, 15 July 1799; to Mr. Stone, 15 July 1799; to Loveland and Smith, 30 August 1799; to Silas Bingham, September 1799; to Thomas Hart, 13 December 1799; and to Loveland and Smith, 1 January 1800, BWC, box 24, folder 2. Blotter, WMCR, vol. 19.

34. Letter book, Dudley Woodbridge Jr. to Simon Converse, 8 February 1804, and to Increase Matthews, 7 December 1804, BWC, box 36, folder 1; ledger, BWC, box 30, folder 1. Dudley Woodbridge Jr. to Joseph F. Munro, 10 December 1803, WWP.

35. See letters to Samuel and George Trotter from Akin and Gomez, William Armstrong, Daniel Brown, Isaac Evans, Frederick Hine, Thomas Haughey, David Kinkead and Co., Alexander McNeil, and William Shannon, in Samuel and George Trotter Co., Lexington, Ky., Business Correspondence, 1805–1819, Cincinnati Historical Society, Cincinnati; and the Daniel R. Southard Papers, FHS. West Union,

Ohio, was built specifically as a settlement with access to Zane's Trace: see John Bernard Ray, "Zane's Trace, 1796–1812: A Study in Historical Geography" (Ph.D. diss., Indiana University, 1968), 189–91.

36. Atherton, *Frontier Merchant,* 115–23; Bruce C. Daniels, *The Connecticut Town: Growth and Development, 1635–1790* (Middletown, Conn.: Wesleyan University Press, 1979), 147–48.

37. Ray, "Zane's Trace," 54, 158–64; letter book, Dudley Woodbridge Jr. to James Converse, 3 February 1804, 22 March 1804, 2 April 1804, and 7 December 1804, BWC, box 36, folder 1.

38. Cuming, "Sketches," in *EWT,* 4:130, 222; Melish, *Travels,* 428–29; Ray, "Zane's Trace," 164.

39. Joseph F. Munro to John Matthews, 30 May 1801, 12 June 1801, 18 December 1801, and 30 December 1801, DML/MC; and Joseph F. Munro to Ephraim Cutler, 22 December 1846, DML/CC.

40. Letter book, Dudley Woodbridge Jr. to Harman Blennerhassett, 4 February 1802; to James Converse, 31 August 1802; and to Royal Converse, 31 August 1802, WMCR, vol. 1. Letter book, Dudley Woodbridge Jr. to Cook and Cresson, 14 February 1810, and to Nathaniel S. Cushing, 6 June and 23 November 1808, BWC, box 43, folder 1; and ledger, BWC, box 30, folder 1.

41. Letter book, Dudley Woodbridge Jr. to James Converse, 21 October 1801, February 1802, 9 March 1802, 7 March 1803, 8 May 1803, and 25 July 1803, WMCR, vol. 1.

42. Letter book, Dudley Woodbridge Jr. to Wright Converse, 9 April 1804, and to Simon Converse, 9 April and 18 May 1804, BWC, box 36, folder 1; second letter book, Dudley Woodbridge Jr. to Simon Converse, 27 November 1805, BWC, box 36, folder 1.

43. Alfred Tischendorf and E. Taylor Parks, eds., *The Diary and Journal of Richard Clough Anderson, Jr., 1814–1826* (Durham, N.C.: Duke University Press, 1964), 31; Miles and Hynes Papers, Murfreesboro, Tenn., FHS; Jonathan H. Hanna to George Wood Meriwether, 27 December 1809, George Wood Meriwether Papers; Daniel Preston, "Market and Mill Town: Hamilton Ohio, 1795–1860" (Ph.D. diss., University of Maryland, 1987), 54–55; Marietta Jennings, *A Pioneer Merchant of St. Louis, 1810–1820: The Business Career of Christian Wilt* (New York: Columbia University Press, 1939), 39, 47, 199; and Ramage, *John Wesley Hunt,* 21–40.

44. Fred Mitchell Jones, "Middlemen in the Domestic Trade of the United States, 1800–1860," *Illinois Studies in the Social Sciences* 21, no. 3 (1937): 44; Dwight L. Smith, ed., *The Western Journals of John May: Ohio Company Agent and Business Adventurer* (Cincinnati: Historical and Philosophical Society of Ohio, 1961), 135–36; Francis Baily, *Journal of a Tour in Unsettled Parts of North America in 1796 and 1797,* ed. Jack D. L. Holmes (Carbondale and Edwardsville, Ill.: Southern Illinois University Press, 1969), 92–93.

45. William Woodbridge to James Backus, 21 June 1807, BWC, box 2, folder 1.

46. Ledger, box 27, folder 1; two ledgers, box 45, folder 1; all of the above in BWC. Prechtel-Kluskens, comp., *Third Census of the United States, 1810 [microform].*

47. Prechtel-Kluskens, comp., *Third Census of the United States, 1810 [microform]*; Isaac Lippincott, *A History of the Manufactures in the Ohio Valley to the Year 1860* (New York: Arno Press, 1973), 67–68, 90–92. A similar pattern of widely scattered mills grew up in Hamilton's hinterland, twenty-five miles north of Cincinnati on the Great Miami River during the early 1800s; see Preston, "Market and Mill Town," 64–66; for an account of Hamilton craftsmen, see pp. 106–10. For the local nature of manufacturing at this stage of development, see Edward K. Muller, "Selective Urban Growth in the Middle Ohio Valley, 1800–1860," *Geographical Review* 66 (April 1976): 182–85.

4. Connecting East and West

1. François André Michaux, "Travels to the West of the Allegheny Mountains," in *EWT*, 3:240; John Melish, *Travels through the United States of America, in the Years 1806 and 1807, and 1809, 1810, and 1811* (New York: Johnson Reprint Corp., 1970), 374; and Thomas Senior Berry, *Western Prices before 1861: A Study of the Cincinnati Market* (Cambridge: Harvard University Press, 1943), 155–63.

2. For an account of merchants who bought and sold western produce on a regular basis in Hamilton's hinterland to the north of Cincinnati, see Daniel Preston, "Market and Mill Town: Hamilton Ohio, 1795–1860" (Ph.D. diss., University of Maryland, 1987), 50–111. Most accounts of Ohio stress that lands in the Miami Valley, lands along the upper Muskingum north of Zanesville, and lands in the congressional lands west of Steubenville proved to be much more fertile than the lower Muskingum of Marietta's hinterland. This may be the reason Woodbridge did so little trade in flour.

3. Leland D. Baldwin, "Shipbuilding on the Western Waters, 1793–1817," *Mississippi Valley Historical Review* 20 (June 1933): 29–39.

4. Letter book, Dudley Woodbridge Jr. to Thomas Soya, 2 November 1801, 17 November 1801; to Harman Blennerhassett, 14 November 1801; to Joseph Clark, not sent, 11 February 1802; to James Backus, 8 February 1802; to Mr. John Fox, 17 May 1802; to Joseph Lewis, 7 December 1802; and to Joel Winchester, 7 February 1803, WMCR, vol. 1.

5. Letter book, Dudley Woodbridge Jr. to H. Mills, 24 February 1803; to Joseph Lewis, 11 September 1803; to Harman Blennerhassett, 18 October and 4 December 1803; and to James Converse, 9 December 1803, WMCR, vol. 1. Ledger, BWC, box 30, folder 1.

6. Baldwin, "Shipbuilding on the Western Waters," 31–32, 36–38, 40–43 (quotation on p. 43).

7. R. Carlyle Buley, *The Old Northwest: Pioneer Period, 1815–1840* (Bloomington, Ind.: Indiana University Press, 1950), 1:411–13.

8. Ibid., 1:413–15.

9. Louis C. Hunter, "Studies in the Economic History of the Ohio Valley: Seasonal Aspects of Industry and Commerce Before the Age of Big Business and the Be-

ginnings of Industrial Combination," *Smith College Studies in History* 19 (October 1933–January 1934): 9; Waterman Palmer to John Mills, 6 March 1818, DML/MC.

10. Letter book, Dudley Woodbridge Jr. to Joseph S. Lewis, 7 August 1799; to Harman Blennerhassett, August 1799; to James Converse, 5 June 1800; to Joseph Clark, 5 June 1800; to James Converse, 11 June 1800; to General Curtis, July 1800; and to John Damon, 16 March 1801; BWC, box 24, folder 2. Letter book, Dudley Woodbridge Jr. to John Damon, February 1802, WMCR, vol. 1. Letter book, Dudley Woodbridge Jr. to Joseph Clark, March 1813, and to Jonathan Creed, February 1813, WMCR, vol. 2. Letter book, Dudley Woodbridge Jr. to S. Scovil and Co., 10 July 1816, and to S. and G. Trotter, 27 July 1816, WMCR, vol. 3.

11. Berry, *Western Prices*, 74; Buley, *Old Northwest*, 1:335–6; Jonathan Goldstein, *Philadelphia and the China Trade, 1682–1846: Commercial, Cultural, and Attitudinal Effects* (University Park, Pa.: Pennsylvania State University Press, 1978), 21; François André Michaux, "Travels," in *EWT*, 3:232–33; Elizabeth A. Perkins, *Border Life: Experience and Memory in the Revolutionary Ohio Valley* (Chapel Hill, N.C.: University of North Carolina Press, 1998), 215; and H. Tyler Blethen and Curtis W. Wood, "A Trader on the Western Carolina Frontier," 159, Tyrel G. Moore, "Economic Development in Appalachian Kentucky, 1800–1860," 222, and Paul Salstrom, "The Agricultural Origins of Economic Dependency, 1840–1880," 264, all in *Appalachian Frontiers: Settlement, Society, and Development in the Preindustrial Era*, ed. Robert D. Mitchell (Lexington, Ky.: University Press of Kentucky, 1991).

12. Goldstein, *Philadelphia and the China Trade*, 2–3, 30.

13. Letter book, Dudley Woodbridge Jr. to Benjamin Ives Gilman, 6 August 1816; to William Robinson Jr., 7 August 1816; to James C. McFarland, 28 October 1816; to Gilman and Ammidon, 9 November and 22 November 1816; and to Mr. Hoskins, 2 December 1816, WMCR, vol. 3.

14. Letter book, Dudley Woodbridge Jr. to Hamilton Kerr, 14 July 1804; to Levi Allen, 9 July 1804; to Denny and Co., 5 July 1805; and to Joseph Lewis, 5 July 1804, BWC, box 36, folder 1.

15. James F. Hopkins, *A History of the Hemp Industry in Kentucky* (Lexington, Ky.: University of Kentucky Press, 1951).

16. Letter book, Dudley Woodbridge Jr. to Samuel Carswell and Co., 17 January 1804; to James Converse, 3 February 1804; to Joseph S. Lewis, 7 February 1804; and to Benjamin Wilson, 27 February 1804, BWC, box 36, folder 1.

17. Dudley Woodbridge Jr. to William Woodbridge, August 1806, WWP.

18. Letter book, Dudley Woodbridge Jr. to Daniel Greene, 27 September and 25 December 1813, and 6 February 1814; to Woodbridge and Pierce, 6 September 1813; to Benjamin Morgan, 29 November 1813; to Paul Fearing, 22 November 1813; to Ebenezer Buckingham, 24 March 1814; to C. and T. Bullett, 14 April 1814; and to Robinson and Barber, 22 March 1814, WMCR, vol. 2. Ledger, BWC, box 45, folder 2.

19. Letter book, letters of July 1816, WMCR, vol. 3.

20. Dudley Woodbridge Jr. to William Woodbridge, 14 January and 25 August 1817, WWP.

21. Preston, "Market and Mill Town," 69–74; Berry, *Western Prices,* 367; François André Michaux, "Travels," in *EWT,* 3:203–205; letter book, Dudley Woodbridge Jr. to Jack, 7 September 1820, WMCR, vol. 4. See also Craig T. Friend, "Merchants and Markethouses: Reflections on Moral Economy in Early Kentucky," *Journal of the Early Republic* 17 (Winter 1997): 553–74.

22. Letter book, Dudley Woodbridge to Silas Bingham, 15 April 1800, BWC, box 24, folder 2. Letter book, Dudley Woodbridge, Jr. to James Converse, 2 July 1805; to Increase Matthews, 8 January 1806; to Jonathan Matthews, 8 July 1806; and to James Converse, 5 February 1807, BWC, box 36, folder 1; and *Fredonian* (Chillicothe newspaper), 14 March 1807.

23. Fred Mitchell Jones, "Middlemen in the Domestic Trade of the United States, 1800–1860," *Illinois Studies in the Social Sciences* 21, no. 3 (1937): 1–14; letter book, Dudley Woodbridge Jr. to Thomas L. Pierce, 16 November 1811, WMCR, vol. 2.

24. Asa R. Runyon to Asa Runyon and Co., 4 June 1815, Runyon Family Papers, FHS.

25. Invoice book, BWC, box 35, folder 2. Other shipments from 1804–1806 include from Clark—lemons, ginger, allspice, nutmeg, almonds, and indigo; from Harvey and Worth—umbrellas, parasols, penknives, vest molds, chisels, marking irons, stirrups, handsaw files, hinges, locks, padlocks, candlesticks, saws, frying pans, combs, kettles, wheel irons, screw augers, and nails; from Gartland—salt and pepper sets, glass salt stands, edge dishes, and wine glasses; from Conrad—chapbooks, paper, inkstands, ink powder, primers, toy books, wafers, sealings, wafer boxes, quills, cyphering books, playing cards, and ruled books; from Carswell and other dry goods merchants—cotton, cambric, muslin, flannel, dimity, velveteen, calico, cashmere, broadcloth, and baize.

26. Ibid.; and invoice book, WMCR, vol. 100.

27. Jack also purchased $980 worth of nails, probably in Pittsburgh; WMCR, vol. 23.

28. For just a few examples, see letter book, Dudley Woodbridge Jr. to Joseph Clark, 5 June 1800, BWC, box 24, folder 2. Letter book, Dudley Woodbridge Jr. to Harvey and Worth, 1 December 1801, and to Joseph Clark, 1 December 1801, WMCR, vol. 1. Letter book, Dudley Woodbridge Jr. to Joseph Clark, 8 May 1804, and to Mrs. Jourdan, 9 July 1804, BWC, box 36, folder 1. Letter book, Dudley Woodbridge Jr. to Richard Ashurst, 18 August 1818, and to William Wilson, 18 August 1818, WMCR, vol. 4.

29. Jones, "Middlemen in the Domestic Trade," 13, 18, 33.

30. Letter book, Dudley Woodbridge Jr. to William Wilson, 13 July 1821; to Richard Ashurst, 10 November 1821; to T. and A. Vinton, 29 November 1821; and to Henry Toland, 30 November 1821, WMCR, vol. 6; letter book, Dudley Woodbridge Jr. to Cooke and Cresson, 26 May 1813, WMCR, vol. 2.

31. R. Pierce Beaver, "Joseph Hough, An Early Miami Merchant," *Ohio Archaeological and Historical Quarterly* 45 (January 1936): 41–42.

32. This paragraph and the ones that follow are based upon the Samuel Meeker Ledger, 1807–1810, Historical Society of Pennsylvania, Philadelphia. A large num-

ber of the 550 names did not have a location listed with their account; I assumed that those represented local (Philadelphia-area) dealings.

For the collection of debts, see Jones, "Middlemen in the Domestic Trade," 18.

33. Thirty-eight under five hundred dollars; fourteen between five hundred one and one thousand dollars; seventeen over one thousand dollars.

34. This and the paragraph that follows are based on Marietta Jennings, *A Pioneer Merchant of St. Louis, 1810–1820: The Business Career of Christian Wilt* (New York: Columbia University Press, 1939), 11–19, 43–48.

35. This and the two paragraphs that follow are informed by Thomas Perkins Abernethy, *The Burr Conspiracy* (Gloucester, Mass.: P. Smith, 1968), 3–118, 199–249.

36. Abernethy, *The Burr Conspiracy*, 66, 107–108; Milton Lomask, *Aaron Burr: The Conspiracy and Years of Exile, 1805–1836* (New York: Farrar, Straus and Giroux, 1982), 129; Walter Flavius McCaleb, *The Aaron Burr Conspiracy* (New York: Wilson-Erickson, 1936), 89.

37. William Woodbridge to James Backus, 21 June 1807, BWC, box 2, folder 1; letter book, Dudley Woodbridge Jr. to Joseph Lewis, 19 November 1808, BWC, box 43, folder 1; Raymond E. Fitch, ed., *Breaking with Burr: Harman Blennerhassett's Journal, 1807* (Athens, Ohio: Ohio University Press, 1988), 62–63, 106, 188–90, 232, 243–45, 250.

38. Dudley Woodbridge Jr. to William Woodbridge, 28 August 1801 and 5 June 1809, WWP.

39. Dudley Woodbridge Jr. to William Woodbridge, 5 June 1809, WWP.

40. Catherine Elizabeth Reiser, *Pittsburgh's Commercial Development, 1800–1850* (Harrisburg, Pa.: Pennsylvania Historical and Museum Commission, 1951), 1–28; Richard C. Wade, *The Urban Frontier: Pioneer Life in Early Pittsburgh, Cincinnati, Lexington, Louisville, and St. Louis* (Chicago: University of Chicago Press, 1964), 43–49.

41. Fortescue Cuming, "Sketches of a Tour of the Western Country," in *EWT*, 4:76–87, 245–55; Thaddeus Mason Harris, "The Journal of a Tour into the Territory Northwest of the Allegheny Mountains," in *EWT*, 3:342; and François André Michaux, "Travels," in *EWT*, 3:156–59.

42. Joseph E. Walker, ed., *Pleasure and Business in Western Pennsylvania: The Journal of Joshua Gilpin, 1809* (Harrisburg, Pa.: Pennsylvania Historical and Museum Commission, 1975), 50, 74, 97.

43. Letter book, Dudley Woodbridge Jr. to Benjamin B. Howell, 24 February 1810, and to Jonathan Creed, 10 March 1810, BWC, box 43, folder 1. In addition see all entries for January to August 1810.

44. Dudley Woodbridge Jr. to William Woodbridge, 12 December 1809, WWP; letter book, Dudley Woodbridge Jr. to Tilford, 23 April 1810 (first 1810 quotation), and to John Woodbridge, 20 April and 11 September 1810, BWC, box 43, folder 1.

45. Letter book, Dudley Woodbridge Jr. to Charles Copeland, 7 April 1810, and to John Woodbridge, 11 September 1810, BWC, box 43, folder 1. William Woodbridge to Dudley Woodbridge Jr., 28 January and 1 March 1810, BWC, box 2, folder 1.

5. The Dimensions of the Riverine Economy

1. Fortescue Cuming, "Sketches of a Tour of the Western Country," in *EWT*, 4:126–127.

2. Dwight L. Smith and Ray Swick, eds., *A Journey through the West: Thomas Rodney's 1803 Journal from Delaware to the Mississippi Territory* (Athens, Ohio: Ohio University Press, 1997), especially 93–98; François André Michaux, "Travels to the West of the Allegheny Mountains," in *EWT*, 3:189.

3. Cuming, "Sketches," in *EWT*, 4:116, 135; George W. Ogden, "Letters From the West: Comprising a Tour through the Western Country," in *EWT*, 19:39 (quotation); John Melish, *Travels through the United States of America, in the Years 1806 and 1807, and 1809, 1810, and 1811* (New York: Johnson Reprint Corp., 1970), 357–58; Smith and Swick, eds., *A Journey through the West*, 76; Mrs. Steele, *A Summer Journey in the West* (New York: J. S. Taylor and Co., 1841), 234; and David Thomas, *Travels through the Western Country in the Summer of 1816* (Auburn, N.Y.: David Rumsey, 1819), 233–34. Invoice book, BWC, box 23, folder 2.

4. J. D. B. DeBow, *Statistical View of the United States* (Washington, D.C.: A. O. P. Nicholson, 1854), 40; François André Michaux, "Travels," in *EWT*, 3:226–27 (quotation); John Woods, "Two Year's Residence in the Settlement on the English Prairie, in the Illinois Country, United States (June 5, 1820–July 3, 1821)," in *EWT*, 10:229; Melish, *Travels through the United States of America*, 415; Francis Baily, *Journal of a Tour in Unsettled Parts of North America in 1796 and 1797*, ed. Jack D. L. Holmes (Carbondale and Edwardsville, Ill.: Southern Illinois University Press, 1969), 121–22. For an account of the settling of Kentucky and its legacy, see Neal O. Hammon, "Land Acquisition on the Kentucky Frontier," *Register of the Kentucky Historical Society* 78 (Autumn 1980): 297–321.

5. Alfred Tischendorf and E. Taylor Parks, eds., *The Diary and Journal of Richard Clough Anderson, Jr., 1814–1826* (Durham, N.C.: Duke University Press, 1964), 31–32, 68; DeBow, *Statistical View*, 40.

6. R. Carlyle Buley, *The Old Northwest: Pioneer Period, 1815–1840* (Bloomington, Ind.: Indiana University Press, 1950), 1:106–109; Benjamin Horace Hibbard, *A History of the Public Land Policies* (Madison, Wis.: University of Wisconsin Press, 1965), 87–100, 175–76, 209–13; William T. Utter, *The Frontier State, 1803–1825* (Columbus: Ohio State Archaeological and Historical Society, 1942), 129–36; Beverley W. Bond Jr., *The Civilization of the Old Northwest: A Study of Political, Social, and Economic Development, 1788–1812* (New York: Macmillan, 1934), 319–20, 334–41; Payson Jackson Treat, *The National Land System, 1785–1820* (New York: E. B. Treat, 1910), 401–410; and George W. Knepper, *Ohio and Its People* (Kent, Ohio: Kent State University Press, 1989), 81–82.

7. Bond, *Civilization of the Old Northwest*, 319–20, 334–41; Buley, *Old Northwest*, 1:106–109; Hibbard, *Public Land Policies*, 209–13; Knepper, *Ohio*, 81–82; Utter, *Frontier State*, 129–36.

8. H. Z. Williams, *History of Washington County, Ohio* (Cleveland: H. Z. Williams and Bro., 1881), 476.

9. Nahum Ward to Thomas W. Ward, 22 February 1813, 28 August 1815, 19 May and 20 June 1817, Ward Family Papers, 1661–1919, Shrewsbury, Mass., American Antiquarian Society, Worcester, Mass., box 3, folder 2.

10. Melish, *Travels*, 595.

11. Max Farrand, ed., *A Journey to Ohio in 1810 as Recorded in the Journal of Margaret Van Horn Dwight* (New Haven, Conn.: Yale University Press, 1914), 36–47, 56–57, quotations on pp. 36–37 and 47. In 1816 David Thomas found the northern route to be just as inconvenient and nearly as crowded; see Thomas, *Travels*, 4–5, 17–22, 56.

12. Buley, *Old Northwest*, 1:415; Ogden, "Letters," 41.

13. Baily, *Journal of a Tour*, 65–69, 79–80, 115, 133, 280–81. For another account of the hazards of ice on the Ohio, see John Cleves Symmes to Jonathan Dayton, 18–20 May 1789, in *The Correspondence of John Cleves Symmes: Founder of the Miami Purchase*, ed. Beverley W. Bond Jr. (New York: Macmillan, 1926), 57–58.

14. This and the paragraph that follows are informed by John Bernard Ray, "Zane's Trace, 1796–1812: A Study in Historical Geography" (Ph.D. diss., Indiana University, 1968), 61–99.

15. Theodore G. Gronert, "Trade in the Early Blue-Grass Region, 1810–1820," *Mississippi Valley Historical Review* 5 (December 1918): 313–17; James A. Ramage, *John Wesley Hunt: Pioneer Merchant, Manufacturer, and Financier* (Lexington, Ky.: University Press of Kentucky, 1974), 6; Richard C. Wade, *The Urban Frontier: Pioneer Life in Early Pittsburgh, Cincinnati, Lexington, Louisville, and St. Louis* (Chicago: University of Chicago Press, 1964), 20, 50.

16. François André Michaux, "Travels," in *EWT*, 3:199–203.

17. Cuming, "Sketches," in *EWT*, 4:181–89.

18. Stephen Aron, *How the West Was Lost: The Transformation of Kentucky from Daniel Boone to Henry Clay* (Baltimore: Johns Hopkins University Press, 1996), 123–33.

19. Baily, *Journal of a Tour*, 110–11; Cuming, "Sketches," in *EWT*, 4:256–57 (quotation); Smith and Swick, eds., *Journey*, 104–105.

20. Melish, *Travels*, 361; Wade, *Urban Frontier*, 54–55 (Drake quotation, p. 55).

21. Letter book, Dudley Woodbridge Jr. to Baum and Perry, May and December 1813, WMCR, vol. 2; Utter, *Frontier State*, 183–87.

22. James Fernon and John Connolly to Richard Ashhurst and Sons, 16 January and 9 February 1816, Claude W. Unger Collection, Historical Society of Pennsylvania, Philadelphia.

23. Henry Bradshaw Fearon, *Sketches of America: A Narrative of a Journey through the Eastern and Western States of America*, 3d ed. (London: Longman, Hurst, Rees, Orme, and Brown, 1819), 199; Elias Pym Fordham, *Personal Narrative of Travels in Virginia, Maryland, Pennsylvania, Ohio, Indiana, Kentucky; and of a Residence in the Illinois Territory: 1817–1818*, ed. Frederic Austin Ogg (Cleveland: A. H. Clark Co., 1906), 192–93; Thomas Hulme, "A Journal Made During a Tour in the Western Countries of America: September 30, 1818–August 7, 1819," in *EWT*, 10:46, 62.

24. Lucy Woodbridge to John Matthews, 30 November 1809, DML/MC.

25. Thomas Senior Berry, *Western Prices before 1861: A Study of the Cincinnati Market* (Cambridge: Harvard University Press, 1943), 27–28; Reginald Horsman, *The Frontier in the Formative Years, 1783–1815* (New York: Holt, Rinehart and Winston, 1970), 162–65.

26. See letter books, BWC, box 24, folder 2, and box 36, folder 1; and WMCR, vol. 1.

27. Letter book, Dudley Woodbridge Jr. to Andrew Miller, 23 December 1811; to Thos. and Jno. Cromwell, 25 November 1811 (quotations), 23 December 1811, 9 March 1812, 8 April 1812, 27 November 1812, and 29 March 1813; to William Hays, 29 March 1813; to G. and C. Anshutz, 17 April 1813; and to James and Thomas St. Clair, 16 July 1813, WMCR, vol. 2. Ledger, BWC, box 45, folder 2.

28. Wade, *Urban Frontier*, 43–48; Catherine Elizabeth Reiser, *Pittsburgh's Commercial Development, 1800–1850* (Harrisburg, Pa.: Pennsylvania Historical and Museum Commission, 1951), 4–15; for contemporary accounts of Pittsburgh, see Cuming, "Sketches," in *EWT*, 4:76–87, 245–55; Fordham, *Personal Narrative*, 71–79; Joseph E. Walker, ed., *Pleasure and Business in Western Pennsylvania: The Journal of Joshua Gilpin, 1809* (Harrisburg, Pa.: Pennsylvania Historical and Museum Commission, 1975), 81–91; Melish, *Travels*, 315–17; Thomas, *Travels*, 51–62.

29. Isaac Lippincott, *A History of the Manufactures in the Ohio Valley to the Year 1860* (New York: Arno Press, 1973), 71–72; Wade, *Urban Frontier*, 43–48, 68–69.

30. Cuming, "Sketches," in *EWT*, 4; R. Douglas Hurt, *The Ohio Frontier: Crucible of the Old Northwest, 1720–1830* (Bloomington, Ind.: Indiana University Press, 1996), 230; Thomas, *Travels*, 63; letter book, Dudley Woodbridge Jr. to Thomas Baker, 1 July 1816, WMCR, vol. 3; ledger, William Robinson Jr. account, WMCR, vol. 90.

31. Louis C. Hunter, "Studies in the Economic History of the Ohio Valley: Seasonal Aspects of Industry and Commerce Before the Age of Big Business and the Beginnings of Industrial Combination," *Smith College Studies in History* 19 (October 1933–January 1934): 51–52; Lippincott, *History of the Manufactures*, 116–20. Letter book, Dudley Woodbridge Jr. to Mr. Stone, 15 July 1799, BWC, box 24, folder 2; letter book, Dudley Woodbridge Jr. to Nathan Kinne, 12 December 1803, WMCR, vol. 1; letter book, Dudley Woodbridge Jr. to S. Spenser, 1 September 1804, and to Nathan Kinne, May and 1 September 1804, BWC, box 36, folder 1; letter book, Dudley Woodbridge Jr. to William Steele, 22 April 1813; to Donally, Steele and Co., 12 July, 24 July, and 3 November 1813; to Richard Beale, 9 September 1819 and 21 January 1820, WMCR, vol. 4; and Donally and Steele, Kanawha Salt Works, Journal (1813–1815), Regional History Collection, West Virginia University, Morgantown, W. Va.; Utter, *Frontier State*, 260.

32. Cuming, "Sketches," in *EWT*, 4:164–65.

33. John Edmund Stealey III, "Virginia's Mercantile-Manufacturing Frontier: Dickinson and Shrewsbury and the Great Kanawha Salt Industry," *Virginia Magazine of History and Biography* 101 (October 1993): 509–34; Hunter, "Studies in the Economic History of the Ohio Valley," 51–52; Lippincott, *History of the Manufactures*, 116–20.

34. Letter book, Dudley Woodbridge Jr. to Trotter, Scott and Company, 28 January and 17 October 1812; to George Trotter Sr., 15 April and 2 June 1813; to J. and D. Maceoun, 24 June 1813, 15 July 1813, 17 July 1813, and 5 August 1813, WMCR, vol. 2.

35. Angelo I. George, "Saltpeter and Gunpowder Manufacturing in Kentucky," *Filson Club Historical Quarterly* 60 (April 1986): 189–208.

36. This and the two paragraphs that follow are informed by Gary A. O'Dell, "The Trotter Family, Gunpowder, and Early Kentucky Entrepreneurship, 1784–1833," *Register of the Kentucky Historical Society* 88 (Autumn 1990): 396–422.

37. George, "Saltpeter and Gunpowder Manufacturing," 189–208.

38. Ramage, *John Wesley Hunt,* 30–68; and Wade, *Urban Frontier,* 49–53.

39. Letter book, Dudley Woodbridge Jr. to S. Cantrell, 12 December 1811, and to Cantrell and Read, 1 April 1812, WMCR, vol. 2.

40. François André Michaux, "Travels," in *EWT,* 3:252–53.

41. Letter book, Dudley Woodbridge Jr. to James H. Overstreet, 13 May 1812, 15 April and 24 April 1813, and 15 January 1814; to Ebenezer Buckingham, 22 May 1812; to A. Bayless, 6 May 1813; and to C. Bullet, 7 June 1813, WMCR, vol. 2. Richard T. Farrell, "Cincinnati, 1800–1830: Economic Development through Trade and Industry," *Ohio History* 77 (Autumn 1968): 111–29; Melish, *Travels,* 377–80.

42. Letter book, Dudley Woodbridge Jr. to Cantrell and Read, 5 June 1812, 12 October 1812, and 21 December 1812; and to James H. Overstreet, 13 May 1812, 15 January and 5 August 1814, WMCR, vol. 2; letter book, Dudley Woodbridge Jr. to S. and G. Trotter, 15 November 1816, WMCR, vol. 3; Dudley Woodbridge Jr. to Paxson, Pearson, and Hatch, 25 October 1818 and 17 January 1819, WWP.

43. Lippincott, *History of the Manufactures,* 124; Walker, ed., *Pleasure and Business,* 87–88; Marietta Jennings, *A Pioneer Merchant of St. Louis, 1810–1820: The Business Career of Christian Wilt* (New York: Columbia University Press, 1939), 84, 89–90, 128. Letter book, Dudley Woodbridge Jr. to S. and G. Trotter, 20 July 1816, WMCR, vol. 3.

44. Ray, "Zane's Trace," 51–54, 76–77, 108, 165–73.

45. Harry N. Scheiber, "Ebenezer Buckingham," *Museum Echoes* 33 (December 1960): 91–94; Lucy Woodbridge to William Woodbridge, 29 May 1802, WWP.

46. Bond, *Civilization of the Old Northwest,* 292; Utter, *Frontier State,* 127.

47. Knepper, *Ohio,* 101; Cuming, "Sketches," in *EWT,* 4:224–25; Melish, *Travels,* 430–32.

48. *Muskingum Messenger,* 30 June 1810; 28 February, 23 May, 4 July, 11 July, and 26 September 1816; and 29 May 1817. Scheiber, "Ebenezer Buckingham"; Hulme, "Journal," 73; *Zanesville Express and Republican Standard,* 31 April 1813.

49. Receipt books, BWC, box 47, folder 2, and box 49, folder 3. Warehouse books, WMCR, vols. 123 and 124, and BWC, box 51, folder 1, and box 55, folder 3. Letter book, Dudley Woodbridge Jr. to Moses Dillon, 9 November and 12 December 1811; see letters to other Zanesville merchants as well, WMCR, vol. 2.

50. Letter book, Dudley Woodbridge Jr. to Woodbridge and Pierce and to Jeffry Price, 12 April 1813, WMCR, vol. 2.

51. Ledger, BWC, box 45, folder 2. The 323 accounts exclude family members, Philadelphia suppliers, business contacts in Pittsburgh, Lexington, Louisville, Cincinnati, and western Virginia, Zanesville customers, and other accounts that are obviously of a business nature.

52. James Weir Ledger, 1813–1815, Greenville, Ky., FHS.

53. Edelin Benedict Account Book, 1816–1819, FHS.

54. John Mills and Co. Account Book, vol. 59, Ohio Historical Society.

55. Waterman Palmer's letters to John Mills can be found in DML/MC.

6. The Western Country

1. L. Loomis to R. J. Meigs, 31 March 1813; J. L. Robinson to Joseph Ficklin, 31 March 1813; Kearney Wharton to Samuel Roberts, 2 April 1813; Benjamin B. Howell to John W. Hunt, 9 April 1813; and Benjamin B. Howell to Abraham S. Barton, 9 April 1913; all of the above in the Isaac H. Jackson Papers, Cincinnati Historical Society, Cincinnati.

2. Letter book, Dudley Woodbridge Jr. to Thomas Boal and Co., Samuel January, and Scudder and A. Hart, 14 June 1812, WMCR, vol. 2.

3. Letter book, Dudley Woodbridge Jr. to Daniel Conner, 15 November and 13 December 1802, and 22 February 1803, WMCR, vol. 1; letter book, Dudley Woodbridge Jr. to Daniel Conner, 21 February 1804, and Joseph Pierce, 17 March 1804, BWC, box 36, folder 1.

4. Letter book, Dudley Woodbridge Jr. to Ebenezer Buckingham, 26 October 1812, WMCR, vol. 2.

5. Leonard Dobbin to Holderman Pearson and Co., 6 February 1821, in John W. Hunt Papers/Holderman Pearson and Co., FHS; Gary A. O'Dell, "The Trotter Family, Gunpowder, and Early Kentucky Entrepreneurship, 1784–1833," *Register of the Kentucky Historical Society* 88 (Autumn 1990): 396–427; and Daniel Preston, "Thomas Kelsey, Hardluck Entrepreneur," *Ohio History* 104 (Summer–Autumn, 1995): 130–41. For business partnerships, see Lewis E. Atherton, *The Frontier Merchant in Mid-America* (Columbia, Mo.: University of Missouri Press, 1971), 115–23.

6. See the Marietta newspaper *American Friend,* 23 March 1821, for a predator hunt and various dates in the 1810s, 1820s, and 1830s for marriage news and election results. For the agricultural society, see *American Friend,* 6 August 1819. Charles M. Putnam to his brothers, 30 October 1820, Putnam Family Papers, Ohio Historical Society, Columbus, box 1, folder 2.

7. Isaac L. Baker to Isaac R. Gwathmey, 1 December 1813, Gwathmey Family Papers, FHS; Luther Dana Barker to John Mills, 13 October 1820, Luther Dana Barker Miscellaneous Papers, FHS. Felix Rennick to unknown, 24 February 1823 and to Daniel McNeill, 15 March 1823, McNeill Family Papers, Regional History Collection, West Virginia University, Morgantown, W. Va.

8. George Rennick to unknown, 22 February 1820, McNeill Family Papers. For accounts of disagreements between northern-born and southern-born residents

of the West, see Andrew R. L. Cayton, "Land, Power, and Reputation: The Cultural Dimensions of Politics in the Ohio Country," *William and Mary Quarterly,* 3d ser., 47 (April 1990): 266–86; Cayton, "'Separate Interests' and the Nation-State: The Washington Administration and the Origins of Regionalism in the Trans-Appalachian West," *Journal of American History* 79 (June 1992): 39–67; and William T. Utter, *The Frontier State, 1803–1825* (Columbus: Ohio State Archaeological and Historical Society, 1942), 397. For an examination of terms and phrases northerners and southerners used to characterize each other on occassion, see Nicole Etcheson, *The Emerging Midwest: Upland Southerners and the Political Culture of the Old Northwest, 1787–1861* (Bloomington, Ind.: Indiana University Press, 1996), 1–14.

9. William Coolidge Jr. Diary and Account Book, 1818–1829, typescript, Department of the Library, Special Collections, Manuscripts, Western Kentucky University, Bowling Green, Ky., and John Sharkey Travel Diary, 1829, FHS. For other examples in the accounts of visitors, see Francis Baily, *Journal of a Tour in Unsettled Parts of North America in 1796 and 1797,* ed. Jack D. L. Holmes (Carbondale and Edwardsville, Ill.: Southern Illinois University Press, 1969), 86; Fortescue Cuming, "Sketches of a Tour of the Western Country," in *EWT,* 4:103, 116, 142, 196, 259; François André Michaux, "Travels to the West of the Allegheny Mountains," in *EWT,* 3:157, 161, 162, 171, 177; Thomas Green Diary, 1825–1827, Regional History Collection, West Virginia University, Morgantown, W. Va., 276; Elias Pym Fordham, *Personal Narrative of Travels in Virginia, Maryland, Pennsylvania, Ohio, Indiana, Kentucky; and of a Residence in the Illinois Territory: 1817–1818,* ed. Frederic Austin Ogg (Cleveland: A. H. Clark Co., 1906), 230; David Thomas, *Travels through the Western Country in the Summer of 1816* (Auburn, N.Y.: David Rumsey, 1819), 110; and Diary 1815–1816, Daniel Banks Papers, FHS.

For references to "the western country" in the correspondence of residents, see the following: American Antiquarian Society, Worcester, Mass.: Ward Family Papers, 1661–1919, Shrewsbury, Mass., Nahum Ward's Correspondence; Ohio Historical Society: Backus-Woodbridge Collection, Putnam Family Collection; Filson Historical Society: Gwathmey Family Papers, John Irwin Papers, Green Family Papers, Buckner Family Papers; Western Kentucky University: Drake Family Papers, John Loving Papers; Western Reserve Historical Society: Caleb Emerson Family Papers. See also Alfred Tischendorf and E. Taylor Parks, eds., *The Diary and Journal of Richard Clough Anderson, Jr., 1814–1826* (Durham, N.C.: Duke University Press, 1964), 55.

10. Gabriel Lewis to Peter Lewis, 25 May 1806, Lewis-Starling Collection, Department of the Library, Special Collections, Western Kentucky University, box 1, folder 5; John Loving to Samuel Loving, 19 August 1812, John Loving Papers; Isaac L. Baker to Isaac R. Gwathmey, 30 January 1814, Gwathmey Family Papers.

11. Caleb Thorniley to Brother, 24 July 1807, typescript, Ohio Historical Society, Columbus.

12. James R. Bentley, "A Letter from Harrodsburg, 1780," *Filson Club Historical Quarterly* 50 (October 1976): 370; Tischendorf and Parks, eds., *The Diary and*

Journal of Richard Clough Anderson, Jr., 64; François André Michaux, "Travels," in *EWT,* 3: 215; James Drake to Albrittain Drake, 2 September 1833, and James Drake to William Drake, 14 July 1840 (quotations), Drake Family Papers.

13. Cuming, "Sketches," in *EWT,* 4:229–30.

14. Gabriel Lewis to Peter, 25 May 1806, Lewis-Starling Collection; and Craig T. Friend, "Merchants and Markethouses: Reflections on Moral Economy in Early Kentucky," *Journal of the Early Republic* 17 (Winter 1997): 553–74.

15. John Melish, *Travels through the United States of America, in the Years 1806 and 1807, and 1809, 1810, and 1811* (New York: Johnson Reprint Corp., 1970), 421, 428; and Fordham, *Personal Narrative,* 164.

16. This and the paragraph that follows are informed by Charles Clifford Huntington, *A History of Banking and Currency in Ohio Before the Civil War* (Columbus: F. J. Heer Printing Co., 1915), 5–37. See also Utter, *Frontier State,* 265.

17. Thomas Senior Berry, *Western Prices before 1861: A Study of the Cincinnati Market* (Cambridge: Harvard University Press, 1943), 370; letter book, Dudley Woodbridge Jr. to S. P. Nevins and Co., 27 October 1813; to Ebenezer Buckingham, 12 January and 3 April 1813; to John Woodbridge, 27 April 1814; to T. L. Pierce, 15 and 17 July 1813; and to J. and. D. Maceoun, 15 and 17 July 1813, WMCR, vol. 2.

18. George W. Knepper, *Ohio and Its People* (Kent, Ohio: Kent State University Press, 1989), 138; Utter, *Frontier State,* 270–71; Richard C. Wade, *The Urban Frontier: Pioneer Life in Early Pittsburgh, Cincinnati, Lexington, Louisville, and St. Louis,* (Chicago: University of Chicago Press, 1964), 66–68; ledger, BWC, box 45, folder 2; letter book, Dudley Woodbridge Jr. to John Woodbridge, 1 November 1812, WMCR, vol. 2; and James Weir Ledger, 1813–1815, Greenville, Ky., FHS. Pittsburgh newspaper quoted in Berry, *Western Prices,* 375.

19. Knepper, *Ohio,* 138; Utter, *Frontier State,* 270–71; Wade, *Urban Frontier,* 66–68; letter book, Dudley Woodbridge Jr. to Joseph Clark and John Woodbridge, 1 November 1812, WMCR, vol. 2.

20. Berry, *Western Prices,* 371–72; R. Carlyle Buley, *The Old Northwest: Pioneer Period, 1815–1840* (Bloomington, Ind.: Indiana University Press, 1950), 1:579–80; Huntington, *History of Banking,* 5, 29–32, 35–37, 43, 51–55; Utter, *Frontier State,* 274–76.

21. Buley, *Old Northwest,* 1:579–80, 587; and Huntington, *History of Banking,* 52–53.

22. Letter book, Dudley Woodbridge Jr. to Richard Bowen and Co., 5 July 1816; to C. and T. Bullett, 30 July 1816; to S. and G. Trotter, 29 August and 11 September 1816; to James H. Overstreet, 17 October 1816; and to Gilman and Ammidon, 4 November 1816, WMCR, vol. 3.

23. Ledger, 1816–1822; and letter book, Robinson to Andrew Hynes, 26 July 1816, Jonathan John Robinson Papers, 1815–1860, Historical Society of Pennsylvania, Philadelphia.

24. Letter book, J. J. Robinson to David Hadden, 4 October 1816; to Wormald, Gott, and Wormald, 18 November 1816; and to N. and F. Phillips and Co., 18 November 1816, Jonathan John Robinson Papers.

25. Letter book, bankbook, journal, personal account book, Jonathan John Robinson Papers.

26. Andrew R. L. Cayton, *The Frontier Republic: Ideology and Politics in the Ohio Country, 1780–1825* (Kent, Ohio: Kent State University Press, 1986), 125–27.

27. Buley, *Old Northwest,* 1:577–78; Huntington, *History of Banking,* 55–56; and Utter, *Frontier State,* 277, 283–88.

28. Buley, *Old Northwest,* 1:581–83; Huntington, *History of Banking,* 60–61; Utter, *Frontier State,* 283–88.

29. Buley, *Old Northwest,* 1:583–84; Huntington, *History of Banking,* 69–72; Utter, *Frontier State,* 278–79, 283–88.

30. Daniel R. Southard to David Starr, 1 July 1819, Daniel R. Southard Papers, FHS; Utter, *Frontier State,* 284–85.

31. Dudley Woodbridge Jr. to William Woodbridge, 26 July and 4 November 1819, and 19 March 1820, WWP.

32. Letter book, Dudley Woodbridge Jr. to Luther Edgerton, 7 July 1819, WMCR, vol. 4.

33. Donald R. Adams Jr., "The Role of Banks in the Economic Development of the Old Northwest," in *Essays in Nineteenth Century Economic History: The Old Northwest,* ed. David C. Klingaman and Richard K. Vedder (Athens, Ohio: Ohio University Press, 1975), 208–45; Buley, *Old Northwest,* 1:565–632, see pp. 577–85 for bank protests; Knepper, *Ohio,* 137–43; Utter, *Frontier State,* 281–83. For more on conflict with easterners as a source of western identity, see Harry N. Scheiber, "Preface: On the Concepts of 'Regionalism' and 'Frontier,'" in *The Old Northwest: Studies in Regional History, 1787–1910,* ed. Scheiber (Lincoln, Nebr.: University of Nebraska Press, 1969), xii.

34. Quoted in Buley, *Old Northwest,* 1:132.

35. Cayton, *Frontier Republic,* 126–27; Wade, *Urban Frontier,* 166–77.

36. Warehouse book, BWC, box 55, folder 3; letter book, Dudley Woodbridge Jr. to Nicholas McCarty, 17 March 1822, box 55, folder 1; both in the BWC. One traveler wrote of meeting a man who suffered from "rheumatic disease," a condition the resident attributed to swimming through high creeks on horseback during his two years in the West; see Orin J. Oliphant, ed., *Through the South and the West with Jeremiah Evarts in 1826* (Lewisburg, Pa.: Bucknell University Press, 1956), 138.

37. Nahum Ward to Thomas W. Ward Jr., 29 October 1827, 14 June 1828, 13 January 1829, and 2 March 1843, Ward Family Papers, box 3, folder 3; Nahum Ward to Thomas W. Ward, 14 May and 18 June 1832, Ward Family Papers, box 3, folder 2.

38. Stephen Aron, *How the West Was Lost: The Transformation of Kentucky from Daniel Boone to Henry Clay* (Baltimore: Johns Hopkins University Press, 1996); Knepper, *Ohio,* 119.

39. Buley, *Old Northwest,* 1:124, 130; Utter, *Frontier State,* 292.

40. Louis C. Hunter, *Steamboats on the Western Rivers: An Economic and Technological History* (Cambridge: Harvard University Press, 1949), 3–14 (quotations on

pp. 4 and 11). See also Tischendorf and Parks, eds., *The Diary and Journal of Richard Clough Anderson, Jr.*, 89.

41. Hunter, *Steamboats on the Western Rivers*, 3–22.

42. Ibid., 22–27; Wade, *Urban Frontier*, 191.

43. Berry, *Western Prices*, 29–34.

44. Ibid., 23–25; Erik F. Haites, James Mak, and Gary M. Walton, *Western River Transportation: The Era of Early Internal Development, 1810–1860* (Baltimore: Johns Hopkins University Press, 1975), 14–25; and Hunter, *Steamboats on the Western Rivers*, 52–60.

45. John Irwin to his brother, 24 September 1836, and to his father, 20 November 1836, John Irwin Papers.

46. Melish, *Travels*, 372; and Donald T. Zimmer, "The Ohio River: Pathway to Settlement," in *Transportation and the Early Nation: Papers Presented at an Indiana American Revolution Bicentennial Symposium* (Indianapolis: Indiana Historical Society, 1982), 65–72.

47. Mrs. Steele, *A Summer Journey in the West* (New York: J. S. Taylor and Co., 1841), 231–32; Thomas, *Travels*, 116–17; and Zimmer, "The Ohio River," 75–78.

48. Berry, *Western Prices*, 39–40; Hunter, *Steamboats on the Western Rivers*, 35–37, 182–86; Martha Kreipke, "The Falls of the Ohio and the Development of the Ohio River Trade, 1810–1860," *Filson Club Historical Quarterly* 54 (April 1980): 196–217; and Wade, *Urban Frontier*, 172, 188, 190, 197–99, 341.

49. Wade, *Urban Frontier*, 170, 182–83, 197–98, 243–47.

Part III. The Buckeye State

1. Andrew R. L. Cayton, *The Frontier Republic: Ideology and Politics in the Ohio Country, 1780–1825* (Kent, Ohio: Kent State University Press, 1986), 151–54.

7. Ohio's Economy Transformed

1. Daybook, Dudley Woodbridge Jr. to C. Schultz, 6 July 1822, BWC, box 55, folder 1; J. D. B. DeBow, *Statistical View of the United States* (Washington, D.C.: A. O. P. Nicholson, 1854), 192.

2. DeBow, *Statistical View*, 192.

3. George Rogers Taylor, *The Transportation Revolution, 1815–1860* (New York: Rinehart, 1951), 32–36. The best recent work on the impact of the Erie Canal on American culture is Carol Sheriff, *The Artificial River: The Erie Canal and the Paradox of Progress, 1817–1862* (New York: Hill and Wang, 1996).

4. Diane Lindstrom, *Economic Development in the Philadelphia Region, 1810–1850* (New York: Columbia University Press, 1978), 85–88.

5. Carville Earle, "Regional Economic Development West of the Appalachians, 1815–1860," in *North America: The Historical Geography of a Changing Continent*, ed. Robert D. Mitchell and Paul A. Groves (Totowa, N.J.: Rowman and Littlefield, 1987), 175; George W. Knepper, *Ohio and Its People* (Kent, Ohio: Kent State Univer-

sity Press, 1989), 157; Peter S. Onuf, *Statehood and Union: A History of the Northwest Ordinance* (Bloomington, Ind.: Indiana University Press, 1987), 146–50; and Harry N. Scheiber, *Ohio Canal Era: A Case Study of Government and the Economy, 1820–1861* (Athens, Ohio: Ohio University Press, 1987), 3–181.

6. This and the paragraph that follows are informed by Scheiber, *Ohio Canal Era*, 88–177.

7. Ibid., 187–245; and Brian P. Birch, "Taking the Breaks and Working the Boats: An English Family's Impressions of Ohio in the 1830s," *Ohio History* 95 (Summer–Autumn 1986): 113–14.

8. DeBow, *Statistical View*, 40, 192; and Knepper, *Ohio*, 225–27.

9. Thomas Senior Berry, *Western Prices before 1861: A Study of the Cincinnati Market* (Cambridge: Harvard University Press, 1943), 38–39; Erik F. Haites, James Mak, and Gary M. Walton, *Western River Transportation: The Era of Early Internal Development, 1810–1860* (Baltimore: Johns Hopkins University Press, 1975), 4–11; Scheiber, *Ohio Canal Era*, 195–98. The best overview of staple grain production remains John G. Clark, *The Grain Trade in the Old Northwest* (Urbana, Ill.: University of Illinois Press, 1966).

10. William Emerson to Caleb Emerson, 8 April (quotation) and 20 August 1837, Caleb Emerson Family Papers, Western Reserve Historical Society, Cleveland, box 1, folder 4.

11. William Emerson to Caleb Emerson, 18 April 1847, Caleb Emerson Family Papers, box 1, folder 5.

12. Richard C. Wade, *The Urban Frontier: Pioneer Life in Early Pittsburgh, Cincinnati, Lexington, Louisville, and St. Louis,* (Chicago: University of Chicago Press, 1964), 187–97; Knepper, *Ohio*, 226; Scheiber, *Ohio Canal Era*, 187–211; Haites et al., *Western River Transportation*, 1–47, 59–73; and Steven J. Ross, *Workers on the Edge: Work, Leisure, and Politics in Industrializing Cincinnati, 1788–1890* (New York: Columbia University Press, 1985), 3–24.

Interestingly, the ratio of 50 percent eastern dry goods matches the ratio dry goods represented of Dudley Woodbridge Jr.'s imports during the first decade of the nineteenth century.

13. Daniel Aaron, *Cincinnati: Queen City of the West, 1819–1838* (Columbus: Ohio State University Press, 1992), 31–37; Walter S. Glazer, "Cincinnati in 1840: A Community Profile" (Ph.D. diss., University of Michigan, 1968), 242; Scheiber, *Ohio Canal Era*, 187–227; and Ross, *Workers on the Edge*, 33–34.

14. Birch, "Taking the Breaks," 101–18 (quotation on p. 106); and Robert P. Swierenga, "The Settlement of the Old Northwest: Ethnic Pluralism in a Featureless Plain," *Journal of the Early Republic* 9 (Spring 1989): 73–105.

15. Aaron, "Cincinnati," 48–54; Jed Dannenbaum, *Drink and Disorder: Temperance Reform in Cincinnati from the Washingtonian Revival to the WCTU* (Urbana, Ill.: University of Illinois Press, 1984); and Ross, *Workers on the Edge*, 74.

16. Irwin F. Flack, "Who Governed Cincinnati? A Comparative Analysis of Government and Social Structure in a Nineteenth Century River City, 1819–1860" (Ph.D. diss., University of Pittsburgh, 1978); and Wade, *Urban Frontier*, 210–20, 243–47.

17. Edward K. Muller, "Selective Urban Growth in the Middle Ohio Valley, 1800–1860," *Geographical Review* 66 (April 1976): 185–92; Scheiber, *Ohio Canal Era,* 189.

18. Muller, "Selective Urban Growth," 185–92. See also Daniel Preston, "Market and Mill Town: Hamilton Ohio, 1795–1860" (Ph.D. diss., University of Maryland, 1987), 164–270, 298–311.

19. James Mak, "Intraregional Trade in the Antebellum West: Ohio, A Case Study," *Agricultural History* 46 (October 1972): 489–97; and Scheiber, *Ohio Canal Era,* 125, 137, 215–16.

20. Louis C. Hunter, *Steamboats on the Western Rivers: An Economic and Technological History* (Cambridge: Harvard University Press, 1949), 42–43; and Scheiber, *Ohio Canal Era,* 110, 122–27, 134, 151, 165–76, 197, 213–18, 230.

Historian Harry S. Scheiber writes,

> A so-called *river improvement* involved construction of locks in the bed of the river itself. This type of construction provided "slackwater" navigation for boats; that is, the flow of water would be controlled by the locks and ancillary dams, so that extreme changes in the pressure of currents might be avoided. Wherever necessary, the natural river banks would be shored up to prevent slides. Moreover, where tributary streams emptied into the main river, dams would be constructed to regulate water flow. The river improvement was designed to be navigable for flatboats, rafts, and steamboats, having no towpath on which animals could be driven to tow canal boats.

See Scheiber, *Ohio Canal Era,* 122.

21. H. Z. Williams, *History of Washington County, Ohio* (Cleveland: H. Z. Williams and Bro., 1881), 370–71, 462–64.

22. Ibid., 484–85; Martin R. Andrews, *History of Marietta and Washington County, Ohio and Representative Citizens* (Chicago: Biographical Publishing Co., 1902), 945; and the Marietta and Harmar City Directory, 1860, Ohio Historical Society.

23. Letter book, Dudley Woodbridge Jr. to Woodbridge and Pierce, 14 May 1814, WMCR, vol. 2.

24. The following discussion of merchants is informed by Glenn Porter and Harold C. Livesay, *Merchants and Manufacturers: Studies in the Changing Structure of Nineteenth-Century Marketing* (Chicago: Elephant Paperbacks, 1989). See also James E. Vance Jr., *The Merchant's World: The Geography of Wholesaling* (Englewood Cliffs, N.J.: Prentice-Hall, 1970).

25. Letter book, Dudley Woodbridge Jr. to Jack, 7 September 1820, WMCR, vol. 5; daybook, Dudley Woodbridge Jr. to John Woodbridge, 18 December 1824, BWC, box 55, folder 1.

26. Credit report of Dudley Woodbridge, Ohio, vol. 193, p. 122, R. G. Dun and Company Collection, Baker Library, Harvard Business School, Boston, Mass.; and Dudley Woodbridge Jr. to William Woodbridge, 5 July 1841, WWP.

27. Dudley Woodbridge Jr. to William Woodbridge, 5 July 1841 and 22 January 1844, WWP.

28. Credit report of George M. Woodbridge, Ohio, vol. 193, p. 87, R. G. Dun and Company Collection; autobiographical notes and other material can be found in the WMCR, vol. 10a.

29. Credit report of W. M. Woodbridge, p. 45, and credit report of Miss L. D. Woodbridge, p. 253, both in Ohio, vol. 193, R. G. Dun and Company Collection. Dudley Woodbridge Jr. to William Woodbridge, 20 December 1848, WWP.

30. Williams, *History of Washington County,* 366, 480; Mills-Woodbridge Agreement, 26 August 1816 and Mills-Woodbridge Agreement, 1 August 1818, both typescript, DML/MC.

31. Andrew R. L. Cayton and Paula R. Riggs, *City into Town: The City of Marietta, Ohio, 1788–1988* (Marietta, Ohio: Marietta College, 1991), 110; and Williams, *History of Washington County,* 340–42, 370–77, 397–402, 445–50, 480–84. Palmer's letters to Mills can be found in DML/MC.

32. Cayton and Riggs, *City into Town,* 123–25; Scheiber, *Ohio Canal Era,* 127–28, 134–35; and Thomas J. Summers, *History of Marietta* (Marietta, Ohio: Leader Publishing Co., 1903), 247–54.

33. Cayton and Riggs, *City into Town,* 129; Robert Leslie Jones, *History of Agriculture in Ohio to 1880* (Kent, Ohio: Kent State University Press, 1983), 3–4, 143–54, 219–20, 244–47, 251–55, 275.

34. Williams, *History of Washington County,* 477; Nahum Ward to Thomas W. Ward, 18 June 1832, Ward Family Papers, 1661–1919, Shrewsbury, Mass., American Antiquarian Society, Worcester, Mass., box 3, folder 2.

35. Bernard Peters, "The German Pioneers," *Ohio Archaeological and Historical Society Publications* 2 (1900): 55–63.

36. United States census, 1830 and 1840; Nahum Ward to Temple Cutler, 24 June 1836, DML/CC; Nahum Ward to Sarah Putnam, 3 July 1842, Ward Family Papers, box 3, folder 3.

8. A New Sense of Place

1. Nahum Ward to Thomas and Elizabeth Ward, 21 May 1812, 7 June 1814, 10 June, 4 March, and 24 November 1832, box 3, folder 2; Nahum Ward to Thomas W. Ward, 3 October 1840, 2 March 1843, 21 June and 9 December 1846, box 3, folder 3; Nahum Ward to Sarah Putnam, 25 June 1849, box 3, folder 3, all in the Ward Family Papers, 1661–1919, Shrewsbury, Mass., American Antiquarian Society, Worcester, Mass.

2. Nicole Etcheson, *The Emerging Midwest: Upland Southerners and the Political Culture of the Old Northwest, 1787–1861* (Bloomington, Ind.: Indiana University Press, 1996), 52–62.

3. This and the two paragraphs that follow are informed by Richard Lyle Power, *Planting Corn Belt Culture: The Impress of the Upland Southerner and Yankee in the Old Northwest* (Indianapolis: Indiana Historical Society, 1953), 5–20, 26–31, 37, 51–56, 92–102 (quotation on p. 7). For an excellent recent study of Yankees in the Old Northwest, see Susan E. Gray, *The Yankee West: Community Life on the Michigan Frontier* (Chapel Hill, N.C.: University of North Carolina Press, 1996).

4. R. Carlyle Buley, *The Old Northwest: Pioneer Period, 1815–1840* (Bloomington, Ind.: Indiana University Press, 1950), 2:17–18; Carville Earle, "Regional Economic Development West of the Appalachians, 1815–1860," in *North America: The Historical Geography of a Changing Continent,* ed. Robert D. Mitchell and Paul A. Groves (Totowa, N.J.: Rowman and Littlefield, 1987), 184–97; and Peter S. Onuf, *Statehood and Union: A History of the Northwest Ordinance* (Bloomington, Ind.: Indiana University Press, 1987), 109–32, 147.

5. Elias Pym Fordham, *Personal Narrative of Travels in Virginia, Maryland, Pennsylvania, Ohio, Indiana, Kentucky; and of a Residence in the Illinois Territory: 1817–1818,* ed. Frederic Austin Ogg (Cleveland: A. H. Clark Co., 1906), 209–229 (quotation on p. 210); Thomas Hulme, "A Journal Made During a Tour in the Western Countries of America: September 30, 1818–August 7, 1819," in *EWT,* 10:64–65; John Melish, *Travels through the United States of America, in the Years 1806 and 1807, and 1809, 1810, and 1811* (New York: Johnson Reprint Corp., 1970), 415; Power, *Planting Corn Belt Culture,* 120.

6. George V. Knepper, *Ohio and Its People* (Kent, Ohio: Kent State University Press, 1989), 207; Stephen Middleton, *The Black Laws in the Old Northwest: A Documentary History* (Westport, Conn.: Greenwood Press, 1993), 13–18, 47–48, 159–61, 271–74, 345–47, 381–83; Joe William Trotter Jr., *River Jordan: African American Urban Life in the Ohio Valley* (Lexington, Ky.: University Press of Kentucky, 1998), 24–25.

7. Stephen A. Vincent provides an excellent account of the migration of free people of color from North Carolina to Indiana in *Southern Seed, Northern Soil: African-American Farm Communities in the Midwest, 1765–1900* (Bloomington, Ind.: Indiana University Press, 1999), 26–45. See also Trotter, *River Jordan,* 26–27; Henry Bradshaw Fearon, *Sketches of America: A Narrative of a Journey through the Eastern and Western States of America,* 3d ed. (London: Longman, Hurst, Rees, Orme, and Brown, 1819), 224; Richard C. Wade, *The Urban Frontier: Pioneer Life in Early Pittsburgh, Cincinnati, Lexington, Louisville, and St. Louis,* (Chicago: University of Chicago Press, 1964), 124–28, 220–25; and John Woods, "Two Year's Residence in the Settlement on the English Prairie, in the Illinois Country, United States (June 5, 1820–July 3, 1821)," in *EWT,* 10:213.

8. Daniel Aaron, *Cincinnati: Queen City of the West, 1819–1838* (Columbus: Ohio State University Press, 1992), 294–314; Leonard L. Richards, *Gentlemen of Property and Standing: Anti-Abolition Mobs in Jacksonian America* (New York: Oxford University Press, 1970); Wade, *Urban Frontier,* 225–29.

9. James L. Dennis, *Washington's Darker Brother: One Hundred Years of Black History in Washington County, Ohio, 1788–1888* (Parkersburg, W.Va.: privately printed, 1986), 8–9, 12, 14; H. Z. Williams, *History of Washington County, Ohio* (Cleveland: H. Z. Williams and Bro., 1881), 100–101, 583–84, 613–14; ledger, WMCR, vol. 91. Recent studies of free blacks in the Old Northwest include Joan E. Cashin, "Black Families in the Old Northwest," *Journal of the Early Republic* 15 (Fall 1995): 449–75; Trotter, *River Jordan;* Vincent, *Southern Seed, Northern Soil;* and

Juliet K. Walker, *Free Frank: A Black Pioneer on the Antebellum Frontier* (Lexington, Ky.: University Press of Kentucky, 1983).

10. Letter book, Dudley Woodbridge Jr. to Reverend Joseph M. Trimble, 5 June 1834, and to William Woodbridge, 13 December 1844, WWP. The letter referring to Nanny implies rather than specifically indicates that she was black.

11. David Putnam to Charles Putnam, 26 March 1844, Putnam Family Papers, box 1, folder 2, Ohio Historical Society, Columbus; Dennis, *Washington's Darker Brother*, 14, 25, 30. For an account of the relations between black pioneers and their white Quaker neighbors in Indiana, see Vincent, *Southern Seed, Northern Soil*, 46–79.

12. Bruce Levine has provided the best synthesis of scholarship on this topic in *Half Slave and Half Free: The Roots of the Civil War* (New York: Hill and Wang, 1992).

13. Stephen Aron, *How the West Was Lost: The Transformation of Kentucky from Daniel Boone to Henry Clay* (Baltimore: Johns Hopkins University Press, 1996), 124–69.

14. James R. Shortridge, *The Middle West: Its Meaning in American Culture* (Lawrence, Kans.: University Press of Kansas, 1989), 104–107; William N. Parker, "From Northwest to Midwest: Social Bases of a Regional History," in *Essays in Nineteenth Century Economic History: The Old Northwest*, ed. David C. Klingaman and Richard K. Vedder (Athens, Ohio: Ohio University Press, 1975), 23–24; Etcheson, *Emerging Midwest*, 108–39; and Onuf, *Statehood and Union*, 151. For early North-South animosity in the West, see Andrew R. L. Cayton, "'Separate Interests' and the Nation-State: The Washington Administration and the Origins of Regionalism in the Trans-Appalachian West," *Journal of American History* 79 (June 1992): 39–67.

Contemporary views of what constitutes the Midwest can be found in the table of contents of *Heartland: Comparative Histories of the Midwestern States* (Bloomington, Ind.: Indiana University Press, 1988), ed. James H. Madison. The book contains chapters on Ohio, Indiana, Illinois, Michigan, Wisconsin, Minnesota, North Dakota, South Dakota, Missouri, Iowa, Kansas, and Nebraska.

For the politics of abolition in Ohio, see Stephen E. Maizlish, *The Triumph of Sectionalism: The Transformation of Ohio Politics, 1844–56* (Kent, Ohio: Kent State University Press, 1983).

15. James Hall, *Statistics of the West at the Close of the Year 1836* (Cincinnati: J. A. James, 1837); Edward D. Mansfield, *On the Railroad Connections of Philadelphia with the Central West* (Philadelphia: J. C. Clark, Printer, 1853); and John Kilbourn, *The Ohio Gazetteer, or, Topographical Dictionary*, 11th ed. (Columbus: Scott and Wright, 1833).

16. See John A. Jackle, *Images of the Ohio Valley: A Historical Geography of Travel, 1740–1860* (New York: Oxford University Press, 1977), 118–21, 160. For an analysis of the backgrounds and biases of early travelers, see William Henry Hildreth, "Travel Literature of the Ohio River Valley (1794–1832)" (Ph.D. diss., Ohio State University, 1944); for comments on remarking favorably on Marietta while ignoring Lexington, see pp. 153–54.

17. Mary Emerson to Caleb Emerson, 13 August and 8 September 1840, box 1, folder 5; and William Emerson to Charles Emerson, 10 September 1838, box 1, folder 4; both in the Caleb Emerson Family Papers, Western Reserve Historical Society, Cleveland; Brian P. Birch, "Taking the Breaks and Working the Boats: An English Family's Impressions of Ohio in the 1830s," *Ohio History* 95 (Summer–Autumn, 1986): 110.

18. Harriet Woodbridge to Amelia Oaks, 4 January 1843; John Woodbridge to Charles Oaks, 18 October 1842, and to Adeliue Barnes, 21 December 1842, Oaks-Woodbridge-Day Family Papers, 1839–1851, Connecticut Historical Society, Hartford, Conn.

19. Aaron, *Cincinnati,* 268–70; Buley, *Old Northwest,* 1:360–61; Walter S. Glazer, "Cincinnati in 1840: A Community Profile" (Ph.D. diss., University of Michigan, 1968), 97–101; Mrs. Steele, *A Summer Journey in the West* (New York: J. S. Taylor and Co., 1841), 249–50.

20. Buley, *Old Northwest,* 1:360–61; Andrew R. L. Cayton, *Frontier Indiana* (Bloomington, Ind.: Indiana University Press, 1996), 288; Power, *Planting Corn Belt Culture,* 26–27, 74–86; Steele, *Summer Journey,* 249–50.

21. Stephen Gutgesell, ed., *Guide to Ohio Newspapers, 1793–1973* (Columbus: Ohio Historical Society, 1974). Towns with one or more "Western" newspapers: Athens, Batavia, Bellefontaine, Bucyrus, Cincinnati, Cleveland, Columbus, Dayton, Eaton, Garretsville, Georgetown, Germantown, Hamilton, Hudson, Lancaster, Lima, Lebanon, Lisbon, Mansfield, Marietta, Marion, Mt. Vernon, Piqua, Portsmouth, Putnam, Ravenna, Sidney, Somerset, Steubenville, Tiffin, Urbana, Warren, Williamsburg, Wilmington, Xenia, and Zanesville. Towns with "Buckeye" newspapers: Columbus, Elyria, Gallipolis, Lisbon, Marietta, Marion, and Ravenna.

22. William Emerson to Caleb Emerson, 20 August 1837, Caleb Emerson Family Papers, box 1, folder 4.

23. David Putnam to Charles Putnam, 26 March 1844, Putnam Family Papers, box 1, folder 2; and Dennis, *Washington's Darker Brother,* 14, 25, 30.

24. Williams, *History of Washington County,* 414–15.

25. See, for example, *Marietta Intelligencer,* 20 March 1840, 15 February 1844, 17 March 1844, 21 March 1844, 11 April 1844, 25 April 1844, 6 June 1844, 20 June 1844, and 10 July 1845.

26. Henry Howe, *Historical Collections of Ohio* (Cincinnati: State of Ohio, 1888), 2:804.

27. Ibid., 2:732–33, 804; *Marietta Intelligencer,* 7 August 1845, 14 August 1845, and 4 September 1845; *Buckeye Newspaper* (Marietta), 21 August 1845.

28. Howe, *Historical Collections,* 2:732–33, 804; *Marietta Intelligencer,* 7 August 1845, 14 August 1845, and 4 September 1845; *Buckeye Newspaper* (Marietta), 21 August 1845.

29. Howe, *Historical Collections,* 2:804.

30. Etcheson, *Emerging Midwest,* 108–39 (quotation on p. 113). See also Aaron, *Cincinnati,* 294–300; Lowell H. Harrison, *The Antislavery Movement in Kentucky* (Lexington, Ky.: University Press of Kentucky, 1978); Carl E. Kramer, "City With a

Vision: Images of Louisville in the 1830s," *Filson Club Historical Quarterly* 60 (October 1986): 427–52; Parker, "From Northwest to Midwest," in Klingaman and Vedder, eds., *Essays in Nineteenth Century Economic History,* 2–24; and Shortridge, *Middle West,* 104–107.

31. Quotation from James Hall, *Letters from the West* (London: H. Colburn, 1828), 63—undoubtedly the Panic of 1819 played a role as well. See also R. Pierce Beaver, "Joseph Hough, An Early Miami Merchant," *Ohio Archaeological and Historical Quarterly* 45 (January 1936): 42; Thomas Senior Berry, *Western Prices before 1861: A Study of the Cincinnati Market* (Cambridge: Harvard University Press, 1943), 60–61; Philip D. Supina, ed., "The Journal of John Brand of Lexington," *Filson Club Historical Quarterly* 58 (January 1984): 57; Louis C. Hunter, "Studies in the Economic History of the Ohio Valley: Seasonal Aspects of Industry and Commerce Before the Age of Big Business and the Beginnings of Industrial Combination," *Smith College Studies in History* 19 (October 1933–January 1934): 7–32; Orin J. Oliphant, ed., *Through the South and the West with Jeremiah Evarts in 1826* (Lewisburg, Pa.: Bucknell University Press, 1956), 140–41; and Steele, *Summer Journey.*

32. Edward K. Muller, "Selective Urban Growth in the Middle Ohio Valley, 1800–1860," *Geographical Review* 66 (April 1976): 192–99.

33. This and the paragraph following are informed by Harry N. Scheiber, *Ohio Canal Era: A Case Study of Government and the Economy, 1820–1861* (Athens, Ohio: Ohio University Press, 1987), 276–79, 318–43. See also Erik F. Haites, James Mak, and Gary M. Walton, *Western River Transportation: The Era of Early Internal Development, 1810–1860* (Baltimore: Johns Hopkins University Press, 1975), chap. 8.

34. Scheiber, *Ohio Canal Era,* 318–43; and Berry, *Western Prices,* 24.

35. Edward K. Muller, "Selective Urban Growth," 188–95; and Donald T. Zimmer, "The Ohio River: Pathway to Settlement," in *Transportation and the Early Nation: Papers Presented at an Indiana American Revolution Bicentennial Symposium* (Indianapolis: Indiana Historical Society, 1982), 77–78.

36. Andrew R. L. Cayton and Paula R. Riggs, *City into Town: The City of Marietta, Ohio, 1788–1988* (Marietta, Ohio: Marietta College, 1991), 126–32.

37. Glenn Porter and Harold C. Livesay, *Merchants and Manufacturers: Studies in the Changing Structure of Nineteenth-Century Marketing* (Chicago: Elephant Paperbacks, 1989).

38. M. H. Dunlop, *Sixty Miles from Contentment: Traveling the Nineteenth-Century American Interior* (New York: Basic Books, 1995), 218–19, and quotation on pp. 198–99. For Chicago and its reliance on railroads, see William Cronon, *Nature's Metropolis: Chicago and the Great West* (New York: W. W. Norton, 1991).

39. Leland R. Johnson, "Engineering the Ohio," in *Always a River: The Ohio River and the American Experience,* ed. Robert L. Reid (Bloomington, Ind.: Indiana University Press, 1991), 180–206 (quotation on p. 206).

40. Etcheson, *Emerging Midwest,* 108–39; Michael Flannery, "Kentucky History Revisited: The Role of the Civil War in Shaping Kentucky's Collective Consciousness," *Filson Club Historical Quarterly* 71 (January 1997): 27–51; James F. Hopkins,

A History of the Hemp Industry in Kentucky (Lexington, Ky.: University of Kentucky Press, 1951), 24–30, 68, 125–32.

Conclusion

1. Patricia U. Bonomi, *Under the Cope of Heaven: Religion, Society, and Politics in Colonial America* (New York: Oxford University Press, 1986); Nathan O. Hatch, *The Democratization of American Christianity* (New Haven, Conn.: Yale University Press, 1989); and Gordon Wood, "The Significance of the Early Republic," *Journal of the Early Republic* 8 (Spring 1988): 1–20.

2. Andrew R. L. Cayton, "'Separate Interests' and the Nation-State: The Washington Administration and the Origins of Regionalism in the Trans-Appalachian West," *Journal of American History* 79 (June 1992): 39–67. For scholars who have examined the clash between North and South within the Old Northwest itself, see Nicole Etcheson, *The Emerging Midwest: Upland Southerners and the Political Culture of the Old Northwest, 1787–1861* (Bloomington, Ind.: Indiana University Press, 1996); Richard Lyle Power, *Planting Corn Belt Culture: The Impress of the Upland Southerner and Yankee in the Old Northwest* (Indianapolis: Indiana Historical Society, 1953); and Hubert G. H. Wilhelm, "Settlement and Selected Landscape Imprints in the Ohio Valley," in *Always a River: The Ohio River and the American Experience,* ed. Robert L. Reid (Bloomington, Ind.: Indiana University Press, 1991), 67–104.

3. Michael P. Conzen, "The American Urban System in the Nineteenth Century," in *Geography and the Urban Environment: Progress in Research and Applications,* ed. D. T. Herbert and R. J. Johnson (New York: John Wiley, 1981), 4:328–30; and Edward K. Muller, "Selective Urban Growth in the Middle Ohio Valley, 1800–1860," *Geographical Review* 66 (April 1976): 178–99.

BIBLIOGRAPHY

Primary Sources

Manuscript Collections

American Antiquarian Society, Worcester, Mass.
    Ward Family Papers, 1661–1919, Shrewsbury, Mass.
Baker Library, Harvard Business School, Boston, Mass.
    R. G. Dun and Company Collection
    Woodbridge-Backus Collection
Cincinnati Historical Society, Cincinnati, Ohio
    Isaac H. Jackson Papers
    James Smith and Findlay Papers
    Samuel and George Trotter Co., Lexington, Ky., Business Correspondence, 1805–1819
Connecticut Historical Society, Hartford, Conn.
    Backus-Woodbridge Records
    Dudley Woodbridge-Roger Griswold Correspondence
    Oaks-Woodbridge-Day Family Papers, 1839–1851
Connecticut State Library, Hartford, Conn.
    Diary of Benjamin Dana
Dawes Memorial Library, Marietta College, Marietta, Ohio
    Cutler Collection, Slack Research Collections
    Manuscripts Collection, Slack Research Collections
Detroit Public Library, Detroit, Mich.
    William Woodbridge Papers, Burton Collection
Filson Historical Society, Louisville, Ky.
    Buckner Family Papers
    Daniel Chapman Banks Papers
    Daniel Halstead Papers
    Daniel R. Southard Papers
    Edelin Benedict Account Book, 1816–1819
    George L. Miles Papers
    George Wood Merriwether Papers
    Green Family Papers
    Gwathmey Family Papers
    James Weir Ledger, 1813–1815, Greenville, Ky.
    John Irwin Papers, 1808–1899
    John W. Hunt Papers
    Louis Tarascon Journal
    Mason County, Ky., Account Book, 1797–1799
    Miles and Hynes, Murfreesboro, Tenn., Papers
    Runyon Family Papers

Historical Society of Pennsylvania, Philadelphia, Pa.
    Claude W. Unger Collection
    Jonathan John Robinson Papers, 1815–1860
    Samuel Meeker Ledger, 1807–1810
Massachusetts Historical Society, Boston, Mass.
    Thomas Wallcut Papers, 1671–1876
Ohio Historical Society, Columbus, Ohio
    Backus-Woodbridge Collection
    Caleb Thorniley to Brother, 24 July 1807
    John Mills and Co. Account Book
    Putnam Family Papers
West Virginia University, Regional History Collection, Morgantown, W. Va.
    McNeill Family Papers
    Thomas Green Diary, 1825–1827
    Woodbridge Mercantile Company Records, 1788–1870
Western Kentucky University, Department of the Library, Special Collections,
    Bowling Green, Ky.
    Drake Family Papers, 1804–1861
    John Loving Papers, Warren County, Ky.
    Lewis-Starling Collection, 1784–1970
    William Coolidge Jr. Diary and Account Book, 1818–1829
Western Reserve Historical Society, Cleveland, Ohio
    Caleb Emerson Family Papers
    Muskingum Bridge

Newspapers

The American Friend (Marietta, Ohio)
The Buckeye Newspaper (Marietta, Ohio)
Fredonian (Chillicothe, Ohio)
Marietta Intelligencer (Marietta, Ohio)
Muskingum Messanger (Zanesville, Ohio)
Zanesville Express and Republican Standard (Zanesville, Ohio)

Published Works

Baily, Francis. *Journal of a Tour in Unsettled Parts of North America in 1796 and 1797.* Edited by Jack D. L. Holmes. Carbondale and Edwardsville, Ill.: Southern Illinois University Press, 1969.
Barker, Joseph. *Recollections of the First Settlement of Ohio.* Edited by George Jordan Blazier. Marietta, Ohio: Richardson Printing Corporation, 1982.
Bentley, James R., ed. "A Letter from Harrodsburg, 1780." *Filson Club Historical Quarterly* 50 (October 1976): 370–71.
Bond, Beverley W., Jr., ed. *The Correspondence of John Cleves Symmes: Founder of the Miami Purchase.* New York: Macmillan, 1926.
Buell, Rowena, ed. *Memoirs of Rufus Putnam.* Boston: Houghton, Mifflin and Co., 1903.

Chief of Engineers, United States Army, comp. *The Ohio River*. 5th ed. Washington, D.C.: Government Prining Office, 1934.

Cutler, Manasseh. *An Explanation of the Map Which Delineates That Part of the Federal Lands*. Salem, Mass.: Dabney and Cushing, 1787.

Cutler, William Parker, and Julia Perkins Cutler, eds. *Life, Journals, and Correspondence of Rev. Manasseh Cutler, LL.D*. 2 vols. Cincinnati: R. Clarke and Co., 1888.

DeBow, J. D. B. *Statistical View of the United States*. Washington, D.C.: A. O. P. Nicholson, 1854.

Farrand, Max, ed. *A Journey to Ohio in 1810 as Recorded in the Journal of Margaret Van Horn Dwight*. New Haven, Conn.: Yale University Press, 1914.

Fearon, Henry Bradshaw. *Sketches of America: A Narrative of a Journey through the Eastern and Western States of America*.3d ed. London: Longman, Hurst, Rees, Orme, and Brown, 1819.

Fitch, Raymond E., ed. *Breaking with Burr: Harman Blennerhassett's Journal, 1807*. Athens, Ohio: Ohio University Press, 1988.

Fordham, Elias Pym. *Personal Narrative of Travels in Virginia, Maryland, Pennsylvania, Ohio, Indiana, Kentucky; and of a Residence in the Illinois Territory: 1817–1818*. Edited by Frederic Austin Ogg. Cleveland: A. H. Clark Co., 1906.

Hall, James. *Letters from the West*. London: H. Colburn, 1828.

———. *Statistics of the West at the Close of the Year 1836*. Cincinnati: J. A. James, 1837.

———. *The West: Its Commerce and Navigation*. Cincinnati: H. W. Derby and Co., 1848.

Hall, Wade, ed. "Along the Wilderness Trail: A Young Lawyer's 1785 Letter From Danville, Kentucky, to Massachusetts." *Filson Club Historical Quarterly* 61 (July 1987): 283–94.

Hulbert, Archer Butler, ed. *The Records of the Original Proceedings of the Ohio Company*. Marietta, Ohio: Marietta Historical Commission, 1917.

Kilbourn, John. *The Ohio Gazetteer, or, Topographical Dictionary*. 11th ed. Columbus: Scott and Wright, 1833.

Mansfield, Edward D. *On the Railroad Connections of Philadelphia with the Central West*. Philadelphia: J. C. Clark, Printer, 1853.

Melish, John. *Travels through the United States of America, in the Years 1806 and 1807, and 1809, 1810, and 1811*. New York: Johnson Reprint Corp., 1970.

Noyes, Mrs. Charles P., ed. *A Family History in Letters and Documents, 1667–1837*. Saint Paul, Minn.: privately printed, 1919.

Oliphant, J. Orin, ed. *Through the South and the West with Jeremiah Evarts in 1826*. Lewisburg, Pa.: Bucknell University Press, 1956.

Petty, Gerald M. *Ohio 1810 Tax Duplicate, Arranged in a State-Wide Alphabetical List of Names of Taxpayers*. Columbus: privately printed, 1976.

Prechtel-Kluskens, Claire, comp. *Third Census of the United States, 1810 [microform]: Population Schedules, Washington County, Ohio*. Washington, D.C.: National Archives, 1994.

Smith, Dwight L., ed. *The Western Journals of John May: Ohio Company Agent and Business Adventurer*. Cincinnati: Historical and Philosophical Society of Ohio, 1961.

Smith, Dwight L., and Ray Swick, eds. *A Journey through the West: Thomas Rodney's 1803 Journal from Delaware to the Mississippi Territory.* Athens, Ohio: Ohio University Press, 1997.

Steele, Mrs. *A Summer Journey in the West.* New York: J. S. Taylor and Co., 1841.

Supina, Philip D., ed. "The Journal of John Brand of Lexington." *Filson Club Historical Quarterly* 58 (January 1984): 54–70.

Thomas, David. *Travels through the Western Country in the Summer of 1816.* Auburn, N.Y.: David Rumsey, 1819.

Thwaites, Reuben Gold, ed. *Early Western Travels, 1748–1846.* 32 vols. Cleveland: A. H. Clark Co., 1904–1907.

Tischendorf, Alfred, and E. Taylor Parks, eds. *The Diary and Journal of Richard Clough Anderson, Jr., 1814–1826.* Durham, N.C.: Duke University Press, 1964.

Walker, Joseph E., ed. *Pleasure and Business in Western Pennsylvania: The Journal of Joshua Gilpin, 1809.* Harrisburg, Pa.: Pennsylvania Historical and Museum Commission, 1975.

Woehrmann, Paul, ed. "The Autobiography of Abraham Snethen, Frontier Preacher." *Filson Club Historical Quarterly* 51 (October 1977): 315–35.

Secondary Sources

Articles and Book Chapters

Baldwin, Leland D. "Shipbuilding on the Western Waters, 1793–1817." *Mississippi Valley Historical Review* 20 (June 1933): 29–44.

Bean, Jonathan J. "Marketing 'the great American commodity': Nathaniel Massie and Land Speculation on the Ohio Frontier, 1783–1813." *Ohio History* 103 (Summer–Autumn 1994): 152–69.

Beaver, R. Pierce. "Joseph Hough, An Early Miami Merchant." *Ohio Archaeological and Historical Quarterly* 45 (January 1936): 37–45.

Birch, Brian P. "Taking the Breaks and Working the Boats: An English Family's Impressions of Ohio in the 1830s." *Ohio History* 95 (Summer–Autumn 1986): 101–18.

Carson, W. Wallace. "Transportation and Traffic on the Ohio and Mississippi before the Steamboat." *Mississippi Valley Historical Review* 7 (June 1920): 26–38.

Cashin, Joan E. "Black Families in the Old Northwest." *Journal of the Early Republic* 15 (Fall 1995): 449–75.

Cayton, Andrew R. L. "Artery and Boundary: The Ambiguous Development of the Ohio Valley in the Early Republic." *Ohio Valley History* 1 (Winter 2001): 19–26.

———. "Land, Power, and Reputation: The Cultural Dimensions of Politics in the Ohio Country." *William and Mary Quarterly,* 3d ser., 47 (April 1990): 266–86.

———. "'Separate Interests' and the Nation-State: The Washington Administration and the Origins of Regionalism in the Trans-Appalachian West." *Journal of American History* 79 (June 1992): 39–67.

Conzen, Michael P. "The American Urban System in the Nineteenth Century." In *Geography and the Urban Environment: Progress in Research and Applications,* edited by D. T. Herbert and R. J. Johnson. Vol. 4. New York: John Wiley, 1981.

Daniels, Bruce C. "Economic Development in Colonial and Revolutionary Connecticut: An Overview." *William and Mary Quarterly,* 3d ser., 37 (July 1980): 429–59.

Earle, Carville. "Regional Economic Development West of the Appalachians, 1815–1860." In *North America: The Historical Geography of a Changing Continent,* edited by Robert D. Mitchell and Paul A. Groves. Totowa, N.J.: Rowman and Littlefield, 1987.

Eslinger, Ellen. "Migration and Kinship on the Trans-Appalachian Frontier: Strode's Station, Kentucky." *Filson Club History Quarterly* 62 (January 1988): 52–66.

Farrell, Richard T. "Cincinnati, 1800–1830: Economic Development through Trade and Industry." *Ohio History* 77 (Autumn 1968): 111–29.

Flannery, Michael. "Kentucky History Revisited: The Role of the Civil War in Shaping Kentucky's Collective Consciousness." *Filson Club Historical Quarterly* 71 (January 1997): 27–51.

Friend, Craig T. "Merchants and Markethouses: Reflections on Moral Economy in Early Kentucky." *Journal of the Early Republic* 17 (Winter 1997): 553–74.

George, Angelo I. "Saltpeter and Gunpowder Manufacturing in Kentucky." *Filson Club Historical Quarterly* 60 (April 1986): 189–217.

Gronert, Theodore G. "Trade in the Blue-Grass Region, 1810–1820." *Mississippi Valley Historical Review* 5 (December 1918): 313–23.

Hammon, Neal O. "Land Acquisition on the Kentucky Frontier." *Register of the Kentucky Historical Society* 78 (Autumn 1980): 297–321.

Hofstra, Warren. "The Virginia Backcountry in the Eighteenth Century: The Question of Origins and the Issue of Outcomes." *Virginia Magazine of History and Biography* 101 (October 1993): 485–508.

Hunter, Louis C. "Studies in the Economic History of the Ohio Valley: Seasonal Aspects of Industry and Commerce Before the Age of Big Business and the Beginnings of Industrial Combination." *Smith College Studies in History* 19 (October 1933–January 1934): 7–130.

Jones, Fred Mitchell. "Middlemen in the Domestic Trade of the United States, 1800–1860." *Illinois Studies in the Social Sciences* 21, no. 3 (1937): 1–81.

Kramer, Carl E. "City With a Vision: Images of Louisville in the 1830s." *Filson Club Historical Quarterly* 60 (October 1986): 427–52.

Kreipke, Martha. "The Falls of the Ohio and the Development of the Ohio River Trade, 1810–1860." *Filson Club Historical Quarterly* 54 (April 1980): 196–217.

Mak, James. "Intraregional Trade in the Antebellum West: Ohio, A Case Study." *Agricultural History* 46 (October 1972): 489–97.

Merrill, Michael. "Putting 'Capitalism' in Its Place: A Review of Recent Literature." *William and Mary Quarterly,* 3d ser., 52 (April 1995): 315–26.

Muller, Edward K. "Selective Urban Growth in the Middle Ohio Valley, 1800–1860." *Geographical Review* 66 (April 1976): 178–99.

Nobles, Gregory C. "Breaking into the Backcountry: New Approaches to the Early American Frontier." *William and Mary Quarterly,* 3d ser., 46 (October 1989): 641–70.

O'Dell, Gary A. "The Trotter Family, Gunpowder, and Early Kentucky Entrepreneurship, 1784–1833." *Register of the Kentucky Historical Society* 88 (Autumn 1990): 394–430.

Perkins, Elizabeth A. "The Consumer Frontier: Household Consumption in Early Kentucky." *Journal of American History* 78 (September 1991): 486–510.

Peters, Bernard. "The German Pioneers." *Ohio Archaeological and Historical Society Publications* 2 (1900): 55–63.

Preston, Daniel. "Thomas Kelsey, Hardluck Entrepreneur." *Ohio History* 104 (Summer–Autumn 1995): 127–41.

Rau, Louise. "Lucy Backus Woodbridge, Pioneer Mother: January 31, 1757–October 6, 1817." *Ohio State Archaeological and Historical Quarterly* 44, no. 4 (1935): 405–42.

Salisbury, Neal. "The Indians' Old World: Native Americans and the Coming of Europeans." *William and Mary Quarterly,* 3d ser., 53 (July 1996): 435–58.

Scheiber, Harry N. "Ebenezer Buckingham." *Museum Echoes* 33 (December 1960): 91–94.

———. "Preface: On the Concepts of 'Regionalism' and 'Frontier.'" In *The Old Northwest: Studies in Regional History, 1787–1910.* Lincoln, Nebr.: University of Nebraska Press, 1969.

Shannon, Timothy J. "The Ohio Company and the Meaning of Opportunity in the American West, 1786–1795." *New England Quarterly* 64 (September 1991): 393–413.

Soltow, Lee. "Inequality Amidst Abundance: Land Ownership in Early Nineteenth Century Ohio." *Ohio History* 88 (Spring 1979): 133–51.

———. "Progress and Mobility Among Ohio Propertyholders, 1810–1825." *Social Science History* 7 (Fall 1983): 405–26.

Stealey, John Edmund, III. "Virginia's Mercantile-Manufacturing Frontier: Dickinson and Shrewsbury and the Great Kanawha Salt Industry." *Virginia Magazine of History and Biography* 101 (October 1993): 509–34.

Swierenga, Robert P. "The Settlement of the Old Northwest: Ethnic Pluralism in a Featureless Plain." *Journal of the Early Republic* 9 (Spring 1989): 73–105.

Vickers, Daniel. "Competency and Competition: Economic Culture in Early America." *William and Mary Quarterly,* 3d ser., 47 (January 1990): 3–29.

Weissbach, Lee Shai. "The Peopling of Lexington, Kentucky: Growth and Mobility in a Frontier Town." *Register of the Kentucky Historical Society* 81 (Spring 1983): 115–33.

Whitaker, Arthur P. "Reed and Forde: Merchant Adventurers of Philadelphia." *Pennsylvania Magazine of History and Biography* 61 (July 1937): 237–62.

Wood, Gordon. "The Significance of the Early Republic." *Journal of the Early Republic* 8 (Spring 1988): 1–20.

Zimmer, Donald T. "The Ohio River: Pathway to Settlement." In *Transportation and the Early Nation: Papers Presented at an Indiana American Revolution Bicentennial Symposium.* Indianapolis: Indiana Historical Society, 1982.

Books and Dissertations

Aaron, Daniel. *Cincinnati: Queen City of the West, 1819–1838.* Columbus: Ohio State University Press, 1992.

Abernethy, Thomas Perkins. *The Burr Conspiracy.* Gloucester, Mass.: P. Smith, 1968.

Anderson, Virginia DeJohn. *New England's Generation: The Great Migration and the Formation of Society and Culture in the Seventeenth Century.* New York: Cambridge University Press, 1991.

Andrews, Martin R. *History of Marietta and Washington County, Ohio and Representative Citizens*. Chicago: Biographical Publishing Co., 1902.

Aron, Stephen. *How the West Was Lost: The Transformation of Kentucky from Daniel Boone to Henry Clay*. Baltimore: Johns Hopkins University Press, 1996.

Atherton, Lewis E. *The Frontier Merchant in Mid-America*. Columbia, Mo.: University of Missouri Press, 1971.

Bakken, Gordon Morris, and Brenda Farrington, eds. *Where Is the West?* New York: Garland Publishing, 2000.

Banta, R. E. *The Ohio*. New York: Rinehart, 1949.

Barnhart, John D. *Valley of Democracy: The Frontier versus the Plantation in the Ohio Valley, 1775–1818*. Bloomington, Ind.: Indiana University Press, 1953.

Bellesiles, Michael A. *Revolutionary Outlaws: Ethan Allen and the Struggle for Independence on the Early American Frontier*. Charlottesville, Va.: University Press of Virginia, 1993.

Berry, Thomas Senior. *Western Prices before 1861: A Study of the Cincinnati Market*. Cambridge: Harvard University Press, 1943.

Bigham, Darrel E. *Towns and Villages of the Lower Ohio*. Lexington, Ky.: University Press of Kentucky, 1998.

Bond, Beverley W., Jr. *The Civilization of the Old Northwest: A Study of Political, Social, and Economic Development, 1788–1812*. New York: Macmillan, 1934.

———. *The Foundations of Ohio*. Columbus: Ohio State Archaeological and Historical Society, 1941.

Bonomi, Patricia U. *Under the Cope of Heaven: Religion, Society, and Politics in Colonial America*. New York: Oxford University Press, 1986.

Buley, R. Carlyle. *The Old Northwest: Pioneer Period, 1815–1840*. 2 vols. Bloomington, Ind.: Indiana University Press, 1950.

Caulkins, Frances Manwaring. *History of Norwich, Connecticut*. Hartford, Conn.: privately printed, 1866.

Cayton, Andrew R. L. *Frontier Indiana*. Bloomington, Ind.: Indiana University Press, 1996.

———. *The Frontier Republic: Ideology and Politics in the Ohio Country, 1780–1825*. Kent, Ohio: Kent State University Press, 1986.

Cayton, Andrew R. L., and Peter S. Onuf. *The Midwest and the Nation: Rethinking the History of an American Region*. Bloomington, Ind.: Indiana University Press, 1990.

Cayton, Andrew R. L., and Paula R. Riggs. *City into Town: The City of Marietta, Ohio, 1788–1988*. Marietta, Ohio: Marietta College, 1991.

Cayton, Andrew R. L., and Fredrika J. Teute, eds. *Contact Points: American Frontiers from the Mohawk Valley to the Mississippi, 1750–1830*. Chapel Hill, N.C.: University of North Carolina Press, 1998.

Clark, Christopher. *The Roots of Rural Capitalism: Western Massachusetts, 1780–1860*. Ithaca, N.Y.: Cornell University Press, 1990.

Clark, John G. *The Grain Trade in the Old Northwest*. Urbana, Ill.: University of Illinois Press, 1966.

Cronon, William. *Nature's Metropolis: Chicago and the Great West*. New York: W. W. Norton, 1991.

Daniels, Bruce C. *The Connecticut Town: Growth and Development, 1635–1790*. Middletown, Conn.: Wesleyan University Press, 1979.

Dannenbaum, Jed. *Drink and Disorder: Temperance Reform in Cincinnati from the Washingtonian Revival to the WCTU*. Urbana, Ill.: University of Illinois Press, 1984.

Davis, James E. *Frontier Illinois*. Bloomington, Ind.: Indiana University Press, 1998.

Dennis, James L. *Washington's Darker Brother: One Hundred Years of Black History in Washington County, Ohio, 1788–1888*. Parkersburg, W. Va.: privately printed, 1986.

Doerflinger, Thomas M. *A Vigorous Spirit of Enterprise: Merchants and Economic Development in Revolutionary Philadelphia*. New York: W. W. Norton, 1986.

Downes, Randolph C. *Council Fires on the Upper Ohio: A Narrative of Indian Affairs in the Upper Ohio Valley until 1795*. Pittsburgh: University of Pittsburgh Press, 1940.

Dunlop, M. H. *Sixty Miles from Contentment: Traveling the Nineteenth-Century American Interior*. New York: Basic Books, 1995.

Eslinger, Ellen. *Citizens of Zion: The Social Origins of Camp Meeting Revivalism*. Knoxville, Tenn.: University of Tennessee Press, 1999.

Etcheson, Nicole. *The Emerging Midwest: Upland Southerners and the Political Culture of the Old Northwest, 1787–1861*. Bloomington, Ind.: Indiana University Press, 1996.

Faragher, John Mack. *Daniel Boone: The Life and Legend of an American Pioneer*. New York: Holt, 1992.

———. *Sugar Creek: Life on the Illinois Prairie*. New Haven, Conn.: Yale University Press, 1986.

Farmer, Charles J. *In the Absence of Towns: Settlement and Country Trade in Southside Virginia, 1730–1800*. Lanham, Md.: Rowman and Littlefield, 1993.

Ferguson, Thomas E., and Thomas Aquinas Burke. *Ohio Lands: A Short History*. Columbus: Ohio Auditor of State, 1987.

Flack, Irwin F. "Who Governed Cincinnati? A Comparative Analysis of Government and Social Structure in a Nineteenth Century River City, 1819–1860." Ph.D. diss., University of Pittsburgh, 1978.

Friend, Craig Thompson, ed. *The Buzzel about Kentuck: Settling the Promised Land*. Lexington, Ky.: University Press of Kentucky, 1999.

Glazer, Walter S. "Cincinnati in 1840: A Community Profile." Ph.D. diss., University of Michigan, 1968.

Goldstein, Jonathan. *Philadelphia and the China Trade, 1682–1846: Commercial, Cultural, and Attitudinal Effects*. University Park, Pa.: Pennsylvania State University Press, 1978.

Gray, Susan E. *The Yankee West: Community Life on the Michigan Frontier*. Chapel Hill, N.C.: University of North Carolina Press, 1996.

Gutgesell, Stephen, ed. *Guide to Ohio Newspapers, 1793–1973*. Columbus: Ohio Historical Society, 1974.

Haites, Erik F., James Mak, and Gary M. Walton. *Western River Transportation: The Era of Early Internal Development, 1810–1860*. Baltimore: Johns Hopkins University Press, 1975.

Harper, R. Eugene. *The Transformation of Western Pennsylvania, 1770–1800*. Pittsburgh: University of Pittsburgh Press, 1991.

Harrison, Lowell H. *The Antislavery Movement in Kentucky*. Lexington, Ky.: University Press of Kentucky, 1978.

Hatch, Nathan O. *The Democratization of American Christianity.* New Haven, Conn.: Yale University Press, 1989.

Havighurst, Walter. *River to the West: Three Centuries of the Ohio.* New York: G. P. Putnam's Sons, 1970.

Hibbard, Benjamin Horace. *A History of the Public Land Policies.* Madison, Wis.: University of Wisconsin Press, 1965.

Hildreth, S. P. *Biographical and Historical Memoirs of the Early Pioneer Settlers of Ohio.* Cincinnati: H. W. Derby and Co., 1852.

———. *Pioneer History.* Cincinnati: H. W. Derby and Co., 1848.

Hildreth, William Henry. "Travel Literature of the Ohio River Valley (1794–1832)." Ph.D. diss., Ohio State University, 1944.

Hinderaker, Eric. *Elusive Empires: Constructing Colonialism in the Ohio Valley, 1673–1800.* New York: Cambridge University Press, 1997.

Hopkins, James F. *A History of the Hemp Industry in Kentucky.* Lexington, Ky.: University of Kentucky Press, 1951.

Horsman, Reginald. *The Frontier in the Formative Years, 1783–1815.* New York: Holt, Rinehart and Winston, 1970.

Howe, Henry. *Historical Collections of Ohio.* 2 vols. Cincinnati: State of Ohio, 1888.

Hulbert, Archer Butler. *The Ohio River: A Course of Empire.* New York: G. P. Putnam's Sons, 1906.

Hunter, Louis C. *Steamboats on the Western Rivers: An Economic and Technological History.* Cambridge: Harvard University Press, 1949.

Huntington, Charles Clifford. *A History of Banking and Currency in Ohio Before the Civil War.* Columbus: F. J. Heer Printing Co., 1915.

Hurt, R. Douglas. *The Ohio Frontier: Crucible of the Old Northwest, 1720–1830.* Bloomington, Ind.: Indiana University Press, 1996.

Jackle, John A. *Images of the Ohio Valley: A Historical Geography of Travel, 1740–1860.* New York: Oxford University Press, 1977.

Jedrey, Christopher M. *The World of John Cleaveland: Family and Community in Eighteenth-Century New England.* New York: W. W. Norton, 1979.

Jennings, Marietta. *A Pioneer Merchant of St. Louis, 1810–1820: The Business Career of Christian Wilt.* New York: Columbia University Press, 1939.

Jones, Robert Leslie. *History of Agriculture in Ohio to 1880.* Kent, Ohio: Kent State University Press, 1983.

Klein, Rachel N. *Unification of a Slave State: The Rise of the Planter Class in the South Carolina Backcountry, 1760–1808.* Chapel Hill, N.C.: University of North Carolina Press, 1990.

Klingaman, David C., and Richard K. Vedder, eds. *Essays in Nineteenth Century Economic History: The Old Northwest.* Athens, Ohio: Ohio University Press, 1975.

———. *Essays on the Economy of the Old Northwest.* Athens, Ohio: Ohio University Press, 1987.

Knepper, George W. *Ohio and Its People.* Kent, Ohio: Kent State University Press, 1989.

Levine, Bruce. *Half Slave and Half Free: The Roots of the Civil War.* New York: Hill and Wang, 1992.

Lindstrom, Diane. *Economic Development in the Philadelphia Region, 1810–1850.* New York: Columbia University Press, 1978.

Lippincott, Isaac. *A History of the Manufactures in the Ohio Valley to the Year 1860*. New York: Arno Press, 1973.

Livermore, Shaw. *Early American Land Companies: Their Influence on Corporate Development*. New York: The Commonwealth Fund, 1939.

Livingood, James Weston. *The Philadelphia-Baltimore Trade Rivalry, 1780–1860*. Harrisburg, Pa.: Pennsylvania Historical and Museum Commission, 1947.

Lomask, Milton. *Aaron Burr: The Conspiracy and Years of Exile, 1805–1836*. New York: Farrar, Straus and Giroux, 1982.

Madison, James H., ed. *Heartland: Comparative Histories of the Midwestern States*. Bloomington, Ind.: Indiana University Press, 1988.

Main, Jackson Turner. *Society and Economy in Colonial Connecticut*. Princeton, N.J.: Princeton University Press, 1985.

Maizlish, Stephen E. *The Triumph of Sectionalism: The Transformation of Ohio Politics, 1844–56*. Kent, Ohio: Kent State University Press, 1983.

Mancall, Peter C. *Valley of Opportunity: Economic Culture along the Upper Susquehanna, 1700–1800*. Ithaca, N.Y.: Cornell University Press, 1991.

McCaleb, Walter Flavius. *The Aaron Burr Conspiracy*. New York: Wilson-Erickson, 1936.

McConnell, Michael N. *A Country Between: The Upper Ohio Valley and Its Peoples, 1724–1774*. Lincoln, Nebr.: University of Nebraska Press, 1992.

Middleton, Stephen. *The Black Laws in the Old Northwest: A Documentary History*. Westport, Conn.: Greenwood Press, 1993.

Mitchell, Robert D. *Commercialism and Frontier: Perspectives on the Early Shenandoah Valley*. Charlottesville, Va.: University Press of Virginia, 1977.

Mitchell, Robert D., ed. *Appalachian Frontiers: Settlement, Society, and Development in the Preindustrial Era*. Lexington, Ky.: University Press of Kentucky, 1991.

Onuf, Peter S. *Statehood and Union: A History of the Northwest Ordinance*. Bloomington, Ind.: Indiana University Press, 1987.

Pathways to the Old Northwest: An Observance of the Bicentennial of the Northwest Ordinance. Indianapolis: Indiana Historical Society, 1988.

Perkins, Edwin J. *The Economy of Colonial America*. 2d ed. New York: Columbia University Press, 1988.

Perkins, Elizabeth A. *Border Life: Experience and Memory in the Revolutionary Ohio Valley*. Chapel Hill, N.C.: University of North Carolina Press, 1998.

Porter, Glenn, and Harold C. Livesay. *Merchants and Manufacturers: Studies in the Changing Structure of Nineteenth-Century Marketing*. Chicago: Elephant Paperbacks, 1989.

Power, Richard Lyle. *Planting Corn Belt Culture: The Impress of the Upland Southerner and Yankee in the Old Northwest*. Indianapolis: Indiana Historical Society, 1953.

Preston, Daniel. "Market and Mill Town: Hamilton Ohio, 1795–1860." Ph.D. diss., University of Maryland, 1987.

Ramage, James A. *John Wesley Hunt: Pioneer Merchant, Manufacturer, and Financier*. Lexington, Ky.: University Press of Kentucky, 1974.

Ratcliffe, Donald J. *Party Spirit in a Frontier Republic: Democratic Politics in Ohio, 1793–1821*. Columbus: Ohio State University Press, 1998.

Ray, John Bernard. "Zane's Trace, 1796–1812: A Study in Historical Geography." Ph.D. diss., Indiana University, 1968.

Reid, Robert L., ed. *Always a River: The Ohio River and the American Experience.* Bloomington, Ind.: Indiana University Press, 1991.

Reiser, Catherine Elizabeth. *Pittsburgh's Commercial Development, 1800–1850.* Harrisburg, Pa.: Pennsylvania Historical and Museum Commission, 1951.

Richards, Leonard L. *Gentlemen of Property and Standing: Anti-Abolition Mobs in Jacksonian America.* New York: Oxford University Press, 1970.

Rohrbough, Malcolm J. *The Land Office Business: The Settlement and Administration of American Public Lands, 1789–1837.* New York: Oxford University Press, 1968.

———. *The Trans-Appalachian Frontier: Peoples, Societies, and Institutions, 1775–1850.* New York: Oxford University Press, 1978.

Ross, Steven J. *Workers on the Edge: Work, Leisure, and Politics in Industrializing Cincinnati, 1788–1890.* New York: Columbia University Press, 1985.

Scheiber, Harry N. *Ohio Canal Era: A Case Study of Government and the Economy, 1820–1861.* Athens, Ohio: Ohio University Press, 1987.

Schneider, Norris F. *The Muskingum River: A History and a Guide.* Columbus: Ohio Historical Society, 1968.

Sheriff, Carol. *The Artificial River: The Erie Canal and the Paradox of Progress, 1817–1862.* New York: Hill and Wang, 1996.

Shortridge, James R. *The Middle West: Its Meaning in American Culture.* Lawrence, Kans.: University Press of Kansas, 1989.

Silverberg, Robert. *The Mound Builders.* Athens, Ohio: University of Ohio Press, 1986.

Soltow, Lee. *Men and Wealth in the United States, 1850–1870.* New Haven, Conn.: Yale University Press, 1975.

Summers, Thomas J. *History of Marietta.* Marietta, Ohio: Leader Publishing Co., 1903.

Taylor, Alan. *Liberty Men and Great Proprietors: The Revolutionary Settlement on the Maine Frontier, 1760–1820.* Chapel Hill, N.C.: University of North Carolina Press, 1990.

———. *William Cooper's Town: Power and Persuasion on the Frontier of the Early American Republic.* New York: Alfred A. Knopf, 1995.

Taylor, George Rogers. *The Transportation Revolution, 1815–1860.* New York: Rinehart, 1951.

Taylor, Robert M., ed. *The Northwest Ordinance, 1787: A Bicentennial Handbook.* Indianapolis: Indiana Historical Society, 1987.

Treat, Payson Jackson. *The National Land System, 1785–1820.* New York: E. B. Treat, 1910.

Trigger, Bruce G., ed. *Handbook of North American Indians.* Vol. 15, *Northeast.* Washington, D.C.: Smithsonian Institution, 1978.

Trotter, Joe William, Jr. *River Jordan: African American Urban Life in the Ohio Valley.* Lexington, Ky.: University Press of Kentucky, 1998.

Tuan, Yi-Fu. *Space and Place: The Perspective of Experience.* Minneapolis: University of Minnesota Press, 1977.

Ulrich, Laurel Thatcher. *Good Wives: Image and Reality in the Lives of Women in Northern New England, 1650–1750.* New York: Vintage Books, 1982.

Utter, William T. *The Frontier State, 1803–1825.* Columbus: Ohio State Archaeological and Historical Society, 1942.

Vance, James E., Jr. *The Merchant's World: The Geography of Wholesaling*. Englewood Cliffs, N.J.: Prentice-Hall, 1970.

Vincent, Stephen A. *Southern Seed, Northern Soil: African American Farm Communities in the Midwest, 1765–1900*. Bloomington, Ind.: Indiana University Press, 1999.

Wade, Richard C. *The Urban Frontier: Pioneer Life in Early Pittsburgh, Cincinnati, Lexington, Louisville, and St. Louis*. Chicago: University of Chicago Press, 1964.

Walker, Juliet K. *Free Frank: A Black Pioneer on the Antebellum Frontier*. Lexington, Ky.: University Press of Kentucky, 1983.

Wheeler, Richard Anson. *History of the Town of Stonington, County of New London, Connecticut*. New London, Conn.: Press of the Day Publishing Co., 1900.

White, Richard. *The Middle Ground: Indians, Empires, and Republics in the Great Lakes Region, 1650–1815*. New York: Cambridge University Press, 1991.

Williams, Frederick D., ed. *The Northwest Ordinance: Essays on Its Formulation, Provisions, and Legacy*. East Lansing, Mich.: Michigan State University Press, 1988.

Williams, H. Z. *History of Washington County, Ohio*. Cleveland: H. Z. Williams and Bro., 1881.

INDEX

Italicized page numbers indicate illustrations.

KIM M. GRUENWALD is Assistant Professor of
History at Kent State University.